VIOLETS FROM OVERSEA

ALSO BY TONIE AND VALMAI HOLT

Picture Postcards of the Golden Age: A Collector's Guide
McGibbon & Kee 1971

Till the Boys Come Home: the Picture Postcards of the First World War
Macdonald & Jane's 1977

The Best Fragments from France by Capt Bruce Bairnsfather
Phin Pub Co 1978

Picture Postcard Artists: Landscapes, Animals and Characters
Longmans 1984

Stanley Gibbons Postcard Catalogue
Stanley Gibbons Publications, 1980

In Search of the Better 'Ole: The Life, the Works and the Collectables of Bruce Bairnsfather
Milestone Publications 1985

Germany Awake!: the Rise of National Socialism Illustrated by Contemporary Postcards
Longmans 1986

I'll Be Seeing You: Picture Postcards of World War II
Moorland Pub Co 1987

Holts' Battlefield Guidebooks
Ypres/Salient
Leo Cooper 1982
Normandy–Overlord
Leo Cooper 1983
Market-Garden Corridor
Leo Cooper 1984
Somme
T & V Holt Assocs 1986

Battlefields of the First World War: A Traveller's Guide
Pavilion 1994

Visitor's Guide: The Normandy Landing Beaches
Moorland Pub Co 1989

Major & Mrs Holt's Battle Maps
T & V Holt Assocs
The Somme 1986
The Ypres Salient 1993
Normandy 1994

Major & Mrs Holt's Battlefield Guide to the Ypres Salient
T & V Holt Assocs 1995

Major & Mrs Holt's Battlefield Guide to the Somme
Leo Cooper 1996

VIOLETS FROM OVERSEA

by

Tonie and Valmai Holt

Charlotte Zeepvat provided the illustrations,
chose the original 20 poems, supplied general
research and comprehensive drafts on Hodgson,
Coulson and Macintosh.

LEO COOPER
LONDON

First published in Great Britain in 1996 by
LEO COOPER
190 Shaftesbury Avenue, London WC2H 8JL
an imprint of
Pen & Sword Books Ltd,
47 Church Street,
Barnsley, South Yorkshire S70 2AS

ISBN 0 85052 406 7

A CIP record for this book is available from
the British Library

Typeset in 10pt Linotype Sabon by
Phoenix Typesetting, Ilkley, West Yorkshire.

Printed in England by Redwood Books, Trowbridge, Wiltshire.

CONTENTS

ACKNOWLEDGEMENTS

Our heartfelt thanks for general advice and for pointing us in the right direction to Peter Simkins, Martin Taylor and Alan Geoffrey of the Imperial War Museum; to the staff of Dover Library for getting hold of obscure books and biographies; to Barry Murphy, Information Officer, and many other helpful members of staff at the Commonwealth War Graves Commission for information about graves and giving us access to records; to Timothy d'Arch Smith, grandson of Gilbert Frankau, for help with the Frankau chapter; and to David Leighton, nephew and literary executor of Roland Leighton, for help with the Leighton chapter and permission to quote from his poetry.

'The Last Post' from *Verses of a VAD* by Vera Brittain is included with the permission of Paul Berry, her literary executor. Our thanks to him and Mark Bostridge, her biographer; to Dr Lewis Burke, graduate of McGill University, for advice with the McCrae chapter; to our special friends and generous researchers Chris Wilson, Rosalie McFerran (especially for Streets), Mike Scott (for Herbert and the RND), Philip Guest (for Owen) and Alf and Jo Jenkins (for Gurney and much else); to Barry Noble for leads on Gibson, and to the library at Hexham and the staff at the Science Museum for information about him; to surviving relatives of Hodgson, other members of the 9th Devons and C.W. Surtees, late archivist of Durham School, for information about Hodgson; the archivists of Brighton College (Martin Jones), St Paul's School (Christopher Dean) and Uppingham (Mr Rudman, also their librarian, Spry Leveton); Colin Campbell and Rosalind Green for information on Mackintosh and Leslie F. Stewart on Coulson; and Les Yaw, who has compiled Streets' poems, letters and diaries under the title *Temple of Truth*, for permission to quote from it, and for additional information on Streets.

Finally our gratitude to Sir Nicholas Hewitt for his confidence in the project and, above all, to Leo Cooper for his tolerance.

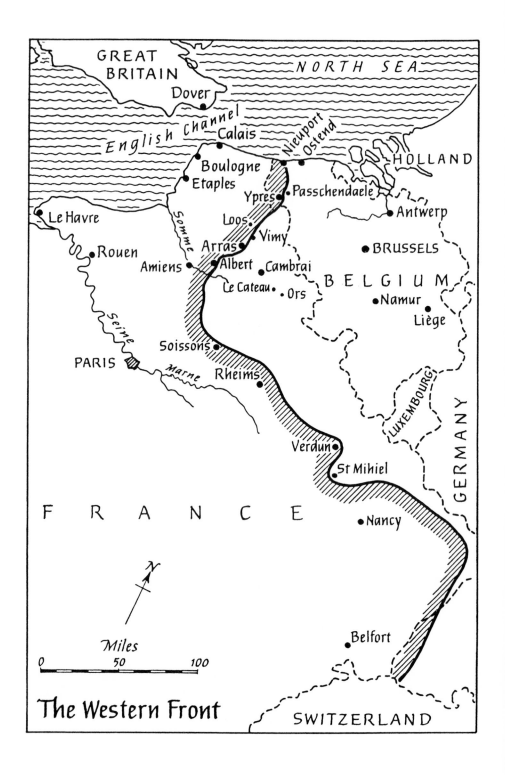

The Western Front

THE POETS
IN ALPHABETICAL ORDER

FOREWORD

Every anthology is, by its very nature, a subjective and personal choice of poets and their works.

This anthology, however, is probably even more subjective than most. It began as an extraordinary gift from the artist and researcher, Charlotte Zeepvat, presented to us on one of our battlefield tours to the Somme in 1980. It was a black display folder which featured exquisite water-colour portraits of twenty poets, a handwritten example of one of their poems and a potted biography of each.

In explaining her choices of poets, poems and their order, Charlotte says:

> I chose an historical sequence because war poetry is interesting as historical evidence; it brings us closer to the experiences of war and helps us to understand. Unfortunately most published anthologies get the history wrong. The standard picture of First World War poetry as a progression from patriotic enthusiasm in 1914, through disillusion in 1916, to bitterness and cynicism at the war's ending is far too simplistic. Hence the choice of 'Lost' to open the collection – and there are plenty of other poems written in 1914, when men were supposedly galloping off to war full of youthful enthusiasm, which express apprehension and doubt, as this does.
>
> I tried to choose the unexpected and unfamiliar, so next you have Grenfell's 'Prayer for Those on the Staff', which is cynical before war poems were supposed to be cynical and shows how front-line officers often felt. Tonie introduced me to Brooke's 'Fragment' and I used it because, again, it is more uncertain and thoughtful than Brooke is supposed to have been. I wanted to include Roland Leighton because he seems to be written off as a character in *Testament of Youth*; even though his poetry is good he never appears in anthologies. This makes your choice of Leighton's *Violets from Oversea* as the title of this book especially pleasing. Giving him a place in his own right became less apparent when I had to include Vera Brittain as well; it was important to me to have at least one woman, and hers was the only picture reference I could find.
>
> Some poems in the book arose directly from the tours. We had often mentioned 'In Flanders Fields' and visited Essex Farm [where

it was written]. Gibson's 'Lament' was for Valmai and 'His Mate' [Studdert Kennedy] for Tonie. Rosalie [McFerran, a regular traveller and knowledgeable enthusiast on the Western Front] discovered Streets that year and I put him in for her, and because it seemed worthwhile to include a self-educated miner among all the public schoolboys. 'A Soldier's Cemetery' seemed appropriate because we had all visited so many cemeteries. We had also visited Wyndham Tennant's grave, so I included an unfamiliar poem of his which I like. Robert Graves was difficult. 'The Dead Fox Hunter' won the day because it was about a real event and a real person.

I wanted Alan Seeger and Leslie Coulson in because of their personal stories – the American volunteer and the journalist who insisted on joining the ranks. Vernède is also here to broaden the range of characters; we are all used to hearing about boys who lied about their age to join up, but he was over-age and filled the 'uncle' role familiar from so many First World War stories [notably R.C. Sherriff's *Journey's End*]. His letters are better than his poems, but I chose 'The Little Sergeant' because it introduced yet another familiar character and showed an appreciation of the courage of 'ordinary' soldiers. 'Rendezvous' and 'The Rainbow' bring in the theme of nature and war, and the vivid awareness soldiers in the trenches had of the world around them.

As you have probably guessed a great deal of research went into this, including several days in the reading room of the Imperial War Museum, and it was there one afternoon that I discovered 'A Lost Leader'. We had talked about the officer with the map ['the most dangerous thing in the British army'] and here he was, bravely leading a column to goodness-knows-where. It made me laugh so much that it demanded to be in the book. Humour was an important part of their experience. The experience of an officer at headquarters with trench maps and telephones was another part of the pattern, and to represent all this I included the Frankau poem which Mike Scott [another First World War enthusiast with an almost encyclopaedic knowledge of the Western Front] introduced me to, which also brings the artillery into the picture.

Mackintosh has always been one of my favourites. I chose 'To Sylvia' because it showed the conflict between home and the front, and the power the trenches had to draw men back, even when they had so much to live for. I was tempted to leave Owen out altogether, because he is given so much attention elsewhere; many critics seem to think that he *is* war poetry and I always wanted to say 'what about the others?' Leaving him out would have gone too far the other way, though, so here he is.

I was reluctant to include Vera Brittain at first, but her poems were good: I chose 'The Last Post' because we had heard so many last posts, and because the poem echoed the uncertainty of Sorley's 'Lost' and started to draw the sequence towards its close. I needed something which was quite clearly an end, which would draw all the threads together and leave an echo in the mind. I therefore chose Sassoon's 'To Leonide Massine'. There are so many poems which might have done it, all more familiar and more obvious than this one. I came across it by chance, having tried others, and it was such a perfect picture of the haunting power of war experience. It is a very beautiful image, it brings in the four years of war and that last line 'be still; you have drained the cup; you have played your part' was a perfect ending and a perfect epitaph for them all, who had played their part, each in the best way that he could, and left their poems like a message in a bottle to the future. That's how I wanted the book to end.

And that is how we have ended it.

The inclusion of Hodgson was inevitable. Charlotte came across 'Before Action' as a very young child and the poem, with its haunting power, introduced her to the idea of First World War poetry. This became a lasting interest. Later she began to research Hodgson's life and works and to collect material for a biography.

Everyone who saw it decreed that the beautiful folder should be developed into a book. Over the years we submitted it to a series of potential publishers. 'Too expensive to produce', 'Too narrow an audience', we were repeatedly told. Finally, we put a proposal to Leo Cooper in 1993. He fell in love with it too and made the wise decision to publish it, provided we included Edmund Blunden, Ivor Gurney, Francis Ledwidge, Isaac Rosenberg and Edward Thomas, who to him seemed serious omissions. This we were pleased to do, and we chose their poems reproduced here for equally idiosyncratic and personal reasons after discussion with Charlotte, who painted their portraits in similar style to the originals.

The reader is advised to read first the poems only, in sequential order, to see the unfolding development of the war and the combatants' attitudes to it, as intended by Charlotte. The essays are 'self-contained' and can be read in any order. Their purpose is to make the poets accessible to the modern reader, bring them alive and put them in their personal and military contexts.

Where incidents and events are common to more than one poet they are described only once in any detail, but cross-reference is made to the relevant chapter. It is extraordinary how often the poets crossed paths or shared experiences. With nearly nine million men of the British Empire under arms, what can have been the odds against Sassoon and Owen being at Craiglockhart at the same time, or that two of the war's greatest poets,

Sassoon and Graves, should serve in the same battalion (1st Royal Welch Fusiliers). To readers unfamiliar with the historical events of the First World War, the section on 'The War the Poets Knew' gives a brief summary and shows where the poets fitted in.

The poets' war can be put further into context by reference to *Major and Mrs Holt's Battlefield Guide to the Somme*, published by Leo Cooper in July, 1996, and *Major and Mrs Holt's Battle Maps of the Somme* and the *Ypres Salient*, published by T & V Holt Associates. They provide a background history to the battles in which many of the poets were engaged or emotionally involved, detailed descriptions of the battlefields and precise locations of the memorials and cemeteries which today mark them.

Tonie and Valmai Holt
Woodnesborough
1996

INTRODUCTION

The poetry of the war that was called 'Great' (it could not be called the First World War until there was a second one) seems to exert an ever-growing fascination on the youth of today. Undoubtedly it is readily available to them, as it is a standard feature of school and university curriculae, but that doesn't necessarily mean that they have to appreciate it.

Perhaps the identification of today's young people with similarly aged youngsters of 1914–18 can be attributed to the similarity of the conditions that surround them: each in a turbulent world where tomorrow is a question mark. Today's uncertainties seem to pale into insignificance when compared to the unspeakable horrors of the Great War, yet the voices from three-quarters of a century ago strike a vibrant, responsive chord. They form a link across the generations, so that one receives a glimmer of understanding of what they experienced to inspire such enduring lines.

They are like the violets from oversea sent by Roland Leighton to his lover, Vera Brittain, from the purgatory of 'Plugstreet' Wood, their faint perfume still perceptible.

The poetic cries from a distant battlefield are as varied as their authors. The received myth is of a moulded figure, modelled on an amalgam of Rupert Brooke, the Grenfells and Edward Tennant. He (not she, of course) is blonde, ethereal, handsome and aristocratic, with the languid energy of his public school, possibly university, background. He is officer material: conversant with the classics, and a superb, gallant leader of men. He has a strong, probably Christian, faith. His generic description is 'golden'. Poetry is his natural second language, with the accent of Henry Newbolt. His style is flower-ridden Georgian, cultivated by Edward Marsh; his ideas high, expressed in the noble language of a bygone, chivalrous age. He is a parfitt knight, above all young and innocent, the boyish crushes of his single-sex schooldays behind him, only momentarily, wistfully regretted.

Some of the chosen poets fit this mould and measure up to this 'ideal'. The majority were commissioned, and six won the MC for gallantry. Of Hodgson and Mackintosh this was almost to be expected from their backgrounds and personalities: sporting scholars with a deep sense of duty. Blunden, the shy, nature-loving poet, would perhaps not appear such an

1

automatic hero. To those who know only their bitter, anti-war poems and not their military careers, Owen's and Sassoon's awards seem more surprising. Sassoon used his when making his famous protest. The fifth was won by an exceptional man, Studdert Kennedy. A VC *manqué* was Julian Grenfell, who won the DSO but would have dearly loved to have emulated his VC cousin, Francis.

Gurney and Rosenberg, perhaps after David Jones and Ian Hiscock the war's most unsuitable and inept soldiers, were, understandably, privates. Yet so was Wilfrid Gibson, who moved in Brooke's circle. More unusual, perhaps, are the three NCO poets – Sergeants Coulson and Streets and Lance-Corporal Ledwidge. The concept of poesy does not seem to accord with one's perceptions of the stolid, hard-working, hard-cursing qualities required to hold a non-commissioned rank in the British (or, for that matter, German) army. This especially applies to the sergeant who, as all subalterns know, runs the whole show. Of these three examples, Streets, who was a Derbyshire miner before the war, and Ledwidge, eighth child of an evicted Irish tenant farmer, could be considered as true, little-educated working class. Coulson was a professional journalist, son of a journalist, who, when he enlisted and was encouraged to obtain a commission, said, 'I will do the thing fairly. I will take my place in the ranks.' We sometimes fail to understand from our world-weary, cynical contemporary attitudes and values that the men of 1914 were simple, utterly sincere and intense in their sense of duty and patriotism. Not only did they speak and write in the language of high devotion and chivalry, they really felt that way. By the time he was killed in October, 1916, Coulson had worked his way up, 'fairly', to the rank of sergeant and had been recommended for a commission.

As for the poets' expected traditional Christian faith, while Hodgson and Studdert Kennedy were Anglican clergymen's sons, Vera Brittain was a self-styled 'sceptic' during the war, and three of the poets (Frankau, Rosenberg and Sassoon) were Jewish. Frankau and Sassoon converted to Catholicism towards the end of their lives, as did Leighton. Although their religion did help many of them through the blackest days, several (even the padre, Studdert Kennedy) would question the justice of a God who permitted such unspeakable horrors and inhumanity as the war progressed, and thence their belief in Him and the role of the Church at the Front: 'The Bishop of Byegumb . . . He preached to our Brigade . . . he made me love Religion less and less' (Sassoon, 'Vicarious Christ', 1919).

Some poets have become icons or symbols of a certain attitude and style, which unfairly makes them two-dimensional and wholly predictable. The main polarization is to link everything patriotic, heroic, noble and unquestioning with Brooke and Grenfell, and everything that is realistic and justifiably bitter with Owen and Sassoon. The implication

2

therefore diminishes the former (as being naive and somewhat insensitive) and elevates the latter (as being able to understand and express the true horror of war). Brooke and Grenfell have earned this misconception with *The War Sonnets* and 'Into Battle' respectively, so the essays on them seek to redress the balance by showing the real men and the range of their work, feelings and attitudes to war. Nevertheless, throughout the book the fact that their names have taken on an adjectival quality is used in comparisons to denote a certain kind of poem, as the custom is so widespread and accepted that the reader immediately understands what is meant by 'a Brooke' or 'a Grenfell' – unfair though that may be to the true poet.

In recent assessments too much (or so it seems to those who understand the intense but pure nature of comradely love in dangerous situations) has been made of the homo-erotic element in First World War poetry. The eminent writer, critic and historian Paul Fussell devotes a whole chapter to the subject in his superbly boat-rocking assessment, *The Great War and Modern Memory*. Martin Taylor's extremely interesting anthology, *Lads*, with many highly original choices of poets and poems, somewhat stretches credulity in discovering a gay in every communal bathing stream and behind every shell-shattered tree.

Graves and Sassoon were undoubtedly both in love with 'Dick Tiltwood' (Lieutenant David Thomas) and perhaps with other youths before they went on to marry. Some of Owen's work is undeniably homo-erotic, that of others (Graves, Gurney and Gibson) would often sound so to the uninitiated. But the supposedly homo-erotic tell-tale images of clean limbs, beautiful youths, expressions of comradely love, and so on can be found in the lines of many uncompromisingly heterosexual poets. Mackintosh's love for his men cries almost unbearably through his searing poem, 'In Memoriam', yet his love for Sylvia, his fiancée, shines as strongly in the poem selected for this volume. But does it really matter whether the poets preferred boys or girls? Does it in any way add or detract from the worth of the poetry itself?

As it happens, the majority of the poets are demonstrably 'normal' in their preferences and allegiances. Vernède was a fond and amusing husband, Thomas a faithful but somewhat neglectful one. Blunden married in 1918, Seeger wrote sultry love poems *à la* Baudelaire, but with women in mind. Two of the poets, Vera Brittain and Roland Leighton, were engaged to each other; and Brooke, while demonstrating many of the supposedly homo-erotic tendencies, expressed the joy and pain of man's love for woman in many of his pre-war poems (and indeed was the authors' favourite love poet in their courtship days, long before they realized his First World War connections).

To several poets a mother figure remained the dominating influence in their young lives. Edward Tennant was writing love poems to his mother, the beautiful Pamela Glenconner, at the age of eight: 'She is something quite divine, And joy, oh joy, this mother's mine!' Julian Grenfell, jealous of the lovers of his demanding and flirtatious mother Ettie, wrote frequently to her from the front. Alan Seeger was a regular writer to his mother. Discussing his chances of returning alive, he admonished her, 'If I should not, you must be proud like a Spartan mother and feel it is your contribution to the triumph of the cause whose righteousness you feel so keenly.' Roland Leighton, despite his love for Vera Brittain, was also strongly attached to his mother. Vera pronounced that, 'A man who cares deeply for his mother can be trusted very far.' Ledwidge, when wounded in hospital, wrote, 'My mother . . . I bless the God/Who such a mother gave/This poor bird-hearted singer of a day'. Coulson wrote longingly of the 'one who'll softly creep/To kiss me ere I fall asleep/And tuck me 'neath the counterpane,/As if I were a boy again.' Owen's mother Susan's legendary possessiveness is well documented in published letters, and one can even be persuaded to subscribe to the facile theory that their relationship influenced his sexuality. But is it not natural that young men, some of them mere boys, many of them far from family and home for the first time in their lives, should think of their mothers' reassuring love when in unfamiliar and dangerous situations, and that public schoolboys, parted from their parents at an early age, should look on their remote and often glamorous mothers with longing and a sort of reverence?

One major influence on the lives of all writers of the era was the 'Georgian' poetry movement. A leading light behind the movement was Edward Marsh, who was a great patron of many struggling young writers and artists. The idea originated with Rupert Brooke, who in September, 1912, half-seriously proposed to Marsh and Wilfrid Gibson that he should play a practical joke on the public by writing a book of poems under twelve pseudonyms and passing them off as the work of a dozen promising writers (Hassall, *Edward Marsh*). Marsh said they should find twelve 'flesh and blood' poets and found himself landed with the real job of editing an anthology. As a start they chose Bottomley, Brooke (of course), de la Mare, Davies, Flecker, Housman and Pound. Then a collective name had to be found. Marsh suggested they take the name of the reigning sovereign, and so the 'Georgians' were born.

They considered themselves modern and innovative, but their pastoral themes made virtually no reference to current events or issues. Dominic Hibberd felt that 'in place of the grand, vague diction of the late Victorians, the new poetry offered plain language, simplicity, sharpness of detail and a commitment to realism that did not duck the unpleasant. Brooke was the prewar leader, with his cool, witty, irreverent style.' Cyril Connolly called their verses 'an explosion of Marsh-gas'. T.S. Eliot, reviewing the 1918 Georgian anthology, said 'the Georgians caress everything they touch' and that their prevailing tone was 'minor-Keatsian'.

Bergonzi felt there is some truth in the description 'the fag-end of late-Victorian romanticism, a nadir before the advent of the triumphant modernists'. Yet they helped to bridge that gap and their legacy, at the very least, is a handful of fine, lyrical poems that have enriched popular anthologies of the inter-war and post-Second World War years. Hibberd also pointed out that 'one of the neglected aspects of First World War poetry is that much of the best of it was either Georgian or Georgian-influenced.'

The first Georgian anthology was published in the New Year of 1913. It was reviewed by Lascelles Abercrombie in the *Manchester Guardian,* Edward Thomas in *The Daily Chronicle,* A.C. Benson in *The Cambridge Review* (he felt Brooke's 'The Fish' among the best of the poems), Edmund Gosse in *The Morning Post,* and the critic of *The Times Literary Supplement,* who singled out Brooke's poems as the only ones to be 'written in just that emotional simplicity which the other poets have eschewed and passion is to be heard in them, even if it is a little shrill.' At least the Georgians had made a considerable mark with their debut collection, and their influence in subsequent years was considerable.

Most of the war poets were brought up to read, enjoy and often memorize the Greek and Latin classics, the King James Bible, *Hymns Ancient and Modern,* the works of Shakespeare, the novels of Sir Walter Scott, 'Morte D'Arthur' (embracing the ideals of chivalry), romantic poets such as Keats and Shelley, and Victorians like Tennyson. They read Kipling, whom they either adored (Frankau) or loathed (Blunden), stirring adventure stories by Henty and Ballantyne, and the *Boy's Own Paper.* Palgrave's *Golden Treasury* was a much-loved anthology and a well-worn copy often accompanied its owner to the front. Housman's *A Shropshire Lad* was also a favourite, as was Hardy – Sassoon read *Tess of the d'Urbervilles* as he watched an attack go in on 1 July, 1916. They were also aware of contemporary poets like Masefield, Flecker and de la Mare, eagerly awaiting each new poem. From these diverse influences, each evolved his own particular and individual mode of expression. They were all writing in the Georgian period, although some can more truly be categorized as Georgian (such as Thomas, Brooke, and Gibson) than others (such as Frankau and Streets).

Another important factor, at least in the lives of the more upper-class poets, was an extraordinarily scintillating and deliberately exclusive group, drawn from the top echelons of British society, known as 'The Souls'. Wilfred Scawen Blunt, the amorous poet, gives the most likely source (there are other, quite different explanations) for this name. Lady Tennant showed him a book about 'Souls . . . the surface soul, the deep soul and the mixed soul, half clever, half childish (the book had something to do, I think, with the name given to the set of which her daughters were such notable members)'.

The Souls were an almost incestuous clique or 'set' confined to a dozen or so 'in' families: Asquith, Balfour, Charteris (Elcho, Wemyss), Curzon, Cust, Grenfell (Desborough), Herbert (Pembroke), Horner, Lister (Ribblesdale), Lyttelton, Manners (Rutland), Tennant (Glenconner) and Wyndham. The men went to school together (mostly at Eton, Harrow or Winchester), the girls were each others' best friends, many families spent the holidays together in the great mansions that were their country residences, and most also had town houses in desirable London squares. There they played sophisticated, witty word games, flirted and fornicated, had endless discussions about their own sparkling unconventionality, created their own 'in' language, ate, drank, wrote elegant poetry and prose, drew and painted (some with great talent), made music, shot game, fished, cycled, played tennis and golf and danced.

Some of their children formed their own set, 'The Coterie', in a somewhat cynical rebellion against the Souls. Brought up in a hothouse of arrogant intellectualism to be aware of their inheritance of excellence and superiority, they seemed poised to fulfil their parents' ambitions for them as the achieving perpetuators of a lifestyle and philosophy. The 1914–18 war was to shatter those hopes and, as happened to no other class of society (except in the pockets of the working-class Northern 'Pals' battalions), was virtually to wipe out a generation, whether they belonged to the Coterie or were on the peripheries of the tight-knit set. (Peter Simkins proves in *Kitchener's Army* that it is sheer myth that a complete generation was eliminated in general terms.) Herbert Asquith's brilliant son Raymond was killed in September, 1916, at 39 the oldest of the Coterie losses. He had been at their very centre. The Wemyss's lost their heir, Hugo Charteris, in April, 1916, and Yvo, the baby of the family, in October, 1915. The Desboroughs (Grenfells) lost Julian in April, 1915, Billy in July, 1915 and twin cousins Riversdale in September, 1914 and Francis, VC, in May, 1915. The Horners (whose daughter Katherine was Raymond Asquith's widow) lost Edward in November, 1917 the Ribblesdales' son Charles Lister died in August, 1915. Lord George Vernon was killed at Suvla Bay, and Patrick Shaw-Stewart was also killed at Gallipoli in December, 1915. And the Glenconners lost Edward Tennant in September, 1916, the youngest death at nineteen. His cousin, Percy Wyndham, was the first of the Coterie to be killed, on 1 September, 1914. From these ranks came two of the poets in this collection, Edward Tennant and Julian Grenfell.

Whatever the dominating personal relationship or literary influence in their lives, the work of the poets included in this anthology, with their different backgrounds, countries and schools and their varied personalities, gives an illuminating insight into the Great War. Their emotions and feelings run a contrasting gamut of reactions to their situation: hopeful, patriotic, dutiful, questioning, bitter, cynical, despairing, angry, lonely, bewildered, sad, humorous, loving – taking one, perhaps, as close as it is possible to be to 1914–18. Their descriptions – of battles, gas attacks, trench raids, time behind the lines, artillery barrages, the battered French and Belgian countryside, losing a pal, being on sentry duty, fearing death – flesh out the military histories, the battalion and divisional war diaries. Their enduring legacy will not fade, as do violets from oversea.

THE WAR THE POETS KNEW

When Archduke Franz Ferdinand was assassinated on 28 June, 1914, the prospect of a major war in Europe filled the minds of most thinking people. Established older poets such as de la Mare, Hardy, Kipling and Yeats doubtless sharpened their pencils in anticipation, but while they were all to contribute to the literature of the war that was to come, it was to be younger, newer poets, many in the front lines, who would record the true immediacy of the struggles ahead.

Hostilities began on the Western Front when German armies invaded neutral Belgium on 3 August, 1914. Following a master plan conceived by General Count Alfred von Schlieffen, they struck first to the west and then turned south and headed for Paris. By the first week in September they were at the outskirts of the city, an advance extraordinary for its speed.

The British public saw the participation of their army in the conflict as help for 'poor little Belgium', to whom Britain was contracted in defence by the Treaty of London. Artists like the Dutch cartoonist Raemakers depicted Belgium as a young, helpless woman being assaulted by a ravening Hun, and the nation enthusiastically responded to the call for volunteers and cheered as the regular soldiers of the British Expeditionary Force went to war.

The BEF met the invader on the Franco–Belgian border at the end of the German strike west, just three weeks after the war began. The site is today marked by a memorial pronouncing that the first shots of the Great War were fired at that spot. It isn't true, of course, because the Belgians and French had been fighting for three weeks. It *is* true to say that the first British shots of the war were fired there, but it indicates a peculiarly British view of the conflict; that it was a struggle between the Germans and the British, with occasional intervention by the French who provided most of the playing field.

The British baptism took place at Mons, and that action and the 'Retreat from Mons' that followed, popularized by Arthur Machen's story of the 'Angels', began the home tradition of chronicling the progress of the war through named battles. It is quite an effective technique, because the thinking of the politicians and military commanders alike tended towards the digital rather than the analogue – or more simply, sometimes they sat and thought and sometimes they just sat. Thus it can be meaningful to relate the story of the war by referring to a series of battles on certain dates, as if nothing went on in between. Something did, of course. Men died by what was euphemistically called 'natural wastage'.

After the Retreat the Allies turned and stood on the River Marne. The Germans were at the gates of Paris, and the five days from 5 to 10 September were perhaps the most important in the last hundred years of the history of Europe. Thanks mainly to the coolness of Joffre, the French Commander-in-Chief, the Allies won a strategic victory, but the world would never be the same again. In just one month of war each side had suffered more than half a million casualties – killed, wounded or missing. And the cause of those casualties was firepower: the use of modern artillery and machine guns, which would come to dictate the culture of the war the poets knew. Because of the terrible efficiency of these new engines of war, men dug into the earth to find shelter, and in so doing created defensive lines of trenches that led to stalemate. The commanders became obsessed with the need to break that impasse.

Unable to penetrate the Allied line on the Marne, the Germans began a retreat. After a pause the Allies followed, in what became known as the Race to the Sea, at the end of which the BEF found itself defending an ancient town in Flanders called Ypres. Its name would become engraved upon the nation's heart as 'Wipers', a place about which Tommy would sing, 'Far, far, from Wipers, I want to be.'

October, 1914, saw the beginning of the three-week battle of First Ypres, at the end of which the British had suffered another 58,000 casualties. During the Christmas that followed, German and British soldiers declared an unofficial truce and played football in no-man's-land while their commanders tried to come to terms with the almost 500 miles of trenches that now separated their armies from the North Sea to Switzerland. They would continue to do so until the end of the war in 1918.

When the BEF went to France (even though the Battle of Mons was in Belgium, most Tommies thought that they were in France) in August, 1914, it was composed mainly of regular soldiers (among them Julian Grenfell) strengthened by 70,000 special reservists called up during August. Three days after Britain declared war on Germany Lord Kitchener issued his call for 100,000 volunteers, with the slogan 'Your King and Country Need You' immortalized by Alfred Leete's dramatic poster. Until early in 1916 all the reinforcements for Britain's forces were volunteers (all the poets in this book except Grenfell), and thereafter they were conscripts. Gibson, unfit for overseas service, served at home in the Army Service Corps.

As 1915 began the Western Front was hardening into two armed camps separated by ever more complicated lines of trenches. Behind each system new populations grew up, populations of soldiers with specialist communities like 'infantry' (Coulson, Graves, Gurney, Hodgson, Leighton,

Mackintosh, Owen, Rosenberg, Sassoon, Seeger, Sorley, Streets, Tennant and Vernède were among them) or 'artillery' (Frankau, McCrae and Thomas), each needing its own form of support yet subject to the same privations. Over the four years of the war the 'strip' developments of the Western Front forced the creation of new systems of supply, command and control for populations numbering millions. The red-hatted staff officer became a hated archetypal figure ('Lord . . .Please keep the extra ADC,/From horrid scenes, and sights of blood' – Grenfell) as he tried to administer to the needs of the fighting soldier, while the soldier himself became alienated from those at home by his inability to communicate to them the appalling conditions in which he had so often to live and fight.

In Britain the growing casualty lists published in the newspapers told the nation that this was total war. The women left behind began to fear the appearance of the telegraph boy on his bicycle. Many wives left the envelope unopened on the table in the hope that if they did not read it the news would go away, a situation dramatically captured after the war by Novak–Varsovie's black-and-white drawing of a mother and child standing at bay from an unopened telegram which radiates a sinister glow.

Yet with all the changes the war was ringing within the societies of the combatants, there is no doubt where the focus of experience lay – in the trenches. Within and around them suffered the soldier. At intervals each side would lumber into a planned assault upon the other and it would be graced with a name – Mons, le Cateau, First Ypres, Neuve Chapelle (the first British-initiated offensive of the war), Second Ypres (when the Germans introduced poison gas), Gallipoli (that brave but doomed Churchillian attempt to outflank the trenches of the Western Front in which Brooke died *en route* and Herbert Coulson, and Ledwidge fought), Loos (when British poison gas blew back upon the Tommies), Verdun (a French affair that actually came to the notice of the British public) and the Somme, the offensive launched on 1 July, 1916, that occasioned almost 60,000 British casualties on its first day. So the chronicle continues via the Canadian success at Vimy, the first mass tank attack at Cambrai, the support to the Italians after Caporetto, the near-disaster of the Kaiser's Battle in March, 1918, and the entry of the Americans at Château Thierry and St Mihiel. Each land battle was launched from trenches, strove to overcome trenches and used soldiers who lived in trenches.

Of all of the battles that chronicle the progress of the war the most in-famous is that of Passchendaele, the second part of the Third Battle of Ypres. Third Ypres opened on 7 June, 1917, with a surprise assault on the Messines Ridge which gained the southern end of the feature that at its northern point expires in the small village of Passchendaele (Studdert Kennedy won his MC during the battle). The ridge joining the two extremes, known as the Passchendaele Ridge, was occupied by the Germans; its capture was the aim of General Haig, the British

Commander-in-Chief. Despite the success of the Messines phase, the generals waited another seven weeks in full view of the enemy before launching the attack known as Passchendaele on 31 July, 1917. Almost immediately the attack stuck in the mud of Flanders and junior commanders advised Haig to stop. He did not. Conditions on the battlefield were so horrendous that one senior officer burst into tears on seeing for the first time the morass of mud, the slick pools of filthy water, the jetsam of dismembered equipment and the swollen remains of countless corpses of men and animals. 'Did we really send men to fight in that?' he asked.

Mud was one trial of the trenches ('you were sodden-wet/With greasy coal-black mud' – Frankau) and the water that often lay knee-deep in them brought its own disease – trench foot, where the feet bulged, making it impossible to wear boots and extremely painful to walk. Then there were rats, bloated to feline size from feeding on the dead; while smaller parasites, the fleas, ticks and cooties (lice), also spread their own disease – trench fever, that sapped a man's strength and held him open to other afflictions. Movement along trenches, wading through a sea of mud, was exhausting. It was unpleasant, too, in that the walls were dovetailed with the dead and arms and legs stuck out everywhere, so men were tempted to climb up upon the parapet to seek firmer ground and were then picked off by snipers. Over all of the degradation of the battlefield thundered the sound of the guns ('the hot shells scream' – Coulson), itself often enough to send men mad.

Yet in the vile atmosphere of battle, love and comradeship found fertile ground. Soldiers truly laid down their lives for their friends ('but they died well,/They charged in line, and, in the same line, fell' – Graves). Officers loved their men ('You were only David's father but I had fifty sons' – Mackintosh); this was not sexual, but the regard for one human being for another when all the social conventions that govern everyday conduct are stripped away by the prospect of imminent death.

The battlefield was a disgusting place, yet men stayed there. Of course there were a few deserters, but the overwhelming majority did what they saw to be their duty to defend King and Country. They stayed in order that their mates would not think ill of them, or because they had been brought up to believe 'Dulce et decorum est, pro patria mori'. The sensations of each day became heightened, colours brighter, and the singing of larks the music of the gods. It was a simple time. Do or die – or, in many cases, do *and* die.

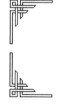 

Charles Hamilton Sorley

CAPTAIN, SUFFOLK REGIMENT

LOST

Across my past imaginings
Has dropped a blindness silent and slow.
My eye is bent on other things
Than those it once did see and know.

I may not think on those dear lands
(O far away and long ago!)
Where the old battered signpost stands
And silently the four roads go

East, west, south and north,
And the cold winter winds do blow.
And what the evening will bring forth
Is not for me nor you to know.

December, 1914

CAPTAIN CHARLES HAMILTON SORLEY

The favourite profitless, but nevertheless irresistible, game of Great War poetry buffs is 'What might he have become if he had lived?' The list of contenders in the game is long, but the winner would probably emerge as Charles Sorley. He was only twenty when he was killed, yet his personality, poetry and letters show a candour, strength and maturity that belie his years. In his short productive period Sorley wrote some of the most memorable verses of the war.

Sorley had all the ingredients of an ideal First World War poet. He was born on 19 May, 1895, to an academic father who became Professor of Moral Philosophy at Cambridge in 1900. His parents were of Scottish extraction and remained resolutely Scottish in outlook despite their English domicile – an attitude passed on to their three children, Charles, his twin brother and elder sister. Charles was proud of the fact that Sorley meant 'wanderer' in Gaelic and tried to live up to the name spiritually. The boys went to King's College Choir School and then, unusually for twins, were sent to separate public schools: Charles, the outgoing achiever, won an open scholarship to Marlborough.

Sorley loved his school, although not unreservedly, and towards the end of his successful career there (he became head of house) was vocally critical of a competitive system which 'deliberately overdevelops the nasty tyrannical instincts'. He is always categorized as a Marlburian, but as far as he was concerned it was *faute de mieux*. 'If I must have an appellation to go through life with . . . it is Marlburian', he wrote to a schoolfriend, explaining that he meant the 'little red-capped town' of Marlborough rather than the school. However, his ties to it remained strong throughout his short life. One of his last letters (5 October, 1915) was to the school's headmaster, and his posthumously-published collected work was called *Marlborough and Other Poems* by his father, which more than anything perpetuated the link.

Sorley was in the Marlborough OTC, but cross-country running was his favourite outdoor occupation. He loved the countryside, and running gave him the opportunity to enjoy the beautiful Wiltshire views as well as the exhilarating exercise. In 'The Song of the Ungirt Runners' he evokes the joy of the schoolboys: 'We swing our ungirt hips,/And lightened are our eyes . . ./We do not run for prize . . ./But we run because

16

we must/Through the great wide air.' He was also active in more academic spheres, belonging to the debating society, contributing articles to the literary society and writing poetry.

Charles was a thoughtful boy and responded to the popular appeal for 'national efficiency', inspired by Captain Scott's gallant death in October, 1912, with the slightly priggish poem, 'A Call to Action', first published in *The Marlburian* (Hibberd, *The First World War*). Honing his craft and crystallizing his attitudes, Sorley had strong, individual opinions, admiring Masefield but considering Tennyson to be 'pre-eminently paltry'. He was getting bored with the classics and the rigid ethos of public school life:

> O come and see, it's such a sight,
> So many boys all doing right:
> To see them underneath the yoke,
> Blindfolded by the older folk,
> Move at a most impressive rate
> Along the way that is called straight.

He developed a strong socialist conscience, regretting that 'poetry up till now has been mainly by and for and about the Upper Classes'. A desire to work with those less privileged than himself by teaching in a working men's college made him eventually leave Marlborough at the end of the 1913 Christmas term, after winning an Oxford scholarship.

In January, 1914, Sorley travelled to Mecklenburg in Germany to perfect his German before enrolling at the University of Jena in April. He revelled in the freedom, in contrast to the constricting school regime, and his letters (happily preserved and published, *Letters*, 1919, the source of most information about Sorley) are exuberant and humorous. 'German soldiers have an unfortunate way of marching, as if there were somebody in front whom they had to kick.' He disliked the aggressive, anti-Semitic behaviour of the students in the university corps, but found the soldiers' wholehearted singing of songs about the Fatherland infectious: 'I felt that perhaps I could die for *Deutschland* – and I have never had an inkling of that feeling about England and never shall.' He even told a schoolfriend, 'I am not a patriotic OM [Old Marlburian],' but perhaps seeing the German student corps made him wonder, somewhat satirically, about his old OTC:

> And is there still a Folly called the corps
> Allowed out twice a week and thinking then
> It's learning how to kill its fellow-men?

He admired the hard-working, enthusiastic and intellectual Germans and his taste in literature developed. He abandoned Masefield and Hardy, enjoying the more demanding works of Ibsen, Goethe and Rilke. His affection for the country author Richard Jefferies stayed with him, however: reading Jefferies transported him to the English countryside he still missed, despite his zest for life in Germany. The schoolboy was quickly growing up into an original, intelligent young man, a bit of a rebel with a hint of cynicism, very much his own person.

When, in the last week of July, 1914, it was becoming obvious that the situation between Germany and Britain was fast deteriorating, Professor Sorley wrote asking Charles to return immediately. But Charles, who was on a walking holiday in Trier, was arrested and briefly imprisoned on 3 August. His feelings must have been in a turmoil when war was declared, his loyalties torn. Nevertheless, he returned home.

He was determined to enlist, but in what, and as what? He considered putting his desire for classlessness into practice by serving as a private soldier, but couldn't resist the regular army commission offered him in the Suffolk Regiment. On the last Wednesday in August he was gazetted a 'Temp 2nd Lieut' in the 7th (Service) Battalion of the Suffolk Regiment. He spent a month at the OTC Training Camp at Churn in Berkshire, and on 18 September joined the regiment at Shorncliffe.

He did not go with the zeal and joy of a Brooke. 'I am full of mute and burning rage and annoyance and sulkiness about it. "Serving one's country" is so unpicturesque and unheroic when it comes to the point . . . But I'm thankful to see that Kipling hasn't written a poem yet.' It was fashionable with young men of Sorley's generation who had poetic pretensions to scorn the old master. Sorley even criticized his hero, Hardy: '"Men Who March Away" is the most arid poem . . . besides being untrue of the sentiments of the ranksman going to war.' Sorley saw, rather, 'A hundred thousand million mites we go'. In 'Poets', written that same September, he takes the role of the inarticulate soldier talking to the privileged poet; 'We have a dumb spirit within:/The exceeding bitter agony/But not the exceeding bitter cry.' He still saw soldiers as potential cannon fodder under 'the old system of hiring your Wellington and a handful of hundred thousand criminals to bleed for you' which he, tongue in cheek, felt 'was, from the point of view of civilization and culture, more beneficial to the country' than allowing scholars and students to 'let out the torch of learning'.

On 14 November he wrote that he was sick of the sound of the word 'England'. Reverting to the theme of 'A Call to Action', he deplored the fact that he was 'training to fight for that deliberate hypocrisy, that terrible middle-class sloth of outlook and appalling "imaginative indolence" that has marked us out from generation to generation . . . I am giving my body . . . to fight against the most enterprising nation in the world.' It took courage to voice such unpopular sentiments, going against the heroic patriotic grain of the first months of the war. In 'To Germany' Sorley continued the almost pro-German theme, but in a less confrontational manner.

In December, 1914, Sorley wrote the poem chosen here to represent the early days of the war. He described it as 'the last of my Marlborough poems': it was looking forward, but the future he saw was uncertain, and might even be death.

Sorley sent several poems written during his training to his parents the month before he went to France in May, 1915, and these tend to be anthologized under that later date. One such is an exceptional poem, untitled by Sorley but sometimes called 'Route March' or, more usually, by its first line, 'All the Hills and Vales Along'. Increasingly critics recognize it as a skilfully crafted work, blending a deceptively jaunty, lilting marching rhythm and pleasing originality with the stark reality that 'the singers are the chaps/Who are going to die perhaps'. I.M. Parsons, in the introduction to his much-read anthology *Men Who March Away*, calls it 'the most remarkable of all the poems' in the early war. He first took it at face value as demonstrating Sorley's 'magnificent zest about nearly everything he wrote, a zest which is frequently betrayed into naïveté by the inadequacy of his technique'; then later re-evaluated it as 'not only singularly moving but, in its beautifully controlled tone, a technical triumph astonishing in a young man who was only twenty when he was killed.'

On 28 April, 1915, Sorley wrote his much-reproduced criticism of Rupert Brooke (see Brooke) on reading his obituary in *The Morning Post*, a paper hitherto critical of Brooke but now 'loud in his praise because he has conformed to their stupid axiom of literary criticism that the only stuff of poetry is violent physical experience, by dying on active service.' It is rarely noted, however, that Sorley did in fact praise 'Sonnet No IV', 'The Fish' and 'Grantchester'.

Unfortunately Sorley himself would soon fulfil that axiom. On 30 May, 1915, his battalion arrived in France, at Acquin, where he wrote with the wry irony that characterized many of his letters, 'in four-score hours we will pull up our braces and fight . . . and I shall march hotly to the firing line, by turn critic, actor, hero, coward and soldier of fortune.' His billets were in Nieppe, where on 12 June he wrote 'Two Sonnets'. 'Sonnet 1' returns to the image of the signpost of 'Lost', now clearly leading him to 'a land I did not know and that I wished to know,' the land of death longed for by romantic poets through the ages. 'Sonnet 2' is more explicit and examines the nature of death. Like Grenfell, for whom death promises 'increase', Sorley sees 'promise' being touched and blossoming 'when you are dead'.

Sorley kept in close touch with his schoolfriends, including Sidney Woodroffe of the Rifle Brigade, who won a posthumous VC when he was killed on 30 July, 1915, just after the Germans' first use of the flame-thrower at Hooge. He is commemorated on the Menin Gate. In his memory Sorley wrote the surprisingly accepting and conventional lament, 'In Memoriam S.C.W., VC' (8 September, 1915).

The battalion served at Ploegsteert Wood at the southern edge of the grim Ypres Salient. The Suffolks' trenches were only seventy yards from the trenches of 'Brother Boche' (as Sorley, like all his fellows, was now calling the Germans). In his letters Sorley described the daily life of censoring the products of the soldiers' indefatigable letter-writing sessions, of creating a tolerant *modus vivendi* with the enemy, of the danger of night patrols by the enemy wire, and the general monotony. He soon began to share the soldiers' healthy distrust and dislike of staff officers and their 'pink-faced ADCs', and to admire Tommy's phlegmatic attitude. 'The British private has this virtue: he will never be impressed.'

His parents wanted to publish the poems (he called them 'contributions') he continued to send with his letters. He thanked them for the suggestion but regretted that he didn't have the opportunity or inclination to revise his works, and that he would rather 'let it be' for either three years 'or the duration'.

At the end of July he planned and led a bombing raid on the heavily-fortified German trenches opposite his own. He meticulously reconnoitred the ground and knew virtually every inch. Just as Sorley and three other bombers were pulling the pins from their grenades, one man dropped his and it exploded under him. The others managed to throw their bombs, but the alerted Germans raked the ground with rifle and machine-gun fire. Sorley pulled the wounded man into a shell-hole, but there were more casualties and to Sorley the man that he brought in felt 'like carrying a piece of living pulp'. He never forgot the hideous image, or the sound the man made when he picked him up.

By the end of August Sorley, now promoted to temporary captain and second-in-command of D Company, was writing about the nauseous relief he felt when he discovered a wounded man had died so that 'we won't have to carry him in . . . One is hardened by now: purged of all false pity: perhaps more selfish than before.' He continued his dangerous patrols to the German wire. 'Thorns in their side we are, often pricking ourselves more than them,' he commented to his mother.

Throughout September preparations were made for a major Allied thrust in the mining area of Loos. The British used poison gas for the first time and it was less than successful, blowing back on to British troops over a considerable part of the front (see Graves). Penetrations of the enemy line just north of Loos failed due to the reserves being held too far in the rear and, despite the use of the newly-formed Guards Division, no real progress was made. The battle began on

25 September, 1915, and three days later Sorley's battalion moved up to relieve the Guards. Battalion diaries confirm the appalling planning in the moving and equipping of reserves, a major factor in the later resignation of the British Commander-in-Chief, Sir John French (connived at by his ambitious second-in-command, Sir Douglas Haig, who took over from him).

Although the major battle was over, fighting continued into October and Sorley coped with the situation by putting his mind into neutral. With the irony that was the hallmark of his letters, he wrote, 'I'm now beginning to think that free thinkers should give up their minds into subjection for we who have given our actions and volitions into subjection gain such marvellous rest thereby. For the present we find high relief in making ourselves soldiers . . .'. On 12 October the battalion moved into the front line opposite the heavily-defended Hohenzollern Redoubt. On 13 October Sorley's company commander was seriously wounded and Sorley was charged with securing the company's defences. In the afternoon the Germans opened up with heavy machine-gun fire and Sorley was hit in the head, perhaps by a sniper. He died instantly. 'Earth . . ./Shall rejoice and blossom too/When the bullet reaches you.'

In his kitbag was the sonnet which, of all his work, might at first glance have been written by Owen, 'When You See Millions of the Mouthless Dead'. The image of the pale, mouthless battalions of dead marching across one's dreams has a shocking impact. The plea to say no 'soft things' to the heedless dead is, according to Moorcroft Wilson, a protest against Brooke's heroic phrases. 'Say only this,' he commands, 'They are dead.' Yet it could equally have been a response to Binyon's 'The Fallen' (published in 1914, so Sorley would almost inevitably have read it), with its same image of marching battalions and the statement, 'We will remember them.'

His body was lost in subsequent fighting, and Sorley is commemorated on the Loos Memorial to the Missing at Dud Corner Cemetery.

Contrary to his expressed wishes, Sorley's father published his slim volume of work, *Marlborough and Other Poems*, in January, 1916. His fellow poets thought highly of them. Blunden described him as 'Another poet who, dying, became famous . . . denied the opportunity to witness and to condemn at length the war of attrition and the attrition of war' (*The Soldier Poets of 1914–1918*, 1930). Graves wrote excitedly to Eddie Marsh, the editor of *Georgian Poetry*, that he had fallen in love with this brilliant young poet whose death was such a waste. Graves identified closely with Sorley: they were born in the same year, spent the same years at public school and came out to France in the same month. He particularly admired 'Sonnet 2'.

Others agreed with Graves; indeed, John Masefield, the Poet

Laureate, is reported as saying 'Sorley was potentially the greatest poet lost to us in that war . . . had Sorley lived, he might have become our greatest dramatist since Shakespeare.' He was thus declaring Sorley the outright winner in the 'What might he have become?' game.

The Hon. Julian Grenfell D.S.O.

CAPTAIN, ROYAL DRAGOONS

PRAYER FOR THOSE ON THE STAFF

Fighting in mud, we turn to Thee
In these dread times of battle, Lord,
To keep us safe, if so may be,
From shrapnel, snipers, shell and sword.

Yet not on us — (for we are men
Of meaner clay, who fight in clay) —
But on the Staff, the Upper Ten,
Depends the issue of the day.

The Staff is working with its brains
While we are sitting in the trench;
The Staff the universe ordains
(Subject to Thee and General French).

God, help the Staff — especially
The young ones, many of them sprung
From our high aristocracy;
Their task is hard, and they are young.

O Lord, who mad'st all things to be
And madest some things very good
Please keep the extra ADC
From horrid scenes, and sights of blood . . .

Belgium, early 1915.

CAPTAIN THE HONOURABLE JULIAN GRENFELL, DSO

Julian Grenfell would seem on the surface the simplest poet to read. He is, in reality, one of the most complicated and difficult to fathom. Many perceive him as a stereotype: a privileged aristocrat who revelled in war and wrote one memorable poem, 'Into Battle'. It is an easily adopted misconception.

Born on 30 March, 1888, Grenfell was Lord Desborough's heir, from a line with a long, distinguished military tradition. His mother, née Ethel (but always known as Ettie) Fane, was a considerable heiress in her own right, descended from Earl Cowper and the Earl of Westmorland. Orphaned at three, she bolstered her self-confidence by surrounding herself with devoted admirers, be they husband, sons or other men. Expected to make a brilliant match, she surprised her friends by marrying the handsome but unexceptional Willy Grenfell, a fine athlete and Oxford graduate who adored her and tolerated her liaisons with other men throughout their long life together. Julian was tormented and made jealous by his capricious, flirtatious and possessive mother: outwardly also an adoring and stimulating parent, she recorded her five children's precocious gems in *Pages From a Family Journal* which she published privately.

Grenfell didn't fit comfortably into the brittle, pretentious, literate society of his parents' generation of the 'Souls', in which Ettie was a star. A sensitive and somewhat serious child who found this milieu artificial and hypocritical, he grew up to distrust relationships and personal involvement. He was indelibly damaged by Ettie's constant demands that her children should be perpetually bright, cheerful, sociable and successful. He learned at an early age to hide any worries, problems, depressions or anxieties from her and to bottle them up, making himself dangerously withdrawn.

Grenfell's childhood was traditional: nanny, governess, prep school at ten, Eton at thirteen. He was a good athlete, a keen hunter, and fond of nature. He was also intelligent and naturally academic, editing the school magazine (and a rival satirical magazine) at Eton. But he refused to conform to Ettie's design for him. In 1905 he wrote in a poem to her, 'I won't become a Social Pet'. Surprisingly and to her credit, Ettie, who often amended entries in her published family journal to make her children sound more loving towards her, included this protest as it stood. Her son's resentment may well have been sparked by her relationship with twenty-year-old Archie Gordon. Imagine the humiliation of a youth being compared unfavourably to his mother's lover (although the Edwardian use of that word would equate to 'suitor' or 'courtier' today), only three years his senior.

When Julian left school for Oxford in 1906 he was in open confrontation with Ettie, calling his protests 'fights for life'. His mental equilibrium suffered and he veered between bouts of unexplained 'illnesses' and periods of frenzied activity with outbursts of violent rage. He shunned the company of his fun-loving friends, and by 1908 complained of 'feeling dead inside' and unable to work. He was suffering from a nervous breakdown, pronounced underweight and overworked, and his planned twenty-first birthday celebrations were cancelled. The family disappointment was sent to rest with an aunt and slept for days on end.

After four months a refreshed Julian felt strong enough to break away from the claustrophobic family atmosphere and make his own friends. He became entranced by the dazzling Manners sisters (Marjorie, Letty and the compulsive siren, Diana), falling hopelessly in love with Marjorie. Ettie thoroughly disapproved of the family, scathingly calling them 'the Hotbed', and did everything she could to discourage Julian from coming under their spell. The new, independent Grenfell rebelled. 'The one set you hate is the Hotbed; the one set I like is the Hotbed,' he wrote. Unfortunately for him, Marjorie married the Marquess of Anglesey and Diana never felt that he was her type.

Hurting from these rejections, Grenfell tried to analyse his confused feelings in a series of highly-critical essays on contemporary society and conventional values. He developed his own creed, individual, far-sighted and modern for his age, but predictably ridiculed by his family. Julian returned to Oxford, but seemed unable to concentrate. Then in December, 1909, his mother's favourite, Archie Gordon, was fatally injured in a car crash and all attention focused on Archie as he lay dying. Ettie was determined that only happy and beautiful thoughts should surround his deathbed. Her theory that a noble death was a joysome thing to a dutiful young man may have influenced Grenfell's philosophy in 'Into Battle' (although it can also be interpreted as the expression of fierce, private delight in giving up everything for the struggle).

Archie's death only depressed Grenfell more, and for two months he lay in a near coma, virtually unnoticed by his family. Such behaviour, they felt, wasn't acceptable, so it simply didn't exist. It was merely 'complete overdoing in every way, after his rapid growth'. He went to convalesce with an aunt in Italy, where he stayed for a year. His parents decided that he should return to Oxford and work for a pass degree (rather than the honours degree he had once been capable of), then enlist in a suitable regiment as quickly as possible. He had always been intended for an army career.

Back at Oxford Grenfell, in another mood swing, joined in some tasteless, boisterous pranks and even showed an unpleasant anti-Semitic prejudice towards, for instance, fellow undergraduate Philip Sassoon. After graduating he was offered a commission in the Royal Dragoons and sailed with them to India in November, 1910. It seemed an ideal escape from the unbearable pressure of his unsuccessful personal relationships.

Grenfell approached army life with mixed feelings. Complying with Ettie's requirement to be always positive and cheery, Julian wrote the type of letter he felt she would like to receive. On this correspondence he has sometimes been judged as a war-loving boor. In fact he continued to suffer from depression, was prey to illness and injury, and shunned potentially hurtful human contact. Horses and dogs were more reliable. Life with a pukka regiment in India allowed him to throw himself into undemanding physical pursuits: riding, hunting, enjoying the countryside. He started to paint again (a childhood talent he hadn't pursued) and continued to write poetry. One of his animal poems of this period, 'To a Black Greyhound', was chosen by Field Marshal Wavell in his charming anthology, *Other Men's Flowers* (1944). It is a vital, original poem with some memorable images.

Grenfell was less happy with army life when the regiment moved to South Africa. He appealed to Arthur Balfour to assist him in investigating how he might stand for Parliament. Then, on home leave in September, 1912, Julian dropped a surprising and unwelcome bombshell on his family: he wanted to study art in Paris. Deflated by their predictable derision, Grenfell returned to his regiment in South Africa in 1913 and tried desperately to throw himself into the social and physical whirl. It didn't work: depression engulfed him once more, and in July, 1914, he made the difficult decision to quit the army for politics.

It was too late. The outbreak of war meant that there was no question of deserting his regiment in the hour of England's need. The 1st Battalion Royal Dragoons arrived back in Britain on 10 September, 1914, and a month later they were in France.

Many men welcomed the war as an escape from unfavourable circumstances. Grenfell was one of them. Time and again he had tried to find his own niche in life and had been deflected from his aim by his parents. Now outside events took the decision out of his hands and gave him a worthy goal to work towards. For the first time since he was a schoolboy he had full parental approval. He threw himself wholeheartedly and enthusiastically into the task, determined to be a good and worthy leader when his ordained hour came.

On the basis of reading only his much-reproduced 'I adore war' battle-cry, Grenfell's critics accuse him of being a crass warmonger and treating war like a game. Certainly there was an element of this attitude in many young men of his upbringing and age – especially before they met the harsh reality of friends being killed and maimed. But there was another, more thoughtful, caring side to Grenfell. Closer study of his letters reveals solicitude for his men, for the local population whose homes and livelihoods were being shattered, and for the devastated countryside itself. He had no doubt but that the war would be long and hard, and showed a healthy disrespect for the staff. This scorn is admirably illustrated in the poem reproduced here, the tongue-in-cheek 'Prayer for Those on the Staff', written early in 1915. Angela Lambert in *Unquiet Souls* (1984) believes that the 'extra ADC' was none other than the Prince of Wales.

Another misconception is that Julian was a 'natural' soldier, perhaps because he was one of the few poets who was a pre-war professional soldier. But the career of army officer had been imposed upon him by his parents and Grenfell made strenuous efforts to quit it, preferring to develop the artistic side of his personality or, failing that, pursue a career in politics.

At the front, however, Julian refused a 'cushy' ADC's job because 'it feels so wrong to be comfortable when others are in the trenches'. He operated as a loner, taking every opportunity to venture from the security of his battalion's trenches to scout or snipe (the latest fashionable sport). This didn't endear him to his fellow officers or men, who felt that his foolhardy bravura would draw enemy fire on them. Nevertheless Grenfell's willingness to expose himself to danger as a runner or scout earned him the DSO in November, 1914, and he was twice mentioned in despatches. He would have preferred to emulate his cousin Francis (who won the first VC in the Salient), but his family were delighted with their hero.

In April, 1915, Julian experienced every young officer's idea of heaven – an 'oh là là' leave in Paris, coupled with a fling with a Parisienne called Peggy, whose photograph was found in his wallet after his death. 'I saw a bit of everything – 'igh society and the artists and the racing set . . . the boxers too and the nuts, and the actresses and the mannequins,' he raved. 'It was the biggest experience of New Things I've ever had in my life, bigger than India.'

Back in the Salient Grenfell was swept up by the hard fighting around Ypres. On 22 April, 1915, the Germans launched their deadly secret weapon of gas over the Pilckem Ridge. If they had exploited the element of surprise they could have advanced through the broken line of terrified French Colonial troops to the very defences of Ypres. But they failed to push forward and Canadian soldiers closed the breach. The Germans launched a second gas attack on 24 April and the Royal Dragoons were brought up to the Poperinghe area. Julian described their daily movements in his diary (which was more realistic than his letters): the shelling, the refugees, the wounded, the aeroplanes and the bombs. Then, on 29 April, appeared the words 'Wrote poem – "Into Battle".' His immortality was assured.

'Into Battle' appears in virtually every anthology of First World War poetry. It is even in the influential *Oxford Book of English Verse, 1250–1918*, published in 1939, hence its familiarity to most poetry lovers. The poem was generally admired by his contemporaries (with the exception of Diana Manners and her fiancé, Duff Cooper, who called it 'a rather over-praised and barbarous poem'). It certainly illustrates the mystic and lyrical side of his nature and his private joy at being at one with the natural world – which isn't always kind or civilized. Nicholas Mosley, Grenfell's biographer, believes 'its luminousness and serenity do not seem false'.

Most people believe it to have been his only poem, and on the strength of it he is often compared to and categorized with Brooke. Bergonzi talks of the romantic 'Brooke-Grenfell' attitude 'that violent action could be regarded as meaningful, even sacred, when it was sanctioned by the traditional canons of heroic behaviour.' He maintains that Captain Yossarian, hero of Heller's *Catch 22*, would have responded, 'Who dies fighting is dead,' to Grenfell's passionate assurance that 'who dies fighting has increase'. Many of Grenfell's peers, like Graves and Sassoon, lived long enough to change their attitudes from those of Grenfell to those of Yossarian. Julian may well have joined them, but when he wrote the poem he only had six weeks to live.

On 13 May, 1915, the 1st Royal Dragoons were in second line trenches on Railway Hill (which Julian called 'the little hill of death') near Hooge. Whilst acting as an observer, as usual seemingly impervious to his own danger (General Pultney described him as strolling around 'as if he were on a river'), Grenfell was knocked over by a shell but managed to return repeatedly to his OP with information about German movements round the Dragoons' flank. Then a shell landed close while he was reporting to the General and a splinter lodged in Julian's skull. His first spoken reactions – 'I think I'm done', said immediately to the General, and, 'Do you know, I think I shall die,' to a fellow officer when sent to No 10 Casualty Clearing Station – expressed his true fears.

He was sent back to base hospital at Wimereux (where his sister, Monica, was a VAD) and wrote the usual cheerful messages: 'My skull is slightly cracked. But I'm getting on splendidly.' With her nursing experience, his sister at first felt that 'he did not seem very ill, and the wound was diagnosed as a scalp wound.' But on 16 May she sent a telegram home advising their parents to go to Julian's side. Pulling influential strings, the frantic parents travelled on an ammunition boat to Boulogne the next day. The family, undeniably close and loving despite Julian's earlier rebellion, were shattered by the thought of his death. Two operations proved unsuccessful, and on 26 May Julian died, as Ettie would have wished, with a 'radiant' smile on his lips, a kiss to her hand, and recent protestations that he had never been so well or happy. Even in the final escape of death he had to keep up the requisite pretence of cheerfulness.

On the day his death was announced 'Into Battle' was published in *The Times*. Julian was buried in what is now Boulogne East Cemetery. Ettie filled his coffin with wild flowers and allowed no mourning to be worn at the funeral. She perpetuated the memory of her hero sons (Julian's brother was killed on 30 July, 1915) in a published memorial book. Raymond Asquith, one of the contributors, wrote an idealized pen portrait, calling Julian 'intelligent and interesting', describing his 'sheer physical vigour' and 'restless and unconquerable energy', while his mind was 'full of fire and fibre, lively, independent'. Asquith confided to his wife that Ettie would probably doctor the book. 'Ettie is a snob . . . . She meant to give her sons the best *mise-en-scène* from a worldly point of view.' So Ettie had the last word and imposed her false image of her son on the future.

Rupert Brooke

SUB-LIEUTENANT, R.N.V.R.

FRAGMENT

I strayed about the deck an hour, to-night
Under a cloudy moonless sky; and peeped
In at the window, watched my friends at table,
Or playing cards, or standing in the doorway,
Or coming out into the darkness. Still
No one could see me.

                I would have thought of them
— Heedless, within a week of battle — in pity,
Pride in their strength and in the weight and firmness
And link'd beauty of bodies, and pity that
This gay machine of splendour'ld soon be broken,
Thought little of, pashed, scattered . . .

                      Only, always,
I could but see them — against the lamplight — pass
Like coloured shadows, thinner than filmy glass,
Slight bubbles, fainter than the wave's faint light,
That broke to phosphorus out in the night,
Perishing things and strange ghosts — soon to die
To other ghosts — this one, or that, or I.

April 1915

SUB-LIEUTENANT RUPERT BROOKE, RNVR

Until the cult of Wilfred Owen sprang up in the last quarter of the twentieth century, Brooke was the icon of the First World War poet: 'the youth of our race in symbol,' as *The Star* claimed. The pendulum of literary fashion swings energetically and Brooke, once almost idolized, is now often ridiculed. To treat him equably he must be judged both in the context of his own Georgian period and from today's more sophisticated viewpoint.

Brooke's physical beauty, correct pedigree and classical education added to his initial success. He was born on 3 August, 1887, the son of a master at Rugby, and naturally entered that illustrious school himself in 1901. Rupert did his father credit: good at games, good at his academic work. It was his natural milieu. 'I had been happier at Rugby than I can find words to say. As I looked back at those five years I seemed to see almost every hour as golden and radiant,' he later wrote. At school he discovered his power to charm, a somewhat theatrical ability to adopt different personae to please the audience he happened to be with. For flirtations with other boys he favoured a slightly decadent, Baudelairean image. But he could also be the manly hero of the cricket XI or rugby XV, or the handsome breaker of female hearts.

In 1906 Brooke won a classical scholarship to King's College, Cambridge. There his head-swivelling good looks – he was about six feet tall, with sensual lips, delicately arched brows, glinting red-gold hair and a vivacious personality – helped to make him the desirable centre of attraction. Henry James, the American novelist, is reported as being relieved to hear that Brooke's poetry was inferior, as 'with that appearance if he had also talent it would be too unfair'. His Cambridge contemporary Frances Cornford crystallized the glamorous myth of the vulnerable golden god:

> A young Apollo, golden-haired,
> Stands dreaming on the verge of strife,
> Magnificently unprepared
> For the long littleness of life.

The popular Adonis was tempted into many absorbing and pleasurable activities. He was a leading light in the Marlowe (dramatic) Society and

34

President of the Fabian Society – he had strong socialist leanings and was an active campaigner, a little-known side of Brooke which is at odds with his received image. He also flitted through a succession of love affairs, boating parties on the Cam and picnics. His degree, a second in the Classical Tripos in May, 1910, was a disappointment and in his fourth year, in a determined effort to excel, Brooke moved from his college rooms to the relative quiet of Grantchester and the Old Vicarage. He switched from Classics to English, specializing in Webster and the Elizabethan dramatists.

Brooke's friends were a glittering array of future achievers in many fields: Hugh Dalton, the Labour MP; writers E.M. Forster, Virginia Woolf and Frances Cornford; economist John Maynard Keynes and his literary brother Geoffrey. But his most passionate attachment was to the unknown Noel Olivier, whom he first met in 1908 when he was twenty and she only fifteen. In 1910 they became secretly engaged, against the wishes of Rupert's dominant mother. Almost immediately he seems to have had ambivalent feelings towards this intelligent, free-thinking soul – or at least towards tying himself to her for the rest of his life. Their agonizing love letters were published in 1991 (*The Letters of Rupert Brooke and Noel Olivier 1909–1915*, edited by Olivier's granddaughter Pippa Harris). Unbelievably, to the otherwise universally desirable Brooke, Noel also had doubts about her feelings. He tried to interest her by making her jealous, but the cool-headed Olivier was adamant: 'It is so strong the feeling that I mustn't marry you,' she wrote.

Travel and writing poetry were Brooke's antidotes to Noel Olivier. In 1910 Rupert's father died and Brooke spent a term at Rugby standing in for his father as a temporary housemaster. He then returned to Cambridge where, interspersed with forays to London and Germany, he continued to write poetry and work on his dissertation on Webster.

On 4 December, 1911, Rupert privately published his first collection, *Poems*. Edward Thomas gave it restrained praise in his *Daily Chronicle* review. Edward Marsh, by now a staunch friend, found the poems 'magnificent', with the 'rapturous beautiful grotesque of the 17th Century'. The 150 poems, written between 1905 and 1911, show an impressive range. Brooke experimented with many different forms, styles and moods. Some were, to quote his friend Geoffrey Keynes in his introduction to *The Poetical Works of Rupert Brooke*, 'juvenilia' written at school. 'The Beginning', for instance, was originally dedicated to 'Antinous' – 'You who I found so fair' – Brooke's pseudonym for a school-friend he had loved at Rugby. Others were sensual love poems inspired by his yearning for Noel Olivier. Many are set in the mystery of night, full of longings and burnings for the sleeping loved one.

Brooke's explicit physical descriptions were shocking to the poetry-reading public of 1911. Even more so was 'Channel Crossing', with its

'Old meat, good meals, brown gobbets, up I throw' realism. It was considered by Marsh 'too disgusting to write about, especially in one's own language'. Brooke was unrepentant about the 'unpleasant poems'. 'The Fish', with its Keatsian cadences, was universally admired, and influential critics gave it an encouraging reception.

Brooke continued travelling – from Munich to the French Riviera in February, 1912. But returning to Rugby he had a mystery 'nervous breakdown' and was 'in a seriously introspective condition'. In May, 1912, he rallied enough to travel again to Berlin, where he wrote his most famous pre-war poem, 'The Sentimental Exile'. Marsh persuaded him to change its title to 'The Old Vicarage, Grantchester' and it has become one of the best-loved, most-quoted poems in the English language. In the good old, bad old days when children were required to learn verses by heart this was always a favourite, and hence remains locked in the memory of generations, to be recalled with fond pleasure in times of need. Brooke's poem has the requisite anodyne factor that makes it particularly suitable for this exercise, the comforting nostalgia of nursery food to the grown public schoolboy. One expects Winnie the Pooh to arrive at any minute to share the honey that is always still there for tea. It is the quintessence of reliable, Edwardian England, but also has life and flashes of amusing originality and eccentricity. Marsh told Brooke that it was 'lovely, my dear . . . the most human thing you've written and the only one that has brought tears to my eyes.'

Brooke was heavily involved with Marsh in the choice of poets and poems for the first Georgian anthology, then in November, 1912, he left again for Berlin where he was amused to read a review of his 'Poems' in *The Oxford Magazine*: 'The book is full of bad taste and at times positively disgusting.' He returned to England in December, where he met the actress Cathleen Nesbitt. His enthusiasm for the Georgian project brought him into contact with everybody on the current literary scene, and he embarked on a frantic social whirl.

Brooke was gratified on 8 March, 1913, to learn that he had been awarded a fellowship at King's for his dissertation on Webster. On 22 May he sailed for America and Canada with a commission from the *Westminster Gazette* (£4 per article for his impressions). The trip was an attempt to allay his restlessness and discontent, but he was soon homesick, making up 'little minor pitiful songs' which he sent to Marsh for attempted publication. Despite this, he continued travelling across the Pacific, spending Christmas in New Zealand. Brooke shied away from the reality of home, preferring to annoy Marsh by disporting 'in a loincloth, brown and wild, in the fair chocolate arms of a Tahitian beauty'. In April his Gauguinesque lifestyle led to 'coral-poisoning' and infected sores on his legs.

He arrived back in London on 5 June, 1914, tanned with sun-bleached hair. His trip had produced fifteen articles for the *Westminster Gazette* and a handful of poems, including 'Clouds' and 'The Great Lover', an instantly attractive poem written with longing for home from Mataiea.

Cathleen Nesbitt still featured in Brooke's life. He had corresponded regularly with her on his great journey of self-discovery, but she had to share him with the usual large circle of poets, politicians and academics fuelling his search for sensation and stimulation. Rupert's charm was as seductive as ever and he was in great demand.

But time was running out. Marsh, in his capacity as private secretary to the First Lord of the Admiralty, Winston Churchill, was swept up in the tide of war, his work on the Georgians having to take a back seat. At the end of July he took Brooke to dine with the Prime Minister, Herbert Asquith, and introduced him to Churchill, who offered to help him get a commission. When war finally broke out Rupert couldn't make up his mind how to react. At one stage he thought of going to France to help get the harvest in. 'If Armageddon is on, I suppose one should be there,' he decided eventually, but getting a commission for active service wasn't as easy as he expected.

Finally Marsh helped him into a new unit, a land force administered by the Admiralty – the Royal Naval Division. On 27 September, 1914, Brooke and his friend Denis Browne went to Betteshanger Park, Lord Northbourne's estate near Eastry in Kent, to join the Anson Battalion, 2nd Naval Brigade, RND. Sub-Lieutenant Rupert Brooke was in charge of training a platoon of thirty men, a motley crew of stokers from northern England, Ireland and Scotland. On Sunday 4 October they marched to Dover to the cheers and encouragement of the local population to embark for France.

At Dunkirk the battalion learned they were bound for Antwerp to check the German advance sweeping towards Lille and Ghent, their artillery already pounding Antwerp. They met the retreating Belgians in disarray and, after a night in a gloomy deserted château at Vieux-Dieu (where they were visited by Winston Churchill), were ordered to relieve the Belgians in trenches at old fortifications nearby. During the day the château received a direct hit and Brooke lost some manuscripts he had left there. Ordered to withdraw, the Anson Battalion was caught up in the stream of fleeing refugees from Antwerp. At Bruges they entrained for Ostend and on 9 October they were back in Dover. The expedition had been a miserable failure. It was Brooke's only taste of real war and he thought it was a 'truer Hell' than Dante's Inferno.

Back in London he started to write the sonnets that would immortalize him. On 18 October he returned to Betteshanger, but on 25 October the battalion moved to Chatham. Their commanding officer, Lieutenant-Colonel George Cornwallis West, was extremely unpopular, and Brooke eventually managed to transfer to a company of Hood Battalion, commanded by Bernard Freyberg.

Brooke was writing to Cathleen and other friends at this time, with much introspection and soul-searching about the significance of the war and his own attitude towards it. Those who were taking part in the war were set apart 'under a curse or a blessing or a vow'. He felt keenly the futility and frivolity of his previous life. To fight Germans was what God wanted of him. The sight of the 'wrong' he had witnessed in Belgium made him 'resolved' in his work, fighting to prevent it happening again. News of wounded or killed friends – 'the rich dead' – started to come in, inspiring his sonnets.

At the end of November the battalion moved to Blandford Camp in Dorset. Conditions were primitive and, although friends provided curtains and furniture to brighten his hut, the fumes from the coke stove made many of the men ill, including Arthur Asquith (the Prime Minister's son) and Brooke. When Violet Asquith arrived to visit her ailing brother just before Christmas Rupert showed her four sonnets in draft stage. The ribaldry of a service Christmas and the drunken celebrations of the stokers amused him, but on Christmas night he stole an hour to work on 'The Soldier'.

On leave over the New Year, he spent some days at Rugby, stayed at Walmer Castle 'among all those Field Marshals' with Violet Asquith, then lunched with her father and Winston Churchill in London. Back at Blandford there were excited rumours that they would soon be sent overseas on active service. Brooke completed his sonnets, his 'five camp children', and sent them to Wilfrid Gibson. In early February he went on sick leave with a feverish cold; the humble sub-lieutenant was nursed in No 10 Downing Street for nine days, where he again met Henry James (who later wrote the preface to the reprint of Brooke's American articles). Brooke was back at Blandford in time for an official visit from the First Lord of the Admiralty, accompanied by Marsh and Clementine Churchill.

On 20 February the news that they were bound for the Dardanelles thrilled the battalion. Brooke exulted at the prospect of breaking through the Hellespont and the Bosphorus and taking Constantinople: what a romantic idea. It was, of course, Churchill's brainchild and there is little doubt that Winston would have discussed his bold plan with Brooke, who was confident that he would be home again by May. Preparations began apace and on 24 February the Churchills, Marsh and Violet Asquith came to Blandford for a march past before the King the next day. It was the last time Brooke would see his friends. On 28 February the Anson and Hood Battalions sailed on the *Grantully Castle* for Gallipoli. 'I have never been so happy,' wrote Rupert to Cathleen, seeing himself in the romantic guise of a crusader.

Also on board were friends like Denis Browne, Patrick Shaw-Stewart,

Arthur 'Oc' Asquith and Charles Lister, members of the exclusive Coterie set. (Asquith was the only one of the friends to survive the war: Browne and Lister were killed at Gallipoli and Shaw-Stewart in France. Asquith was wounded and never totally recovered.) They enjoyed the voyage, dining at the Union Club in Malta and watching a performance of *Tosca* before finally anchoring in Mudros Bay at the Greek island of Lemnos. Through his field-glasses Brooke glimpsed Mount Olympus. 'And my eyes fell on the holy land of Attica. So I can die,' he wrote to Cathleen. On 18 March came the order to sail for the Dardanelles, but the expedition was aborted and they returned to Lemnos; six days later they sailed to Port Said. On 30 March they arrived in Cairo by train, stayed in Shepheard's Hotel and made a bizarre upper-class expedition to the Pyramids and Sphynx with Lord and Lady Howard de Walden and Aubrey and Mary Herbert.

The next day was gruelling: route marches in the hot sun. Shaw-Stewart got gyppy tummy and Brooke felt unwell. During the night he was sick, and lay on his camp bed with a raging headache during an inspection by General Sir Ian Hamilton the following morning. Hamilton, an admirer of Brooke's poetry, offered him a staff job on his headquarters ship *Queen Elizabeth*, perhaps prompted by Marsh and Churchill. Brooke refused, although he had a high opinion of Hamilton, calling him 'our greatest poet-soldier and our greatest soldier-poet'. He dragged himself up from his bed to visit Shaw-Stewart but was obviously unwell, and the MO confined the pair to a diet of arrowroot for several days, during which Brooke wrote 'The Dance' for Denis Browne to set to music. He had developed a sore on his upper lip, but it seemed to disappear as he got better. On 10 April the *Grantully Castle* sailed back to Lemnos. Brooke, although still weak, insisted on going. His strength gradually returned and he went back to duty. On 17 April, anchored in the Bay of Skyros, Rupert received a letter from Marsh with a cutting from *The Times* of 5 April reporting that Dean Inge had read his sonnet 'The Soldier', during his sermon at St Paul's Cathedral. It was the start of the process known by his detractors (and by his true friends, as they felt it diminished the real man) as the 'canonization' of Brooke.

At a divisional field day on 20 April Brooke, having spent four hours on watch the previous night, was already tired. During the afternoon Brooke, Browne, Lister and Shaw-Stewart rested in the peaceful atmosphere of a shady olive grove. That evening at dinner he retired early, complaining of the old swelling on his lip. The next day it was worse, he ached all over, and his condition deteriorated rapidly. His temperature rose to 103°F and from time to time he lost consciousness.

The battalion surgeon called in the fleet surgeon, the divisional staff medical officer and the brigade medical officer. After a consultation they agreed that the problem was coming from an infected mosquito bite and the infection was spreading. It was decided to move him to a French hospital ship, where he was the only patient among twelve surgeons. Asquith informed them that this was 'our best poet and the apple of Winston's and Sir Ian's eye'. Frantic messages winged their way to Churchill and Hamilton; equally frantic messages responded. The experienced French surgeon decided to operate to cauterize the infected area. Asquith and Browne were desperate. Their friend was dying before their eyes and the combined expertise of all these doctors seemed powerless to save him. At 4.46 in the afternoon of 23 April, 1915, St George's Day, two days before the Gallipoli landings, Rupert Brooke died. The god was not immortal.

His friends decided to bury him on Skyros, in the olive grove he had enjoyed. It had to be a hasty affair; the *Grantully Castle* was due to sail for Gallipoli at dawn the next day. Shaw-Stewart commanded the guard of honour; Brooke's friends had his epitaph inscribed in Greek on a wooden cross and piled small marble rocks into a cairn. Brooke's poem 'Fragment', reproduced here, gives an impression of the affection in which he held these friends during his last voyage.

Today the grave bears a stone surmounted by a crusader's sword, green-painted wrought iron railings surround it and wild flowers grow in profusion nearby. In 1930 a well-meaning Greek sculptor carved a large, naked statue of a muscular male figure on Skyros and dedicated it to Brooke. Frances Cornford commented that it looked 'like an advertisement for Elliman's embrocation' (Hassall, *Rupert Brooke*). Modern postcards call it 'The Roupert Brooke'.

But there were other memorials, the most important being his poems. *1914 and Other Poems* was published in 1915, featuring an idealized photograph of the bare-shouldered poet taken by Sherril Schell in 1913. Bergonzi called it a 'deplorable' photograph; Brooke's friends called it 'Your favourite Actress'. Geoffrey Keynes, introducing *The Poetical Works of Rupert Brooke*, feels the pencil drawings in that volume by Rupert's close friends, Jacques and Gwen Raverat, 'convey the essence of Brooke's personality, the gay and golden qualities, both physical and mental'. An admirer wrote to Brooke's mother, 'I have never met so entirely likeable a chap . . . . Your son was not merely a genius; what is more important, he had a charm that was literally like sunshine.' De la Mare said, 'Indeed the good things simply softly shimmered out of him.'

The sonnets were more or less universally acclaimed. Most critics felt Brooke would have gone on to equal Owen or Sassoon had he endured more battle. Gurney differed: 'It seems to me that Rupert Brooke would not have improved with age, would not have broadened; his manner had become mannerism, both in rhythm and diction.' Charles Sorley found the sonnets 'overpraised. He is far too obsessed with his own sacrifice regarding the going to war of himself (and others) . . . . He has clothed his attitude in fine words: but he has taken the sentimental attitude.'

In contrast, Winston Churchill perpetuated what some call the hagiography of Brooke. In *The Times* on 26 April, 1915, he wrote, 'A voice had become audible, a note had been struck, more true, more thrilling more able to do justice to the nobility of our youth in arms engaged in this present war than any other . . . he was all that one would wish England's noblest sons to be in the days when no sacrifice but the most precious is acceptable.' Walter de la Mare maintained that 'His surely was the intellectual imagination possessed in a rare degree. Nothing in his work is more conspicuous than its preoccupation with actual experience, its adventurousness, its daring, its keen curiosity and interest in ideas, its life-giving youthfulness . . . . What place in English literature the caprices of time and taste will at length accord him does not concern us.'

Indisputably the *War Sonnets* were a distillation of the spirit of 1914. Their publication bottled that essence: on reading them today we uncork the flask and release the authentic whiff of a country when young men were still proud to die for it.

Roland Aubrey Leighton

LIEUTENANT, 7TH WORCESTERS

VILLANELLE

Violets from Plug Street Wood,
Sweet, I send you oversea.
(It is strange they should be blue,
Blue, when his soaked blood was red,
For they grew around his head;
It is strange they should be blue.)

Violets from Plug Street Wood —
Think what they have meant to me —
Life and Hope and Love and You
(And you did not see them grow
Where his mangled body lay,
Hiding horror from the day;
Sweetest, it was better so.)

Violets from oversea,
To your dear, far, forgetting land
These I send in memory,
Knowing You will understand.

Ploegsteert Wood, April 1915

LIEUTENANT ROLAND AUBREY LEIGHTON

It is difficult to consider Roland Leighton in his own right because of his strong links with Vera Brittain and the shortness of his unfulfilled academic and literary life contrasted with her own long and prolific career. Most of what is known about him comes from Vera's writings: *Testament of Youth* and *Chronicle of Youth*.

Roland was born in March, 1895, the eldest of three children, to the journalist and writer of adventure stories for boys, Robert Leighton, and the flamboyant novelist, Marie Connor Leighton. Mother and elder son had a strong rapport and deep affection for each other. His sister Clare became a well-known woodcut illustrator of books and wrote the preface to *Chronicle*, in which Roland first appears on 27 June, 1913, when Vera went to the annual old boys' day at Leighton's school, Uppingham. Leighton, a house captain, was 'one of the cleverest boys at Uppingham .... I like him immensely, he seems so clever & amusing & hardly shy at all.'

Vera was struck by Roland's physical appearance when he came to stay for part of the Easter, 1914, holidays: 'impressive rather than handsome . . . powerful frame and big head with its stiff, thick hair gave him the appearance of a very large person; [in] strange contrast with his fair head and pale face, his large dark eyes looked contemplatively at the world from beneath black strongly marked eyebrows.' But his mind and reputation appealed more to her at this stage than physical aspects.

To the intellectually aspiring young girl from provincial Buxton, Leighton, with his 'reputation for brilliance and unapproachableness', his excitingly Bohemian family, his 'maturity and sophistication', was almost unbearably appealing. They had long discussions, mainly about the nature of God, and Leighton recorded his reactions in a poem called '*Nachklang*' ('Reminiscence'). Although he could not easily express his emotions, and had initial feelings of embarrassment and uncertainty, he had already fallen for this unusual, attractive and opinionated girl. 'Sweetest sceptic, we were born for living./Life is Love, and Love is –/You, dear, you.' They discussed their attempts at writing poetry and examined each other's works critically. Roland wrote out 'Lines on a Picture by Herbert Schmaltz' and 'Triolet'.

Leighton was co-editor of the school magazine and his editorial for

June, 1914, bears all the hallmarks of an exceptional classics scholar and budding poet:

> Gold and green and blue; sunlight and grass and sky; all the subtle joys of Middle cricket, and of clean headers into shadowed water, and of dilettante ice-eating, and of languorous afternoon-schools; – all the luxurious pleasantness of a Summer Term have long since enwrapped us in a Lethean doze.

The following issue of the magazine reports on Uppingham's Speech Day, including details of Roland's seven prizes and the fact that he had won the Senior Open Classical Postmastership to Merton College, Oxford, for the following autumn. He was anxious for Vera to attend, as naturally he wished to show off a bit with this impressive list of achievements. Afterwards she and Roland found time to talk again and cement their attraction for each other. Roland was in his OTC colour-sergeant's uniform. Vera noted that he took the OTC 'very seriously' and was going on a fortnight's camp in Aldershot.

On 17 July Roland sent Vera another 'deservedly prizeless Prize poem', 'The Crescent and the Cross', which she dismissed as 'derivative' with 'the personal element somewhat lacking'.

After war was declared on 4 August Roland tried to enlist, but was initially turned down by the army because of his poor eyesight. (He was very self-conscious about wearing glasses: on a visit to the theatre with Vera she records, 'Roland tried to avoid putting on his glasses as he did not want me to notice them, but when he found he could not see without them, he asked me if I minded his putting them on & when I said that of course he must he did so & begged me not to look.') Vera had passed her Oxford entrance exam, so it seemed they would be studying together.

In the meantime Roland took a temporary post as assistant recruiting officer and soon decided that he could not go to Oxford for 'a life of scholarly vegetation at such a time as this'. He was gazetted to the Norfolk Regiment and in November became a Territorial second lieutenant. He told Vera that he still felt that his eyesight would keep him from going to the front.

In December Roland and Vera exchanged photographs and at the end of the month Vera went to stay with her grandmother in Purley to see Roland and meet his mother. Vera was entranced by this 'brilliant, strong-willed, utterly lovable mother' with her 'unusual appearance', and they discussed Roland almost as if he were not present. Vera said that she didn't understand Roland and he maintained that his mother did 'more than anyone else'. The closeness and friendliness between mother and son was very apparent.

Following this successful meeting between mother and prospective (although not yet declared) daughter-in-law, the couple dined at the Comedy Restaurant and afterwards Roland tried to buy Vera some violets – which she refused. But the following day he bought her a bunch, 'Sweet-smelling & very fresh.' Violets became their flowers. At dinner that night Vera asked Roland if he would like to be killed in action. 'Yes, I should; I don't want to die, but if I must, I should like to die that way,' he replied.

On 16 January, 1915, they met in London and he accompanied her back to Oxford. For the first time he kissed her hand. On 24 January he wrote that his regiment was to be posted to Lowestoft and on 1 February that he had volunteered to go to the front at once with the 4th Suffolks. 'When men whom I have once despised as effeminate are being sent back wounded from the front, when nearly everyone I know is either going or has gone, can I think of this with anything but rage and shame?' On 6 February his offer had still not been taken up, but he was promoted to first lieutenant. Then, while Vera was in Buxton recovering from influenza, Roland transferred to the 7th Worcesters: they were off to the front in ten days' time. He was invited to Buxton to stay for the night, though the boorish Mr Brittain wondered 'why on earth Vera was making all this fuss of that youth without a farthing to his name'!

This last meeting before Leighton went to France is graphically described in *Testament of Youth*. They felt they already had an ideal marriage of minds, so many ideas in common, but at this stage the torment of their unconsummated love, when each feared they might never see the other again, was almost unbearable – they dared not even touch fingers, 'for fear that the love between us should render what we both believed to be decent behaviour suddenly unendurable.' How unnatural that strict self-control seems today – and would seem to many before the end of the war. They agreed, however, to marry. Roland confessed that 'he had no love for the army at all, and admitted that he wished he were at Oxford occupied with classics and books. He seemed to find that part of the reason was vanity . . . The real reason seems to be the vague moral sense of acting up to his faith in, his highest opinion of, himself.'

When he left the next day Vera consoled herself with reading Shelley's 'Adonais', and some of Roland's own poems, especially the lines,

> Goodbye, sweet friend, what matters it that you
> Have found Love's death in joy and I in sorrow?
> For hand in hand, just as we used to do,
> We too shall live our passionate poem through
> On God's serene tomorrow.

As a farewell present Roland sent Vera an amethyst (the colour of violets) brooch and a card saying 'In Memoriam. March 18, 1915'. To his mother he announced, *'Je suis fiancé; c'est le guerre.'* At this stage, despite earlier uncertainties on both scores, he was committed to Vera and to the war. On 31 March he entrained to Folkstone, sailed on SS *Onward* to Boulogne and then marched to St Martin's Camp on the hill above. The following day the battalion went by train to Cassel and took up billets at Hardifort. On 3 April they were inspected by General Sir Horace Smith-Dorrien and three days later marched twenty miles to billets near Bailleul, and subsequently to Armentières. Roland wrote from Armentières, amazed at thriving shops so close to the front line; then, as he moved nearer, described the sound of heavy artillery and the sky lit by flares.

The battalion reached the trenches on 12 April, in the labyrinth that was Ploegsteert ('Plugstreet' to Tommy) Wood. Leighton's experiences were like those of so many new officers – life in the troglodite city of a maze of trenches and dug-outs, mud, not washing, seeing to the men's welfare, keeping one's head down to avoid sniper fire. He was particularly moved to find three German graves: 'Somebody once loved the man lying there.'

On 14 April the battalion came out of the trenches and Roland almost missed the strange life. It was a feeling common to many soldiers, who came to believe that the only real world was the dangerous one of the front line. Later he was to comment that 'there is nothing glorious in trench warfare'.

At about this time Leighton sent Vera four violets he had picked in Ploegsteert Wood. When she wrote *Testament of Youth*, in 1933 she still had them: 'the blue is brown now, and crinkled, but the flower shapes remain unspoilt.' He wrote a poem to accompany them in the form of a villanelle (a pastoral poem or ancient dance form accompanied by song), but typically wasn't satisfied with it and kept it back for revision. The finished product is reproduced here. It is a haunting poem, juxtaposing the incongruous concepts of a love poem and a graphic description of the horror of a dead soldier (probably inspired by the unburied body of a British soldier which so upset Leighton that he ordered it to be covered).

The life of trench warfare continued throughout the summer: days of rest behind the lines, concert parties and duets with young French girls, comrades killed in gallant actions, birds singing in Ploegsteert Wood, close escapes from snipers' bullets, ration parties, sheltering from shells in craters, mine explosions, experimenting with new grenades. Vera went through the old Uppingham magazines that Roland had edited and which contained his poems, notably '*Clair de Lune*', a pastoral Georgian poem. She also found an untitled poem he had written just before the war: 'And so, farewell./All our sweet songs are sung,/Our red rose-garlands withered;/The sun-bright day –/Silver and blue and gold –/Wearied to sleep.' She sent him a volume of Brooke's poems which made him 'want to sit down and write things myself instead of doing what I have to do here.'

On 3 July Vera heard that Roland had cut his fingers, she assumed on the barbed wire. He was moving south and in consequence leave had been cancelled. The 7th Worcesters moved through the mining district near Loos to Maroc, distinguished themselves by marching seventeen miles through rough terrain to Lillers station with not a man falling out, and thence north of the Somme to billets in the Bois de Warnimont and on to St Léger on 7 August. Their trenches near Hébuterne were in what was known as a 'quiet area' and most of their time was spent, in deteriorating weather, in building up their defences.

During the move south Roland could not write and Vera, by now a VAD, was mad with worry. At last a letter came: Leighton had a temporary staff job at VII Corps HQ. After a further spell in the trenches, the longed-for leave came on 18 August. Roland assured Vera that 'All along I have felt I shan't be killed. In fact I may almost say I know it.'

The couple, feeling rather strained in each other's company, travelled to Buxton, to Lowestoft and to see Roland's mother. He gave Vera the poem he had written when he picked the violets in Ploegsteert Wood. She thought it was a perfect literary gem, 'the union of brilliance of intellect with personal love'. They decided to make their engagement official, but not to buy a ring. Their farewell at St Pancras was like every wartime couple's before or since: words difficult, the last desperate kiss, the whispered goodbye. They would never see each other again.

On a date noted as 26 September in *Testament* and 17 September in *Chronicle*, Leighton sent Vera the code that meant he would be going into action: '*Hinc illae lacrimae*' ('Hence those tears', Terence). On 1 October he told her it was a false alarm: they had been stood down twice after being told to prepare to go over the top. To his great pride he was made acting adjutant and hoped for leave on 31 December 'if he didn't get hit by something in the meantime'. He was temporarily transferred to the Somerset Light Infantry, but back with the 7th Worcesters he heard that his leave had been brought forward to 24 December, arriving home on Christmas Day. An excited Vera managed to get leave too, and waited anxiously throughout Christmas Day and Boxing Day. On 27 December there was a telephone call. The Leighton family had received a telegram: 'Regret to inform you that Lieut R.A. Leighton 7th Worcesters died of wounds December 23rd.'

From then on Roland is described with a Capital H for 'Him' in *Testament* and *Chronicle*, almost as if he had become deified.

He was wounded on the night of 22–23 December, when the 7th Worcesters had just taken over new trenches which had been left in a dilapidated condition. Leighton's platoon was detailed to repair the broken wire in front of them and during a recce Roland was hit in the stomach by machine-gun fire when approaching a gap in the wire well known to the enemy, a fact which the previous occupants of the trench failed to point out to their successors. His company commander and a sergeant bravely rushed out to bring him in and twenty minutes later at the casualty clearing station he was given a large dose of morphine. Despite an ambitious abdominal operation the next day (which showed that his spine had been injured and he was paralysed) by the senior surgeon at Louvencourt, Roland only regained consciousness long enough to receive Extreme Unction from a Jesuit priest who, the family learned later, had been instrumental in his conversion to Roman Catholicism earlier that year. He died at 11.00pm on the night of 23 December. A service was held for him in the village church and he was buried, and still lies, in Louvencourt Cemetery, where violets are often placed by admirers.

At the end of January Roland's kit was returned and Vera visited his mother and sister as they unwrapped the tragic parcel. It was a harrowing sight: his uniform caked with mud and blood from his mortal wound. In her preface to *Chronicle*, Clare describes burying the 'blood-stained and bullet-riddled tunic that Father has hidden from the packages' so as not to upset her mother. The December earth was frozen so hard that they had to boil kettles of water to thaw it. Roland's black notebook in which he wrote his poems was there, containing '*Nachklang*', 'In the Rose Garden', 'I Walk Alone', 'Villanelle' and his last poem, headed 'Hédauville. November 1915'. Vera found it a complete mystery, but passed the village when she made a pilgrimage to Roland's grave in 1920. She thought she saw a resemblance to the road near Buxton where they had walked together before the war.

The poem may contain some clues to what Roland's family were convinced were his changing feelings about his relationship to Vera:

> . . . You may meet
> Another stranger, Sweet.
> And if he is not quite so old
> As the boy you used to know,
> And less proud, too, and worthier,
> You may not let him go – . . .
> It will be better so.

'What did he mean, I wondered, as I read and re-read the poem, puzzled and tormented,' Vera confided to her diary. Was Roland hinting that she would be happier with another? David Leighton, Roland's nephew and literary executor, also sees some possible clues in the fragment, 'Ploegsteert', that the relationship would have to end. 'Agony', maintains Mr Leighton, 'has a subsidiary meaning of the death-struggle. *Agonie* in French still has the meaning of mortal agony. Roland with his linguistic background would certainly have been aware of this. Did he indeed even wish to die, perhaps as a way out of the terrible conflict between hurting the one he loved and marrying the one he knew he could not stay with? I don't suppose we shall ever know . . . . Perhaps it is as well that Vera did not appear to suspect.'

'Roundel', found in the black notebook, contained yet more lines describing the lonely, tormenting path he was treading:

> I walk alone although the way is long
> And with gaunt briars and nettles overgrown.

The comfort and assurance offered by the Roman Catholic church, and what must have been a very understanding priest, may well have impelled Roland's conversion. Certainly it is extremely strange that this man, devoted to two women, his mother and, supposedly, Vera, should not have told them about what must have been a major decision. It indicates a distancing, certainly from Vera, the self-confessed sceptic. The idea of a death-wish to release him from his agony is echoed in Vera's painful cry, 'Oh, my love! – so proud, so confident, so contemptuous of humiliation . . . . Why did you go so boldly, so heedlessly, into No Man's Land when you knew that your leave was so near? . . . it seemed as though he had gone down to the grave consciously indifferent to all of us who loved him so much.' Perhaps he could not bear the thought of having to face Vera with his change of heart.

Roland's brother Evelyn's view was that 'if they had married they would have been "at each others throats" within a very short time.' Each knew, and was a large enough person to admit, that they could be difficult: 'It is not good for autocratic persons always to get what they want from other people,' Roland wrote, and Vera felt that, as the letter was 'rather bitter and cynical . . . he must be catching it from me.' Although Vera often notes the loving phrases in his letters, there is also a reference to 'a row' when she complained at the scarceness of his letters. He apologized, explaining that 'I have felt myself justified in forgetting everything and everybody except my own Infallible Majesty.'

The speculation about the continuance or not of the relationship between these two interesting young people may never be resolved, but how does Leighton, the brilliant Classics scholar, Uppingham's record prize-winner, the disconcerting conversationalist, the young man who only lived through the pages of a passionate girl's diary, rate as a poet? Why do his few known works appear so infrequently (if at all) in anthologies?

Leighton and Vera were aware of, and admired in each other, the fact that they were intellectual snobs, delighting in their erudition. A certain pretentiousness shows in Leighton's poems. He chose foreign titles ('Clair de Lune', 'Nachklang') and esoteric poetic forms (such as 'Villanelle' and 'Roundel' – a fifteenth century French form with fourteen lines and two rhymes). A prophetic poem which makes an appropriate epitaph was written in 1913 in the form of a triolet: an octet, usually with octosyllabic lines (this one does not comply), with two rhymes, the first, third, fourth, fifth, and seventh lines and the second, sixth and eighth lines, with the eighth line repeating the second.

> There's a sob on the sea
> And the Old Year is dying,
> Borne on night wings to me.
> There's a sob on the sea,
> And for what could not be
> The Great world-heart is sighing.
> There's a sob on the sea
> And the Old Year is dying.

Certainly Leighton wrote in the rather stereotyped style imposed by his era and education, but his verses have a charm and a hint of originality that warrant a place in their own right.

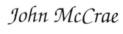

John McCrae

LIEUTENANT-COLONEL, CANADIAN ARMY MEDICAL CORPS

IN FLANDERS FIELDS

In Flanders fields the poppies blow
Between the crosses, row on row,
That mark our place; and in the sky
The larks, still bravely singing, fly
Scarce heard amid the guns below.

We are the Dead. Short days ago
We lived, felt dawn, saw sunset glow,
Loved and were loved, and now we lie,
  In Flanders fields.

Take up our quarrel with the foe:
To you from failing hands we throw
The torch; be yours to hold it high.
If ye break faith with us who die
We shall not sleep, though poppies grow
  In Flanders fields.

Near Ypres, Spring, 1915

LIEUTENANT-COLONEL JOHN McCRAE

If one had to choose a single poem that epitomized the spirit of the Great War it would have to be 'In Flanders Fields', written not by an English public schoolboy subaltern in a flush of patriotism but by a forty-three-year-old Canadian colonel, John McCrae. And just as it is erroneously assumed that Julian Grenfell wrote only one poem, so McCrae is now only remembered for 'In Flanders Fields'. Yet in his youth, and even in an earlier war, he had composed other fine verses.

McCrae was born in a stone cottage in Guelph, Ontario, on 30 November 1872, to second generation Canadian parents of Scottish Presbyterian origins. The family had a strong tradition of service to medicine, and a feeling for Gaelic poetry. McCrae's father also loved the military, having been commissioned into the 47th Foot and served with the 16th Foot, the Wellington Rifles and the 1st Brigade of Field Artillery. In 1915, at the age of seventy, this doughty old gentleman recruited a battery (the 43rd), sailed to England, and was greatly disappointed not to be allowed to go to France with them. From his mother John inherited a great love of literature, which was enhanced by his English teacher at school. A strong religious belief bound his family and formed an important part of John's life.

At fourteen John joined the Highland Cadet Corps and learned drill from a Crimean War veteran, winning a gold medal for being the best-drilled cadet in Ontario. The next year he became a bugler in his father's battery, at sixteen became the first Guelph pupil to win a scholarship to Toronto University and at eighteen joined the artillery.

At university he was a model student, hard-working and dutiful. Fellow students remember a tall, good-looking boy with an infectious smile but appalling dress sense! However, he became asthmatic and his ill health prevented him from achieving the academic heights he sought. As a result McCrae spent an unhappy year at the agricultural college in Guelph as an assistant teacher. Internal jealousies and power struggles were rife, and John was not really qualified or confident enough to fulfil his teaching rôle with credit. The students demonstrated against him and the system in general, and eventually the government appointed a commission of enquiry. It was a difficult and uncomfortable period for the sensitive twenty-year-old, his unhappiness compounded by an unrequited love affair.

He was relieved to return to Toronto in 1893 to complete his BA in natural sciences before studying medicine from 1894 to 1898 at the University of Toronto Medical School, gaining his degree and again winning a gold medal. He found time, however, to write poetry, publishing more than at any later period in his life, and short stories (in 1897 he even had one published in *Blackwood's Magazine* in the UK).

The poetry of this period was inspired by his unhappy love affair (about 'a little maiden fair/With locks of gold') but show the strength he derived from his religion ('God's kind words come . . .'). As with so many young poets, the idea of death privately preoccupied him, but he projected the image of a jolly man who enjoyed life. As a postgraduate he had been fortunate to study under the innovative and charismatic William Osler, 'the best-known and loved physician of his generation in North America' (Prescott), at the Johns Hopkins Hospital in Baltimore where McCrae's brother also worked. It was a stimulating and exciting experience.

When the Boer War was about to erupt in 1899, McCrae showed a militaristic view in his poem, 'Disarmament', published in the *Toronto Globe* in reaction to the International Disarmament Conference in the Hague. Once Britain was at war, Canada agreed to supply 1,000 men who sailed for South Africa on 18 October, 1899. McCrae, enjoying his work under Osler, was torn between joining the colours and staying at his job. Then defeat followed defeat for the British and, when Ladysmith was besieged, McCrae's strongly developed sense of duty impelled him to go to her aid. He had been awarded a fellowship in pathology at McGill University, Montreal, which he managed to postpone when he was commissioned into D Battery of the Royal Canadian Artillery.

'I shall not pray for peace in our time,' he wrote to his mother on enlisting during 'Black Week' in December, 1899, when the reverses at Stormberg, Magersfontein and Colenso all took place. 'One campaign might cure me, but nothing else ever will unless it should be old age.'

McCrae was put in charge of a section and sailed from Halifax on *The Laurentian* on 20 January, 1900. The Canadians landed in Cape Town shortly after Kimberley was relieved. There the young lover of literature was thrilled to meet his hero, Rudyard Kipling, and to become part of a stirring episode in the Empire which seemed so glamorous to this young man from the Dominions. He felt fit and fulfilled, especially when the Canadian contingent was despatched to quell a rebellion in the Karoo. But it was an inglorious expedition and the inexperienced Canadians did not acquit themselves well. They were then sent to Bloemfontein, where McCrae complained of tedium. Visiting the military hospital at De Aar he was disquieted at the poor standards: 'For absolute neglect and rotten administration it is a model.' He saw fierce active service with his battery against Christiaan de Wet as part of (General) Cunningham's Column. McCrae was exhilarated, even earning the soubriquet 'McCrae and his Covenanters' and praise from Lord Roberts. The Canadians' active participation in the war continued until January, 1901, when they sailed back to Halifax.

McCrae received high praise for his participation from his commanding officer: 'An exceptionally clever officer and perfect gentleman,' who was 'the constant companion and friend of the men. The life of the camp . . . the most popular officer of the lot.' McCrae felt that 'the red patch on the map of South Africa has grown, the addition having been purchased at a price.' In 1901 he was promoted to captain in the 16th Battery and the following year to major. In 1904 he resigned and, it is said, never talked about his Boer War experiences.

He returned to his medical studies at McGill, where a school of pathology was being founded under John Adami. As a research scientist McCrae was deemed to have 'neither the mind nor the hands'. Nevertheless he was appointed resident pathologist at Montreal General Hospital in 1902 where he was able to 'visualise clinical events', wrote Adami, 'and then from our findings he would bring some co-ordination of the several views.' 'Jack' McCrae's reputation as a lecturer not to be missed on bacteriology and pathology grew. He could be stern, with occasional outbursts of temper, but was loved by his students as a born teacher who could 'make easy a subject which at first was difficult'.

In 1904 he went to study in the UK and gained his Royal College of Physicians qualifications. The next year he set up practice in Montreal while continuing to lecture – and to write poetry. In 1908 he was appointed physician to the Royal Alexandra Hospital for Infectious Diseases.

It was a productive and arduous period for a man friends described as 'a social figure' (Sir Andrew Macphail). 'A man of the greatest in eating and drinking, his amusements abhorred late hours and he kept himself mind and body in the training of an athlete,' wrote another friend, the humourist Stephen Leacock. The man seemed almost too good to be true – a regular workaholic – but his humour, vitality and gift of fun and mimicry seem to have made him a joy to know. 'I have so damned many things on my soul at present that I can't sit down and be ordinarily gay without my conscience say "my dear fellow, art is long and time is fleeting" and you ought to be doing this and that,' he wrote to Macphail in 1909. His cultural life was important to his sanity, and he belonged to several intellectual and social clubs.

Between 1906 and 1909 McCrae published five poems in the McGill University magazine. 'The Unconquered Dead', recalling the 1899 Battle of Magersfontein, and with its echoes of Kipling, pre-empted 'In Flanders Fields'. 'Isandlwana', published in 1910, was inspired by a visit to Brecon, home of the 24th Foot who were massacred by Cetswayo's Zulu Impi, where he met an old lady whose mind had been unhinged by her son's death.

McCrae remained a traditionalist, associating with friends who preferred Canada's links with the old country to what they considered to be the threat of moral contamination from close ties with their brash commercial neighbour, America. Britain still represented all that was fine, noble, just and legal. Yet they felt strongly proud and nationalistic about their own country, safe in the benevolent family of the Empire. Another friend at this time was Lord Grey, the Governor General of Canada. McCrae served as MO to his expedition across Lake Winnipeg to Hudson Bay in August, 1910, and again was 'the life of the party'. Grey was a traditional English aristocrat, but a likeable human being and McCrae continued to communicate with him during the Great War.

From 1911 to 1914 McCrae's reputation as one of the busiest, most able, most likeable teachers and physicians in Montreal continued to grow. With Adami he wrote *A Textbook of Pathology for Students of Medicine*, published in 1912. He also wrote papers for the *American Journal of Medical Science*. He was happy at McGill and resisted all temptations to move. The only unsuccessful aspect of his life was his inability to find a compatible wife. In 1910 he fell in love with a woman he refers to as 'Lady R' in correspondence with friends. Although she married another, he continued to yearn for her until 1914. Nevertheless he was a desirable bachelor and several women were to claim that they were engaged to him when he went to France in 1914.

McCrae enjoyed broadening his horizons with travel, frequently sailing to Europe. In 1913, concerned about the war clouds threatening Europe, he wrote 'The Captain', when a modern ship was so named after Britain's famous fighting ship. The poem was published in the university magazine.

On 29 July, 1914, McCrae left again for England. War was declared while he was still aboard ship. 'I am afraid that my holiday trip is knocked galley west,' he commented. Canada followed Britain in declaring war on Germany on 4 August, 1914. Her Prime Minister, Robert Borden, recognized the war as 'ours'. In three weeks 45,000 volunteers enlisted. McCrae cabled home his willingness to serve, was offered the appointment of brigade surgeon and sailed home again at the end of August.

The militia was disappointed that the old regimental units were abolished and numbered battalions of the Canadian Expeditionary Force were being raised. The Director of Artillery, E.W.B. Morrison, wished to grant McCrae the rank of lieutenant-colonel and give him command of an artillery brigade. Officially McCrae was too old at forty-one, so he was given the title of brigade surgeon, the rank of major and the position of second-in-command.

During his brief return to Canada McCrae did not visit his family, but he saw friends in Montreal and told them he felt bachelors like himself with experience of war were duty-bound to go. On 3 October, 1914, the first Canadian contingent of 1,424 officers and 29,197 other ranks left for Plymouth, including Major John McCrae and his new horse, Bonfire, a present from a friend. The Canadians were enthusiastic but untrained, and spent a wet and miserable time on Salisbury Plain, raring to do their bit in France but bogged down in mud and drill. Somehow the Canadians felt that they cared more passionately about the conduct of war across the Channel than the seemingly lethargic Britons.

In December McCrae visited his old teacher, Sir William Osler, who was living in Oxford. Osler abhorred war, but was energetic in organizing the medical services. In February, 1915, the Canadian division finally moved to France, where they were attached to a unit of the Royal Field Artillery near Armentières. They first saw action in the Battle of Neuve Chapelle on 10–13 March. John wrote to his parents and friends about the battle, relieved that a sniper took a pot shot at him 'but he made a good miss'. He was pleased that his men were fit and 'medically, work is light'. But by 30 March in one of his regular (usually twice-weekly) letters to his mother he was concerned that 'Our Canadian plots fill up rapidly.'

McCrae seems to have performed dual functions, using his experience as both a physician and an artillery officer. He was hauled over the coals for using too much ammunition in putting out a German battery during the great shell shortage, and it was reported that 'he nearly caused a mutiny by giving artillery orders on the authority of his medical rank'. He was just as concerned with sanitation and the omnipresent lice. One day, while scrubbing down with lye soap, the explosion of a German shell nearby made him run naked down the road from his billet.

On 6 April the Canadian Division moved to the Ypres Salient to relieve the French to the north-east of Ypres. They were just in time to experience the use of the Germans' new weapon, chlorine gas, which was in contravention of the 1899 and 1906 Hague Conventions. First released at about noon on 22 April, the greenish-yellow cloud struck excitable French Colonial forces, who ran in terror, leaving a yawning three-mile gap in the line. Had the Germans exploited this success the war might have had a different outcome. As it was, darkness and confusion saved the day for the Allies and the Canadians were called in to plug the gap.

McCrae described the scene in a letter: 'As we sat on the road we began to see the French stragglers – men with arms [some versions say 'without arms' and this is more likely], wounded men, teams, wagons, civilians, refugees – some by the roads, some across country, all talking, shouting – the very picture of débâcle . . . . Of one's feelings all this night – of the asphyxiated French soldiers – of the women and children – of the cheery steady British reinforcements that moved up quietly past us going up, not back – I could write, but you can imagine.'

Soon his medical skills were in demand. On 24 April he was in his dressing station on the banks of the Ypres Canal, describing the road outside. His account of the Second Battle of Ypres is one of the most moving and vivid ever written. The shelling was severe and relentless. Wounded men, stragglers and horses were constantly hit. 'It got to be a nightmare.' While desperately trying to keep up with the stream of casualties, he had time to assess the military situation. 'For 36 hours we had not an infantryman between us and the Germans and this gap was 1,200 to 1,500 yards wide. God knows why the G [Germans] did not put in a big force to eat us up. We really expected to die.' By 25 April the Canadians had lost 6,000 of their strength of 10,000.

McCrae's accounts continue in his letters. The shelling was unremitting, the small cemetery beside his dressing station grew daily. On 2 May Lieutenant Alex Helmer died, virtually blown to pieces by a direct hit by an eight-inch shell. McCrae was moved by the last words in Helmer's diary: 'It has quieted a little and I shall try to get a good sleep.' McCrae said the committal service over Helmer's body. 'A soldier's death,' he commented. A wooden cross was put over his grave, but it must have been lost in subsequent fighting: in Essex Farm Cemetery that today stands by the still extant bunker that was McCrae's dressing station, there is no headstone bearing Helmer's name. He is commemorated on the vast Menin Gate which bears the names of 55,000 men 'missing with no known grave'. This death was reputedly the inspiration for McCrae's immortal poem, 'In Flanders Fields'.

Accounts vary enormously as to the exact circumstances when the poem was written: one witness remembers McCrae before 7.30am on 2 May, 1915, sitting writing on the rearstep of an ambulance overlooking Helmer's grave; another that he wrote the poem in twenty minutes, overcome with grief just after Helmer's burial. Yet another maintains that McCrae crumpled up the paper he wrote the poem on but a fellow officer rescued it and persuaded him to send it for publication.

The Second Battle of Ypres continued, meticulously documented by McCrae. On 10 May he wrote to his mother, 'How tired we are! Weary in body and wearier in mind. None of our men went off their heads, but men in nearby units did – and no wonder.'

On 2 June McCrae sadly left his battery to join the Canadian Army Medical Corps. The casualty rate was mounting and MOs were desperately needed. The Oslers, whom he visited during his leave that month, were disturbed at his haggard and weary appearance. On 17 June he proceeded to No 3 Canadian General Hospital at Dannes-Camiers near Boulogne, which had been raised and equipped by McGill University. McCrae was promoted to lieutenant-colonel in charge of medicine and was pleased to meet up with several old friends.

The busy hospital (which treated 1,000 casualties during the Battle of

Loos in the last week of September, 1915) was often visited by celebrities, such as the newspaperman, Sir Max Aitken, and the English bacteriologist, Sir Almroth Wright and his assistant Alexander Fleming, who desperately felt the lack of an effective treatment for infected wounds. Fleming was already working on penicillin, although it would not be perfected until the inter-war years, and not be into significant production until the Second World War. In October No 3 Hospital's tented wards were damaged by heavy storms; with winter approaching, the hospital moved to the Jesuit College in Boulogne.

Rejected by *The Spectator*, 'In Flanders Fields' was published, anonymously, in *Punch* on 8 December, 1915. It immediately struck a chord, both at home and in the front lines, for the sincerity and simplicity of its message: the tragic sacrifice of young lives being made by the thousands must not be in vain. The appeal to those who followed to take up the cause was irresistible. But the poem succeeded because of its two strong symbols: the blood-red poppy and the torch that must be passed on.

The Flanders poppy, taken after the war as the symbol of remembrance, gave the poem its immortality and universality. An American YMCA worker, Moina Michael, on reading the poem, was inspired to write a reply, 'The Victory Emblem'. She responded to the challenge to catch the torch and suggested that those who wished to keep the faith with those who died should wear 'the Poppy red . . . in honour of our dead'. On 9 November, 1918, she used some donations to buy twenty-five red poppies, wearing one herself and selling the rest to overseas War Secretaries at a Conference she was attending. Madame Guérin, the French Secretary, made the practical suggestion that the making and selling of artificial poppies could raise money for ex-servicemen.

The first Poppy Day was held in Britain on Armistice Day, 11 November, 1921. It raised £106,000. Earl Haig had recently been appointed Founder-President of the newly-formed British Legion (which was not granted the designation 'Royal' until 1971) and vigorously promoted the poppy as a fund-raising emblem. Some said the energy with which he fulfilled his presidency was a conscience-salving expiation of his guilt for the horrendous loss of life, for which he had been responsible as Commander-in-Chief of the BEF and which earned him the name 'Butcher Haig'. Today the five disabled ex-servicemen who started the Poppy Factory's work in Bermondsey in 1922 have been replaced by nearly 200 at the Royal British Legion Village near Maidstone. They make 45 million poppies and 70,000 wreaths a year for the annual appeal, which raises £4.5 million and benefits 50,000 ex-servicemen and women.

The supremely human and compassionate Canadian doctor and soldier who inspired this perfect symbol of respect, thanksgiving and eternal remembrance did not live to see its enduring universality. But even during his lifetime the poem became a rallying cry, much loved and quoted. It was particularly popular in the United States and was translated into many languages, even Latin. McCrae commented to his mother, 'It only needs Chinese now, surely!'

After the poem's publication McCrae's efforts continued undiminished and his health and vigour suffered in proportion. Friends noticed the change in his personality, the loss of his natural gaiety, the guilt he felt at surviving battle after battle, patching together the wounded or seeing them die. His horse, Bonfire, and dog, Bonneau, were faithful and comforting companions. In October, 1916, after treating the horrendous casualties from the Somme, McCrae's asthma recurred and he was hospitalized in nearby Wimereux. In 1917 he was unwillingly embroiled in the politics of Sir Sam Hughes, the Canadian Minister for Defence, who wished to segregate Canadian wounded in Canadian hospitals and keep the Canadian Corps separate from the BEF. McCrae's friends Osler and Adami resigned in protest at the policy (which was impracticable in medical terms) and Hughes was forced to quit his office.

McCrae, who had a simple affinity with his men, was also irritated (despite his strong religious beliefs) by the sanctimonious army padres whose message, 'Jesus saves', seemed irrelevant to men living in hellish conditions and whose comrades were constantly being killed. 'At times I get past words,' he exploded to his mother.

In April, 1917, after a refreshing leave in the UK, McCrae felt particularly proud to be treating the wounded from the brilliant Canadian success at Vimy Ridge, where on 9 April they cleared the strongly-held ridge after the French had failed in the attempt after two years of costly fighting. It became known as 'the day Canada became a nation', much as 25 April, 1915, was known as the day the Australians came of age in Gallipoli.

On 20 June, 1917, another of McCrae's poems, 'The Anxious Dead' was published in *The Spectator*. He was right in judging that 'it will hardly go as far as "Flanders Fields".'

From July to November, 1917, his hospital treated the wounded from the Third Battle of Ypres, Passchendaele. That autumn McCrae was disappointed not to get promotion and command of No 3 Hospital. His ill health continued, with some debilitating asthma attacks, and he was bedridden and severely depressed when the news came through on 24 January, 1918, that he was to be the consulting physician to the First British Army. But McCrae did not recover, and died at 1.30am on 28 January, 1918.

Dr Harvey Cushing, a distinguished neurosurgeon serving as operating surgeon with the BEF, recorded in his diary: 'I saw poor Jack McCrae with Elder at No 14 General last night – the last time. A bright flame rapidly burning out. He died early this morning. Just made consulting Physician to the 1st Army – the only Canadian so far to be thus honored. Never strong, he gave his all with the Canadian Artillery during the prolonged second battle of Ypres and after, at which time he wrote his imperishable verses. Since those frightful days he has never been his old gay and companionable self, but has rather sought solitude. A soldier from top to toe – how he would have hated to die in bed. A three days' illness – an atypical pneumonia with extensive pneumococcus meningitis, as we learned this afternoon . . . . They will bury him tomorrow. Some of the older members of the McGill Unit who still remain here were scouring the fields this afternoon to try and find some chance winter poppies to put on his grave – to remind him of Flanders where he would have preferred to lie. Was anyone ever more respected and loved than he? Someone has said that "children and animals followed him as shadows follow other men".'

McCrae's death was a shocking blow to his many devoted friends and colleagues by whom he was infinitely loved and respected. They gave him an impressive funeral with full military honours, attended by his grieving staff, in Wimereux Cemetery, high on a hill overlooking the Channel. The funeral procession was led by his horse, Bonfire, his master's boots reversed in his stirrups. John McCrae, dedicated and loyal, intelligent, critical and questioning, epitomized the ideal son of the Empire he loved and served so well. To him we owe the eternal symbol of faith and remembrance, the scarlet Flanders poppy and one of the Great War's best-loved poems.

Edward Thomas

SECOND LIEUTENANT, ROYAL GARRISON ARTILLERY

TEARS

It seems I have no tears left. They should have fallen —
Their ghosts, if tears have ghosts, did fall — that day
When twenty hounds streamed by me, not yet combed
    out
But still all equals in their rage of gladness
Upon the scent, made one, like a great dragon
In Blooming Meadow that bends towards the sun
And once bore hops: and on that other day
When I stepped out from the double-shadowed Tower
Into an April morning, stirring and sweet
And warm. Strange solitude was there and silence.
A mightier charm than any in the Tower
Possessed the courtyard. They were changing guard,
Soldiers in line, young English countrymen,
Fair-haired and ruddy, in white tunics. Drums
And fifes were playing 'The British Grenadiers'.
The men, the music piercing that solitude
And silence, told me truths I had not dreamed,
And have forgotten since their beauty passed.

1915

SECOND LIEUTENANT
EDWARD THOMAS

The received image of Edward Thomas is of a man of the English soil, steeped in country ways from birth, an established poet before 1914 whose wartime poetry avoids all mention of the war.

The facts are very different. Thomas was born on 3 March 1878, and brought up in the London suburbs of Lambeth and Battersea. His boyhood playground was the urban criss-cross of narrow streets where young Londoners played the normal gang game of raids and counter-attacks. The closest Edward came to a green, open space was Wandsworth Common, where this nature-lover watched, with almost hypnotic fascination, as older boys dissected live frogs. His knowledge of the real countryside came from holiday visits to Swindon, where his mother's artisan family introduced him to rambling and fishing. Edward's Wiltshire uncles and Welsh grandmother had a strong influence on the young townie, and his love of nature stems from these early, impressionable days.

The source of this information is the first part of Thomas's unfinished autobiography, *The Childhood of Edward Thomas*, a critical self-assessment from which a picture of a somewhat priggish loner emerges. Thomas's father was a prosperous civil servant, and young Edward was aware of his superiority to the 'roughs' he played and fought with. 'The majority . . . came from homes poorer or less refined than my own.' Of his 'Board-school' (a school governed by a school board) he revealingly wrote, 'I had my own way. It was usually easy for me to get it. While I was at the Board-school I was conscious of possessing some power over my physical superiors, though the use of it was unconscious.' At the age of ten he was sent to private school, where he mingled with the 'sons of tradesmen, professional men, moderately well-to-do clerks and men of small independent means'. Next came day school in Battersea, where he wrote of his schoolmates, 'on the whole they were a coarse, rough lot'. At the age of twelve Edward won a scholarship to yet another school.

Thomas was a typical Edwardian boy, somewhat aggressive and – to today's sensibilities – brutal in a way that was then considered normal and 'manly'. His reading, which influenced his games, was of Indians and Mexican bandits. He kept pigeons, white rats and rabbits and made their cages himself. Holidays were shared between Eastbourne, Wales and

Swindon – which he always preferred – and where he was drawn more and more to animals and the countryside. Paradoxically, he had a strange, sadistic streak and was taken by the 'novelty' of seeing calves being killed at the abattoir, of stamping violently on the fish he caught or driving his 'thumbnail through the neck or into the back' (traditional ways of killing fish). But this macho behaviour was thought normal enough in an age which did not see the need for the preservation of species. So Edward happily blew birds' eggs and skewered moths and butterflies. His mentor and hero was an old countryman he called 'Dad', whose skills at fishing, tales of poaching, knowledge of bird song and Wiltshire accent delighted him. 'Dad' was immortalized as 'Lob' in Thomas's poem of that name.

Parallel with this rough, masculine side, Thomas showed an affinity to women. He would always be attracted by and attractive to them. The playmates he remembers are mostly girls: Tottie Armour of the 'black curly hair, dark eyes and cherry lips'; Mabel, 'the perfect loving friend of the light brown hair and round face'; Laura the 'dark, sturdy beauty' to whom he was 'more or less faithful for several years'; the 'buxom Welsh cousin named Florence'. His first descriptions of his mother, remembered *en déshabillé*, are sensual. 'She is plainest to me not quite dressed, in white bodice and petticoat, her arms and shoulders rounded and creamy smooth . . . I liked the scent of her fresh warm skin.' As he grew up sex remained an intriguing mystery about which he often speculated.

At his new school Thomas found a master with 'a tender feminine smile', who encouraged him to write and extend his reading to Shakespeare and the *Aeneid*. He also developed a precocious interest in politics and social matters, following his father's Liberal inclinations and even going with him to political meetings. He learned to care about 'the downtrodden in Ireland, in London slums and elsewhere' and to champion Home Rule. Exerting his own personality and testing his beliefs, he became a bit of a rebel against his bourgeois parents. He delighted to shock by swearing most foully, lying, staying out late, rebelling against the boring Sunday sermons and continuing to get himself embroiled in punch-ups. A close friendship with a boy called John, 'a staunch Conservative' from a wealthy background, seemed to steady him.

At this stage Edward discovered the writer who was to become perhaps the greatest influence on his work and life, Richard Jefferies. His 'free open-air life' and 'spice of illegality' was alluring. In the Jefferies's countryside, Thomas created an imaginary idealistic land to which he could flee from the pressures of urban and domestic life: a Never Never Land that he sought in his perpetual moves in later life.

Thomas also found new pleasure in poetry, especially in the works of Tennyson. This coincided with yet another move, at the age of fifteen, to St Paul's public school. 'The whole school impressed and alarmed me,' he wrote. He was ill at ease with his confident, privileged fellow pupils and withdrew even more into his own inner world. Writing became a balm, almost a compulsion, and his first articles, or 'essays', were published. He met the writer and critic James Ashcroft Noble, who encouraged him and found magazines to publish his work. Edward responded by falling in love with Noble's daughter Helen. The teenage love affair, despite heavy parental disapproval, was consummated before Thomas went up to Oxford to read History at Lincoln College. They were married at Fulham Registry Office on 20 June, 1899, and their son, Merfyn, was born early the next year. With a family to support, Thomas continued to write throughout his undergraduate years, and was disappointed with his second-class degree.

Then came a period of self-doubt, conflict with his father, who urged a career in the Civil Service, a punishing work schedule of reading (he managed to get work as a reviewer) and writing, and miserable lodgings in suburban London. His frustration and feelings of inadequacy were taken out on Helen, whose unwavering love and support never failed to pull him through. A second child, Bronwen, was born in October, 1902, and the family moved to more congenial surroundings at Bearsted in Kent.

The dreary life of a literary hack was interspersed with frequent moves, which Thomas always hoped would improve his circumstances, bring him closer to his Never Never Land: to Sevenoaks, then to Hampshire – Ashford, Petersfield and Steep. Certainly the countryside brought solace and gradually his reputation as a reviewer and critic grew. He was stimulated by meeting the writers whose work he helped to publicize and whom he came to count as friends, like Walter de la Mare, W.H. Davies and John Drinkwater. In December, 1911, Thomas reviewed Rupert Brooke's first collection, *Poems*, in the *Daily Chronicle*; although somewhat brief and guarded, he prophesied a poetic future for him.

On 5 March, 1912, Thomas was invited to breakfast with Edward Marsh, the Georgian poets' patron. He did not acquit himself well. Many years later Marsh wrote to the poet Gordon Bottomley, 'It must have been one of his less good days – he was unforthcoming and constricted, perhaps dyspeptic, and seemed to look down his nose at both of us as well as at the food, so it led to nothing. I wish we could have met him in the country and known the man whom you describe.'

But Thomas's literary career began to take off. His biographies of Richard Jefferies and George Borrow were published and his books about the English countryside, *The South Country* and *In Pursuit of Spring*. Edward and Helen were befriended by the American poet, Robert Frost. Their circle expanded to include Rupert Brooke, Hilaire Belloc and the writer Eleanor Farjeon, who fell in love with Thomas and never married. This was probably his happiest period. Although difficult and moody, even at times suicidally depressed, he loved his family dearly (a third child, Myfanwy, was born in 1910) and enjoyed the stimulus of other creative minds. The Gloucestershire village of Dymock became the focal point for the discussions, readings and carousings of a group of Georgian poets, including Brooke, Lascelles Abercrombie, Wilfrid Gibson, Farjeon and Frost.

It is extraordinary that although Thomas was a valued member of the group, at the beginning of 1914 he had still never published a poem. C. Day Lewis credits Robert Frost with transforming 'Thomas the Doubter' into 'Thomas the Rhymer'. Edward was in the depths of one of his black moods of melancholia which 'sent him flinging out of the house to tramp the countryside all night'. Frost 'referred him to paragraphs in his book *In Pursuit of Spring* and told him to write it in verse form in exactly the same cadences. That's all there was to it.'

When war was declared, Thomas at thirty-six was over the statutory age for enlistment. He did not share the prevalent jingoistic war fever. 'I hate not Germans nor grow hot/With love of Englishmen, to please the newspapers' ('This is No Petty Case of Right or Wrong'). In the December, 1914, edition of *Poetry and Drama* he wrote a dismissive article 'On Poets and Poetry in time of war'. He mocked the poets who 'also serve who only sit and write' and were inspired to rush into verse for the first time. 'No other class of poetry vanishes so rapidly, has so little chosen from it for posterity,' he opined. How wrong he was, especially and ironically as far as his own poetry was concerned.

For suddenly the floodgates opened and all the pent-up poetry in Thomas's agonized soul started to pour forth. He wrote about his wife and children; his difficult relationship with his father; the Wiltshire man he called 'Dad'. He sang of home and lovers, mothers and children, star-lings and cuckoos, goldfinch and thrush, lichen, ivy and moss, wind and mist, roads and lakes, clouds and rain. The themes are Georgian, but his approach was original, pleasing and surprising, with a beauty and felicity of phrase and image that have caused his poetry to be regarded as among the finest written during the First World War. And contrary to popular misconception, the war did infiltrate those bucolic and domestic themes. 'The Trumpet' is a call to arms, not in the strident tones of Jessie Pope or the heroic terms of Brooke, but Thomas's horn is 'lovelier than any mysteries' and might have been played by Grenfell to whom 'death has increase'. Yet the poem was written, not as the others of its genre, in the first flush of excited patriotism, but two years into the war.

Perhaps the most extraordinary fact about Edward Thomas's brilliant cascade of 144 poems is that they were all written in the two years between 1914 and his going to France in 1916. His daughter Myfanwy wrote, 'My father wrote no poems while at the Front; the poems to his wife and chil-dren were written in April, 1916.' Many anthologists fall into the trap of assuming that Thomas, like Gurney, Blunden and Ledwidge, wrote poetry about the peaceful countryside as therapy for the violence and destruction surrounding him. But poems like 'In Memoriam Easter 1915', which seems to identify Thomas with soldiers who would not return from the war, were written before he joined up.

In Thomas's masterpiece of narrative writing, 'As the Team's Head-Brass', the ploughman asks the narrator if he'd been out to the front. 'If I could only come back again, I should,' is the reply. The war began for Thomas when he enlisted in the Artists' Rifles in July, 1915. His family moved to High Beech near Epping Forest to be close to Edward as he trained as a map-reading instructor with the Royal Artillery. On map-reading exercises he discovered fascinating place names – Childerditch, Margaretting, Pyrgo and Havering – which, according to Myfanwy 'were woven into the poems written for his family before he left for France in 1917'. Another unusual name, Adelstrop, seen from a train window, became the title of what is perhaps his best-known poem (probably because of its inclusion in the *Oxford Book of English Verse*). It was written on the same day as 'Tears', the haunting poem reproduced here. Both poems describe a typical English incident: the singing of a blackbird and hounds streaming after a fox, but the gentle pastoral scene painted in 'Adelstrop' contrasts with the sharp sorrow for 'the young English countrymen,/Fair-haired and ruddy, in white tunics' whose beauty would pass in 'Tears'.

Thomas spent Christmas, 1916, with his family, their last time together. Helen and the girls decorated the 'horrible house' with 'a festive bower of holly and ivy and boughs'. For Myfanwy, afraid of the dark and the beasties that may lurk in it, Thomas wrote 'Out in the Dark', where nothing more fearsome than 'Fallow fawns' invisibly go. At the end of January, 1917, he left for France, with cheques for the next six months prudently written, his goodbyes made to Helen, the children and Eleanor Farjeon.

Once at the front his diary describes his arrival in the snow at Le Havre, where the battery 'had to be specially warned against venereal', and entraining for Doullens. The fragmented entries give the flavour, often 'merry', of army life – swearing, dirty stories, singing 'There's a long, long trail a-winding', 'jaunty talk full of old army proverbs and metaphors' from a fellow officer. Thomas chose billets for the men and was mess secretary. Then they moved, through Warlus to Dainville and billets on the Arras road, towards Beaurains. He inspected OPs (observation posts – a dangerous occupation as they are usually far forward) above Agny, Wailly, Achicourt and Beaurains. As always, letters were a highlight – '750 letters for men; 17 for me'. He was a prodigious letter writer and received as many as he wrote.

Posted as Orderly Officer to Group 35 HA (Heavy Artillery) in Arras, he loved the town. 'In class it was like Bath.' But soon Thomas chafed, 'Am I to stay on here and do nothing but have cold feet?' He could not understand why the Germans ('Huns') did not attack the British guns at Arras. 'Some day this will be one of the hottest places this side of Hell.' As spring stirred in April he noticed the blackbirds singing as the bombardment from his battery hotted up, and 'larks, partridges, hedge sparrows, magpies by OP'. On Easter Day he reported shelling on their positions and a lucky near miss. The next day, 9 April, 1917, Edward Thomas was killed at his OP by the blast from a shell. 'His body was quite untouched,' wrote Myfanwy, 'and the war diary in his pocket bore strange sea-shell-like markings as though it had undergone tremendous and violent pressure.' Thomas was buried in Agny Cemetery.

After the war Helen, whose anguish at his death was almost unbearable, worked indefatigably to gain recognition for Edward's undoubted poetic genius and organized the publication of his *Collected Works*. His admirer, Walter de la Mare, wrote a laudatory but realistic introduction to the book, describing his nature, the hard 'journey-work' he had to put in, the occasional desperation. 'His poems were a release from that bondage,' he commented, explaining how Thomas found sheer joy in writing them. De la Mare gives a vivid physical description of Thomas at their first meeting: an out-of-place Gulliver in the Lilliput of London, with a long, narrow face and a grave expression, 'a glint of gold in his sun-baked hair', blue eyes under long lashes, wide lips, square chin, large feet and 'powerful and bony' hands, a low and gentle voice with 'stylish' talk. 'His smile could be whimsical, stealthy, shy, ardent, mocking, or drily ironical; he seldom laughed.' When Thomas was killed, de la Mare felt that 'a mirror of England was shattered of so pure and true a crystal that a clearer and tenderer reflection of it can be found no other where than in these poems.'

Full appreciation for the quality of his work came late. Edward Marsh refused to include any of his poems in the second volume of *Georgian Poets* (although de la Mare volunteered to stand down to make room) as he had made it a rule not to publish for the first time a poem submitted to him posthumously: so many bereaved parents were trying to make his anthology a memorial for their poetic sons. But in recent times recognition of his work is universal. C. Day Lewis felt that he wrote 'an extraordinarily honest kind of poetry. It has both the awkwardness and the irresistibleness of absolute sincerity. It is very much in character; for Thomas was a shy, reticent man, with great personal charm and an honesty that could at times be ruthless.' The critic Philip Hobsbaum maintained in 1961 that the mainstream of modern literature ran not through T.S. Eliot, but from Hardy through Edward Thomas to contemporary poets like Larkin.

When his name was included with fifteen other poets of the First World

War on a great stone in Poets' Corner in Westminster Abbey in 1990, his daughter Myfanwy wrote that this man who spent so much of his life in discontented striving would have been 'amazed indeed, but fulfilled and content'.

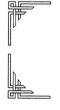

Robert Graves

CAPTAIN, ROYAL WELCH FUSILIERS

THE DEAD FOX HUNTER

*(In memory of Captain A.L. Samson, 2nd Battalion Royal
Welch Fusiliers, killed near Cuinchey, September 25th 1915)*

We found the little captain at the head,
His men lay, well aligned.
We touched his hand — stone cold — and he was dead,
And they, all dead, behind
Had never reached their goal, but they died well.
They charged in line, and, in the same line, fell.

The well known rosy colours of his face
Were almost lost in grey.
We saw that dying, and in hopeless case,
For others' sake that day
He'd smothered all rebellious groans; in death
His fingers were tight-clenched between his teeth.

For those who live uprightly and die true
Heaven has no bars or locks.
And serves all tastes . . . or what's for him to do
Up there, but hunt the fox?
Angelic choirs? No, Justice must provide
For one who rode straight, and in hunting died.

So if Heaven had no hunt before he came,
Why, it must find one now.
If any shirk, or doubt they know the game,
There's one to teach them how,
And the whole host of Seraphim complete
Must jog in scarlet to his opening Meet.

CAPTAIN ROBERT
VON RANKE GRAVES

'The men who had died . . . were not particularly virtuous or wicked, but just average soldiers, and the survivors should thank God they were alive and do their best to avoid wars in the future.'

This sensible truism was penned by one of the most colourful and extravagant writers to emerge from the war, Robert Graves. Graves is mostly known from his autobiographical account, *Goodbye to All That*, the most entertaining book to come out of the Great War. In many passages the fictional aspects of the book overwhelm the autobiographical: its author was prone to embroider, 'improve' or simply invent for dramatic or comic effect. But in his 1931 essay, 'P.S. to *Goodbye to All That*', Graves blatantly claimed that he deliberately set out to write a money-spinning best-seller to overcome his severe financial problems. He even listed the components he knew would interest the general public: references to food and drink; murders and ghosts; personalities like T.E. Lawrence and the Prince of Wales, poets, prime ministers and kings; sport, love affairs, wounds, weddings. Complete accuracy was not a claim he made for the book, and it should be savoured for what it is: an account which, although exaggerated and inaccurate in parts, nevertheless gives a personal insight into a young officer's war and provides entertaining cameos of many of the characters he encountered.

Graves's contemporaries and friends saw it otherwise. According to Martin Seymour-Smith in his authorized biography, Graves's publishers wrote to him in a panic, having been contacted by an indignant Sassoon, egged on by Blunden, who 'feels so strongly about the whole book that in order to quieten him down and prevent him taking some drastic legal action' they proposed to delete whole sections and insert asterisks! Some palliative amendments were made, but Blunden, the more vituperative of the pair, went through the published tome with Sassoon with a fine, mean toothcomb and annotated 250 of the 448 pages with a view to lodging the amended book at the British Museum to give posterity a correct version of events. He wrote to a friend, 'Robert Graves has published, for money and to create a sensation, a most ugly and untruthful autobiography. It is the season of gross and silly war books, and he has succeeded in selling his. But he has lost all the respect . . . left in the minds of Sassoon and other old friends.' Captain J.C. Dunn, MO of the 2nd Welch Fusiliers, also took exception to some parts and told Graves that 'legends are always livelier than facts'. Dunn complained to Sassoon that he was sorry Graves had found a publisher for the work. Sassoon also told Graves, probably sarcastically, that he was glad that he was making 'a lot of money'.

Graves was born on 24 July, 1895, to Alfred Perceval Graves and Amalia Elizabeth Sophie, née von Ranke. Alfred ('A.P.') was an intelligent, light-hearted poet and minstrel, and a widower bringing up five children when he married the sanctimonious, humourless 'Amy'. She gave him five more children, of whom Robert was the third, and converted him to teetotalism, thereby killing his sense of fun. A.P.'s family was Irish, with a tradition of clerics and academics; Amy's family was German, her most famous ancestor being the historian Leopold von Ranke to whom Robert felt he owed his 'clumsy largeness, endurance, energy, seriousness, and thick hair'.

Graves attended a succession of prep schools, staying for three years at Wimbledon where he 'began playing games seriously, grew quarrelsome, boastful and domineering.' His public school was Charterhouse, where his experiences were not consistently pleasurable and his von Ranke middle name caused trouble. He was no Brooke, enjoying golden, happy schooldays, but an awkward and ungainly young boy. 'From my first moment at Charterhouse I suffered an oppression of spirit that I hesitate to recall in its full intensity,' he wrote.

A large part of his unhappiness was rooted in his terror of sexuality. 'In English preparatory and public schools romance is necessarily homosexual.' His mother had instilled in him her traditional religious prudishness, yet in his fourth year Graves 'fell in love' with a boy he called 'Dick' in Goodbye to All That (actually G.H. Johnstone, later Baron Derwent). The love on Graves's side was 'pure'. He claimed to be among the 'pseudo-homosexuals' created by the public school system: boys who were not homosexual by nature but experimented with it, physically or mentally, at school before growing out of it when they discovered girls.

Another great influence on Graves during his later years at Charterhouse was a master, George Mallory (who became every schoolboy's hero when he disappeared while only 800 feet from the summit of Mount Everest in June, 1924), whose enthusiasm for literature was imparted to Graves. Robert had been writing poetry since he was thirteen, was a member of the Poetry Society and contributed poems to the school magazine, which he co-edited in 1913. Mallory introduced Graves to Edward Marsh, who read some of his verses and declared them to be written 'in the poetic diction of fifty years ago'. Marsh and Mallory introduced Graves to the poetry of Brooke, W.H. Davies, Flecker and other modern Georgians, which excited him. He was also fascinated by ancient Celtic poetry.

His last year at school was happier, mostly because he 'did everything possible to show how little respect [he] had for school tradition'. He gained (with the Dutch courage of illicit 'cherry whisky') a reputation as an invincible boxer, won a classical exhibition to St John's College, Oxford, and cared most for 'poetry and Dick'. He was, however, embroiled in an unsavoury episode (which might have warned him of Dick's lack of innocence) when, ever the prude, he caused the dismissal of a master for kissing Dick (which the duplicitous Dick later denied).

Early family holidays were spent with his mother's aristocratic German relations and Robert learned to speak the language (a skill he hid when teased at school for being 'German'). He much preferred later holidays in North Wales, where Mallory took him climbing on Snowdon and taught him to become a skilful and daring mountaineer. On leaving Charterhouse in 1914 he went to the Welsh hills around the family holiday house in Harlech, nervous about going to Oxford.

The outbreak of war came as an honourable let-out; encouraged by the secretary of Harlech golf club he joined the Royal Welch Fusiliers at Wrexham, getting a commission only because he had been in the Charterhouse OTC. (In fact he resigned from it 'in revolt against the theory of implicit obedience to orders'.) In training he was intimidated by the experienced old soldiers in his platoon, but survived his induction and moved to an internment camp for aliens in Lancaster guarding 'harmless German commercial travellers and shopkeepers' and forty waiters from the Midland Hotel in Manchester, who were handed over to Graves. Spy mania was running high.

The fifty Welsh reservists whom he commanded were reprobates, a continual headache to the inexperienced Graves. He chafed to go to France, but the adjutant refused him until he had overhauled his wardrobe and 'looked more like a soldier'. Boxing came to his rescue again: he acquitted himself well against a sergeant who later won a welterweight Lonsdale Belt. The adjutant put him down for a draft due to go to France the following week.

The days of training at Wrexham and the antics of the inventive and ribald Welsh rogues are hilariously and bawdily described in *Goodbye to All That*. Graves was astounded by, and somewhat admiring of, their obscene language, their sexual prowess, their inventive lies and misdemeanours. Graves was taught his regiment's proud history, learned the techniques of the Boer War and how to conduct himself on formal occasions. The regiment had some idiosyncratic customs and traditions, considering themselves 'second to none, even to the Guards'. Imagine his disappointment, therefore, when firstly he wasn't sent to France until May, 1915, and secondly was sent not to the revered RWF but to the 'tough and rough' Welsh Regiment.

His first platoon of forty men was a motley crew, a mixture of the over-age (including a sixty-three-year-old Boer War veteran) and the under-age (some boys of fifteen). They had a hot welcome to the front line, coming under shellfire even as they marched from the railhead at Cambrin singing – in perfect tune, of course – 'Aberystwyth'. Graves kept, or later retrieved, copies of letters he wrote at the time, and from them built up a record of these early days in the trenches. Interspersed with the near factual account are apocryphal stories, like the two young miners who shot their hated sergeant, gave themselves up to the adjutant and reported their 'accident'. 'What do you mean, you damn fools?', the adjutant asked. 'Did you mistake him for a spy?' 'No, sir. We mistook him for our platoon sergeant.'

They were billeted at first at Béthune, then on 24 June moved to Vermelles in the mining area near Loos. At the end of July Graves was sent to join the 2nd Battalion of the RWF at Laventie. On the way he met the Prince of Wales in Béthune's public baths: their conversation consisted of remarks about how bloody cold the water was. At battalion HQ Graves was given an indifferent welcome. It was a regimental custom to ignore new junior officers (known as 'warts') for the first six months. He was warned not to make any undue noise in the mess, not to drink whisky or play the gramophone. Polo matches were played and non-riders were expected to attend riding school. Amazed at these 'childish' rituals, Graves wondered whether the battalion was aware there was a war on. 'The Royal Welch don't recognize it socially,' responded an officer from the East Surreys. Graves privately whispered under his breath. 'You damned snobs! I'll survive you all!' He virtually did.

Graves gained valuable experience and learned practical survival techniques until, on 9 September, he went on leave. Like many front-line soldiers, he found the home front unreal, his family and friends impossible to relate to, and sought solace in the Welsh hills before returning to the front in time for the preparations for the Battle of Loos. His account of the mismanagement of the 'accessory' (gas) and the bungling ineptitude of bringing up reserves through retreating and wounded troops is a classic passage in *Goodbye to All That*. The descriptive 'bloody balls-up' summarizes it perfectly, but the account is poignant. Graves lost many friends he had grown fond of – only five company officers survived in the Royal Welch. The poem reproduced here, 'The Dead Fox Hunter, In memory of Captain L. Samson' (who died on 29 May, 1915, and is buried in Cambrin Churchyard Extension) shows his sense of personal loss.

On 15 October Graves was gazetted a special reserve captain. He was just twenty. A few days later came the shocking revelation seen by chance in a copy of Horatio Bottomley's *John Bull*, that the object of his Charterhouse crush, Dick, had made 'a certain proposal' to a Canadian soldier and had been convicted in a police court of sexual delinquency. 'The news nearly finished me,' Graves commented. It caused him to evolve his own theory of progressive neurasthenia: it gradually rendered a man unfit for trench warfare. It was explained, he maintained, by Dr William Rivers as being 'the action of one of the ductless glands . . . in failing at a certain point to pump its sedative chemical into the blood'. Graves reckoned it took some ten years for his own system to recover.

In November Graves was sent to Locon, north of Cambrin, to join the 1st Battalion. There he met Siegfried Sassoon, and they soon discovered that each was writing. Sassoon had had some 'privately-printed pastoral pieces of eighteen-ninetyish flavour'; Graves was preparing his first book of poems, *Over the Brazier*, for publication. Sassoon gives a vivid portrait of Graves, who appears in *Memoirs of an Infantry Officer* as David Cromlech. He was 'big and impulsive', with a 'sallow, crooked and whimsical face . . . deplorably untidy', known as 'a queer bird' by fellow officers, 'an expert at putting people's backs up unintentionally. . . far too fond of butting in with his opinion before he's asked for it.' He would 'grow up into the most bumptious young prig God ever invented.'

Sassoon became extremely fond of Graves, with a lasting affection that even outrode the *Goodbye to All That* brouhaha. They were kindred spirits and delighted in discussing literature. Each wrote to Edward Marsh about the other, Sassoon saying that he was 'rather disappointed about his [Graves's] poems' and questioning Marsh's wisdom in wanting to publish them. Marsh, although not liking all of them, found some to be 'fresh, pleasant things'.

Sassoon and Graves became friendly with a young Welshman, David Thomas, a second lieutenant from the 3rd Battalion who transferred to the 1st Battalion on 29 November, 1915. In *Memoirs* Sassoon refers to him as 'Dick Tiltwood'. After a spell acting as an instructor in the Bull Ring at Harfleur, Graves returned to the battalion in March, 1916. On the evening of 17 March, A Company, led by Graves, and C Company under Thomas went out on a working party, putting sandbags in position. At about 10.30 Thomas was hit by a rifle bullet in the neck. To Graves's relief he was able to walk to the dressing station, but a tracheotomy failed to save him from choking. Graves was devastated. 'I felt David's death worse than any other since I had been in France,' he said, and wrote a moving tribute, 'Goliath and David. For Lieut David Thomas, 1st Batt. Royal Welch Fusiliers killed at Fricourt, March, 1916', which reversed the outcome of the Bible story. German might was too powerful for the 'shepherd boy who stood out fine and young'. Sassoon's reaction was one of anger. He 'went out on patrol looking for Germans to kill,' but also expressed his grief in poetry.

Graves had leave in April, 1916, during which he had an operation on his boxing-modified nose (but maintained that it was bungled). He then walked in the hills around Harlech and, returning to London, met Lloyd George. 'The power of his rhetoric amazed me,' commented Graves, who felt himself swept up in the hypnotic power of his oratory. Graves was then sent to the 3rd Battalion at Litherland, thereby missing the first few days of the July, 1916, Somme offensive and probably saving his life. He returned to France on 5 July, all available men having been rushed out to replace the horrendous casualties of 1 July. His disappointment was bitter when he was sent to the 2nd Battalion, rather than to his own 1st Battalion, arriving in the middle of a raid at Givenchy. The only officer he liked in the 2nd was the MO, Captain Dunn. Graves's rank of captain was resented by some junior officers and the suspicion of his German origins was brought up again. Dunn refers to 'von R Graves' in his diary.

Moving back to the Somme area, Graves was relieved to find Sassoon still alive. They both wrote about the bitter fighting by the 38th Welsh Division in Mametz Wood, Graves describing the nauseous corpses which remained after the 8–10 July battle as he bivouacked in the wood several days later. The horrific sights were 'a certain cure for lust of blood'.

On 19 July the battalion was held in reserve, Graves and his company sheltering in Bazentin churchyard, for the early morning attack on High Wood on 20 July. A 5.9-inch shell burst among them and Graves was hit with 'a bad chest wound of the kind that few recover from', recorded Dunn in his diary. He was in fact reported killed, as, being unconscious, he was given up for dead and only rescued as he was being taken for burial when he was observed to be breathing. His parents even received the customary letter, which confused them as it arrived after one from Robert saying he was recovering! Graves, naturally, exploited this bizarre situation for all the comedy and drama he could derive from it. He wrote to his CO 'that the shock of learning how much he is esteemed has recalled him from the grave and that he has decided to live for the sake of those whose warm feelings he has misunderstood.' The incident inspired his poem 'Escape'.

There is no doubt that the wound, the narrow escape from death, his participation in the two great battles of Loos and the second stages of the Somme, added to his grief at the death of David Thomas, all conspired to shatter his nerves. Coincidentally Sassoon was in England at the same time, and they cemented their friendship and discussed their changing attitudes to the war. In November they were still together, in Litherland, but Graves insisted on returning to France, and in January was again in the Bull Ring at Harfleur. He then rejoined the 2nd Battalion on the Somme, and had the unpleasant duty of sitting on a field general court-martial. During the First World War 346 British officers and men were executed for cowardice, desertion and other offences (*For the Sake of Example*, Anthony Babington). The acts were mostly suppressed until after the war and Graves was concerned at the cover-ups he knew were taking place at the time.

Graves's lungs, damaged by his wound, continued to give trouble and resulted in bronchitis. Dunn pronounced him unfit for active service and sent him back to the hospital at Rouen where he had been treated for his injury. He requested to be sent to hospital in Oxford, joining the University Officer Cadet Battalion as an instructor. There, or on trips to London, he met Bertrand Russell, Aldous Huxley, Lytton Strachey, Philip and Ottoline Morrell, Arnold Bennett and H.G. Wells – 'more well-known writer than ever before or since' – and Ivor Novello, 'wearing a silk dressing gown in an atmosphere of incense and cocktails'. It was the end of his active war.

Then came the extraordinary episode of Sassoon's notorious protest, his hospitalization at Craiglockhart and meeting with Owen (see Sassoon). It is interesting that Graves described Owen as a 'weakling', with 'that passive homosexual streak in him which is even more disgusting than the active streak in Auden'. Owen found Graves 'a big, rather plain fellow, the last man on earth apparently capable of the extraordinarily delicate fancies of his books.' Graves's collection *Fairies and Fusiliers* was published in 1917, following *Over the Brazier* in 1916. They were typically Georgian poems, some showing real emotion towards dead comrades, but after the war Graves tried to forget and ignore them.

His reputation is mostly built on his post-war work: the poems that Seymour-Smith maintains are 'the most remarkable love poems in the language', forged from his difficult relationships with his unsuitable wife Nancy (whom he married in 1918) and the flamboyant poet Laura Riding; the *I Claudius* and *Claudius the God* series, whose television production brought him popular fame in 1976, and other prolific outpourings until his death in 1985.

The American academic Randall Jarrell wrote that *I Claudius* was 'a good book singular enough to be immortal'. Graves himself is, he aptly said, 'First and last . . . a poet; in between he is a Graves'.

The Hon. Edward Wyndham Tennant

LIEUTENANT, GRENADIER GUARDS

LIGHT AND DARKNESS

Once more the Night like some great dark drop scene
Eclipsing horrors for a brief entr' acte
Descends, lead-weighty. Now the space between,
Fringed with the eager eyes of men, is racked
By spark-tailed lights, curvetting far and high,
Swift smoke-flecked coursers, raking the dark sky.

But as each sinks in ashes grey, one more
Rises to fall, and so through all the hours
They strive like petty empires by the score.
Each confident of its success and powers,
And hovering at its zenith each will show
Pale rigid faces lying dead, below.

There shall they lie, tainting the innocent air,
Until the Dawn, deep veiled in mournful grey,
Sadly and quietly shall lay them bare,
The broken heralds of a doleful day.

Hulluch Road, October 1915

LIEUTENANT THE HONOURABLE EDWARD WYNDHAM TENNANT

Edward Tennant, known as 'Bim' by family and friends, could – apart from his dark hair – have been the prototype for the ideal First World War poet. Of impeccable pedigree, his portrait shows an aristocratic, handsome, languid face with sensually full lips and sad eyes that belied his fun-loving spirit and natural energy.

He was born on 1 July, 1897; his mother, née Pamela Wyndham, had a passionate love affair in her youth before settling down to marry Edward Tennant, later Lord Glenconner. It was not a successful marriage and Pamela turned her affections to Sir Edward Grey, Foreign Secretary at the outbreak of the war, and to her first-born, Edward. Pamela was a central figure in the sparkling Souls clique, and, coming from this intellectual milieu, the young Edward was a precocious author (see Introduction). Even before he could write he was dictating infantile verses. His childhood was idyllic: in an era when children were only just beginning to be seen (let alone heard) by their parents, Bim had a mother who delighted in his company and who encouraged (and preserved for posterity) his every written word.

He was a resourceful, self-contained child, often taking long solitary walks, innovative in his games of pirates and soldiers and organizing his playmates. A typical gung-ho poem of this era was 'The Night Attack: A Poem of Bravery'. In 1907 Edward went to West Downs preparatory school, which he loved – as much as any ten-year-old who was inordinately attached to his mother could. His headmaster said he was 'Full of light and shade . . . hating to inflict or to suffer pain, loving the gentle and the beautiful in life, turning instinctively to sunshine and warmth . . .the life and soul of his school-fellows . . . He loved high-spirited fun.'

Edward was less happy with the rigid formula of life at Winchester. Although he continued to enjoy writing poetry, he was not academic and persuaded his parents to allow him to leave school a year early, in 1913, at the age of sixteen. The outbreak of war a month after his seventeenth birthday put paid to plans to send him to Germany to learn the language in preparation for a diplomatic career. From all that one reads of his character and nature he might have made an ideal ambassador for the country he loved. No one had a bad word to say about Bim; his uncle George described him as 'Full of initiative and resource, quite modest, absolutely spontaneous and with all his "finished manner", a genuine boy.' The fondness was mutual. When George, his hero and to whom he bore a remarkable resemblance, died in June, 1913, Bim wrote 'Le Voyageur' in tribute to him.

Osbert Sitwell, who described Bim as 'my most intimate friend', said, 'To be in his company was like having an electric battery in the room, invigorating without being in the least tiring. Literary expression was as easy to him as talk to other people. He had great verbal ingenuity, and jokes of endless variety, from those concerned with ideas down to puns, poured from him.' Sitwell saw Bim as being 'consumed with a raging generosity, brave, spontaneous, quick in word and deed, with the heart of a Christian and with a spirit higher than any I have ever known.' The generosity was quite classless and Bim was occasionally known to invite people he took pity on in the streets 'to dinner, to meet his girlfriends, the "hell-kittens" . . . sometimes with a startling . . . lack of success. Fellow-guests of each team were outraged.'

Tennant was equally popular with his fellow officers when he joined the 4th Battalion of the Grenadier Guards in August, 1914, and became known as the 'Boy Wonder'. He found the first year of the war, spent in Chelsea Barracks, exhilarating: training for the great knightly tournament and engaging in a hectic social whirl. It was also a time of great poetic activity, especially when he was home on sick leave with jaundice early in 1915. In July his battalion moved to Bovington for final training before going overseas, and the under-age Bim had to have special parental permission to go to France – nineteen was the official minimum age. In France the Grenadiers followed the familiar pattern, disembarking from the *Empress Queen* at Le Havre – 'a delightful town, and I had a splendid bathe in the sea,' Bim wrote. They then travelled by train to Saint Omer and marched the final leg to billets at Blendecques.

Edward wrote every two or three days to his 'Darling Moth', excited to be in this grown-up adventure – 'I am on the high-road of my life'. Friends were on hand, formal Guards mess dinners were sumptuous affairs and rations were supplemented with hampers from Fortnum & Mason, 'the soldier's twin saints'. On 31 August Bim, still infatuated with his mother, wrote 'please put our special message in your next letter, as it is our hall-mark of love, isn't it? And nothing will ever make me love another woman more than I love you, I swear it. At any rate till after I am married.' He missed her very much, but life was still 'great fun': tennis with pretty little French girls, champagne and rounders watched by the Prince of Wales.

But preparations for the great offensive at Loos then got under way. The boy soldier, who wrote to his brother of the 'fun' of snaring Germans in the wire entanglements and then turning a machine gun on them, was about to grow up. On 19 September Bim proudly told Pamela that his battalion was now in the newly-formed Guards Division and that when 'this great advance starts, it is pretty certain to succeed at first'. Battalion diaries describe the move to Vermelles on 23 September, where Bim wrote, 'I have the feeling of Immortality very strongly,' as did so many of his peers who were about to be killed. On 27 September he was detailed to stay back with the transport and artillery while his battalion took Hill 70. It was a lucky escape. Eleven out of eighteen officers were casualties and Tennant was horrified by his first glimpse of the bloody and ghastly realities of war. Already he had lost friends.

Bim's poetry reflected his changing views. In 'A Bas La Glorie' he wrote 'good men go, we lose our friends and kith,/The men who sink knee-deep in boosted fame/Prove that "rewarded courage" is a myth'. His attitude to the staff changed too. Before Loos he described 'Brigadier General Hayworth, General Lord Cavan, General Haking, and Haig at the head of the list' as 'all very fine generals and I could wish for no one else'. In his new poem he scathingly talked of the men who 'sat in cars,/And whizzed about with red-band caps, awry,/Exuding brandy and the best cigars./With bands and tabs of red.'

In October, on the Hulluch Road, Bim wrote the poem reproduced here, 'Light and Darkness'. Some of its images are striking, and the description of the dead as 'The broken heralds of a doleful day' shows a strong Shakespearian influence. Tennant knew all the speeches from *Henry V* by heart and loved to use noble and archaic terms.

Exhausted by lack of sleep and the prolonged thunderous crashings of the guns after a period of continuous active service, a 'run-down' Bim was sent in October to an ODS (Officers' Dressing Station) at Béthune. In November he had a fun-filled home leave, dancing with adoring 'hell-kittens' and soaking in the remedial atmosphere. Back in France the Battalion saw action around Chapigny before resting in Laventie which, despite its battered state, he loved. The joy of finding a garden still bright with jasmine, daffodils and sweet-smelling daphne prompted his most competent and best-known poem, 'Home Thoughts in Laventie', which lyrically recalls the homesickness he first experienced at prep school. Bim was most concerned about his mother's reaction to his 'pomes', which he sent home to her as they were written.

In the new year of 1916 the battalion prepared to move to the dreaded Ypres Salient, passing through 'Popinjay' (Poperinghe), which provided some light relief and non-ration food. On 16 March Bim described coming up by train to Ypres, occupying uncomfortable but safe dug-outs in the canal bank, being heavily shelled and indulging in the current craze for souvenir hunting: 'We found some rather good Dutch tiles . . . and some heavy gargoyles from the Cloth-hall.' Life in the Salient was a ' "through the looking-glass" experience'. Another home leave came at the end of March (Tennant seemed to do better than most for leave), during which he had flu and passed his convalescence correcting the proofs of his own letters, carefully kept for posterity by his mother. He celebrated Easter with a poem 'to send [my] love across the English Channel'. Just after the holiday Pamela Glenconner lost her day-old baby daughter; Bim hastened to send her a 'love-line' to comfort her.

In 'Popinjay' he wrote contrasting poems: 'Worple Flit', a 'fanciful, bizarre, old-world ballad', 'The Nightingale', the 'glamorous love story adapted from Boccaccio' (Adcock), and 'The Mad Soldier'. Untypical, this is his most adult poem, closer in style to Owen, Sassoon or Rosenberg. It is a monologue, written in soldier's language which doesn't shirk stark images of rats eating 'Body-meat', by a man who has been marooned in a shell-hole for three or four weeks with four or five dead comrades. It was not intended to be included in the collection he was preparing for publication, *Worple Flit and Other Poems* (some written long before the war), but in an anthology being assembled by his friends the Sitwells, who published it and two of Tennant's other war poems.

In sending it in all its explicit brutality to Pamela, Bim broke his policy of shielding her from the worst of his appalling experiences. Letters at this time are full of his normal fun and optimism, nostalgia for the golden days of his childhood, and doubts about the publishability of his poems. Bim was honest in his self-appraisal: 'I know my poetry is not complex and impressionistic enough to suit the modern style of criticism.'

His charmed life continued when his battalion missed the slaughter of 1 July, 1916, his nineteenth birthday. They moved to the Somme halfway through August, first to trenches at Beaumont Hamel, then to Ville-sur-Ancre. After a period of rest the battalion joined the front line at Carnoy and Edward's letters became more descriptive of the real 'grisly' conditions. His religious faith remained a strong support for him: 'I pray I may be all right, but in case "Where is death's sting?" ' he wrote on 12 September.

On 18 September he said, 'Thank Heaven I have come safely out of this battle after two days and two nights of it'. He had experienced terrifying shellfire, sheltering for a day and a cold, uncomfortable night in a shell-hole with the CO, the adjutant and the doctor. He was then detailed to take 'messages down the line of trenches to different captains. The trenches were full of men, so I had to go over the open. Several people who were in the trench say they expected every shell to blow me to bits,' he reported.

Others were not so lucky. 'I suppose you have heard who are dead? Guy Baring [Lieutenant-Colonel the Honourable Guy Baring, son of Lord Ashburton, twice mentioned in despatches], Raymond Asquith, Sloper Mackenzie [Captain Allan Mackenzie, son of the late Sir Allan

Mackenzie] and many others. It is a terrible list.' Asquith, the Prime Minister's son, and these other close friends had been killed on 15 September, the first day of the Guards' Division's attack on Lesboeufs.

Bim's last letter on 20 September, full of presentiments about his impending death, assured his mother that he carried four 'photies' of her when he went into action. He prayed that he would be worthy of his 'fighting ancestors' and went into battle steeled with the philosophy, 'not what I will but what Thou willest'. He was killed on 22 September and is buried close to one of his heroes, Raymond Asquith (who made no mention of Bim in his published letters), in Guillemont Road Cemetery.

'Sometimes I think that if I live I shall be a poet one day,' he wrote. Perhaps he would have been.

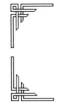

Alan Seeger

LEGIONNAIRE, 2ME REGIMENT ETRANGER

I HAVE A RENDEZVOUS WITH DEATH . . .

I have a rendezvous with Death
At some disputed barricade,
When Spring comes back with rustling shade
And apple blossoms fill the air —
I have a rendezvous with Death
When Spring brings back blue days and fair.

It may be he shall take my hand
And lead me into his dark land
And close my eyes and quench my breath —
It may be I shall pass him still.
I have a rendezvous with Death
On some scarred slope of battered hill,
When Spring comes round again this year
And the first meadow-flowers appear.

God knows 'twere better to be deep
Pillowed in silk and scented down,
Where love throbs out in blissful sleep,
Pulse nigh to pulse, and breath to breath,
Where hushed awakenings are dear . . .
But I've a rendezvous with Death
At midnight in some flaming town,
When Spring trips north again this year,
And I to my pledged word am true,
I shall not fail that rendezvous.

LEGIONNAIRE ALAN SEEGER

When the first American doughboys landed at Saint Nazaire on 28 June, 1917, one of their countrymen had already been fighting a lone crusade for almost two years. A young idealist and budding poet, Alan Seeger took an interesting path to France and enlistment.

Seeger has often been dogged with the tag of 'the American Rupert Brooke'. There are many superficial similarities: born within a year of each other, both came from privileged and cultured families, travelled extensively, were educated at private school and university and were voracious readers, attracted to literature and poetry at an early age. They were both handsome – Seeger as dark as Brooke was fair. But it is their eager adoption of a cause, expressed in their 1914 poetry, that links them. Adcock felt that they, with Julian Grenfell, shared Sir Philip Sidney's devotion to 'three idols – Love and Arms and Song', as Seeger wrote in 'Sonnet 1'.

Alan was born on 22 June, 1888, in New York. At the age of twelve he travelled with his family to Mexico City where the children (he had an older brother and a younger sister) were educated by a tutor who stimulated their taste for reading. The Seegers were a literate family and one of their greatest pleasures was the production of an in-house magazine, to which Alan was an enthusiastic contributor. It was a happy period which left a strong and affectionate impression on the young Seeger: the warm climate, the magnificent scenery, the exciting history of the Conquistadores. The family returned to live in New York, but spent their holidays in Mexico. Alan later wrote of the southern seas in 'Ode to Antares', and the search for beauty would be a driving force for the rest of his life.

After school, Seeger went to Harvard in 1906. It was a brilliant intake, as sparkling in its trans-Atlantic way as Brooke's Cambridge circle. Amongst Seeger's contemporaries were T.S. Eliot and Walter Lippmann, the eminent political commentator. After two years of single-minded reading and studying – he later called it 'learning for learning's sake' – when he gained a reputation as an arrogant loner, Seeger launched into a gay social whirl, much like Brooke. But he continued to explore different cultures, falling under the spell of Celtic literature, and edited and contributed poetry to the *Harvard Monthly*.

After graduating, Seeger seemed to lose his sense of purpose. He virtually dropped out of the traditional society in which he had been brought up, existing on money scrounged from friends. He lived in Greenwich Village, adopted an eccentric and Bohemian mode of dress – flowing black cloak and what is now called 'designer stubble', which was then just as much calculated to make a statement – and desired to live for art's sake. His parents were dismayed and in 1912 sent him to study in Paris, a move which might have been calculated to prolong his nonconformist rebellion. He lived in the Latin Quarter, revelling in *la vie de bohème*, and fell madly in love with the '*singende, springende, schöne Paris*'. Although his attendance at the Sorbonne was spasmodic, it was a period of intense poetic activity with a theme of *carpe diem*.

Poetry poured out of him, joyous hymns to life, to love and lust, to nudes, to the seduction of Paris itself: the chestnut trees and polyglot jostle of students on the Boul' Mich'; Mimi and Manon promenading; the strains of rag-time; the brasseries – where all 'the fervid pulse of pleasure beats' ('Paris'). For a while he was diverted from his ambition to be a successful writer. 'There was a time when I thought much of Fame,' he wrote in 'Fragments II', but 'I scarce regret the temple unachieved'. The sonnet was his favourite form and he wrote a numbered series of sixteen as well as several named sonnets. Some were inspired by events – 'At the Tomb of Napoleon Before the Election in America – November 1912' and 'To England at the Outbreak of the Balkan War' for example. He was even tempted, in his desire to 'live dangerously', to join in. 'I have been so excited over the war, it would have needed a very small opportunity to have taken me over there,' he wrote to his mother.

By 1914 Seeger had produced enough poems to think of publication. In his introduction to the *Poems* of 1916 William Archer called them 'the work of a young man enamoured of his youth, enthusiastically grateful for the gift of life'. Mature enough to stand back from them himself, however, Seeger called the collection *Juvenilia*. No one wanted to publish it and Seeger felt disillusioned and depressed, ready to make a bonfire of his work. Friends chivvied him into going to England (even paying his fare) and in London he rallied at the stimulation of another great capital. He spent hours in the British Museum, socalized with friends, but seemed to have made little or no effort to find a publisher. In July his father came to visit, spending a week of friendship and 'intimacy as we had hardly had since he was a boy in Mexico,' wrote the father. They parted on 25 July. It was the last time he would see his son.

At the outbreak of war Seeger rushed back to France, travelling via Bruges to leave his manuscript with a potential publisher. In Paris war fever was running high. Seeger caught the infectious disease and, holding aloft an American flag, he marched with forty or so of his compatriots to enlist. In an article written for *The New Republic* magazine from the Aisne on 22 May, 1915, Seeger explained why he and other foreigners felt impelled to volunteer. 'Paris . . . – to whom they owed the happiest moments of their lives – was in peril. Were they not under a moral obligation . . . to put their breasts between her and destruction?' He could not stand the thought of his French companions coming back and asking, 'Where have you been all the time, and what have you been doing?' To Seeger the war was a 'stately drama', in which fate had written him a part.

As American citizens could not swear allegiance to the French flag, Seeger joined the French Foreign Legion. He was assigned to C Battalion, 1st Company, 3rd Section of the 2nd Foreign Regiment. By 28 September, 1914, he was training in Toulouse and wrote to his mother, 'We rise at 5, and work stops in the afternoon at 5. A twelve-hours' day at one sou a day. I hope to earn higher wages than this in time to come, but I never expect to work harder . . . I hope you see things as I do, and think that I have done well . . . doing my share for the side that I think right.' The regiment soon moved to the Reims sector and his 10 October postcard home enthused, 'I am in excellent health and spirits . . . I am happy and full of excitement over the wonderful days that are ahead.' The message was repeated on 23 October, from '17 kil. south-east of Reims . . . I am . . . in my element, for I have always thirsted for this kind of thing, to be present always where the pulsations are liveliest. Every minute here is worth weeks of ordinary experience.'

During the grape harvest Alan was struck by the incongruity of unperturbed grape-pickers going about their annual task on one side of a slope while on the other side batteries were roaring. In 'Champagne (1914–15)' Seeger appealed to revellers drinking 'the sweet wine of France' to 'Drink sometimes . . . to those whose blood, in pious duty shed,/Hallows the soil where that same wine had birth.'

Some of Seeger's letters were published in the New York *Sun* and on 8 December, 1914, he described a cheerless, cold and monotonous life of trench warfare, far removed from the heady glamour he had anticipated. Food was becoming an obsession and a corporal told him that 'there wasn't a man in the squad that wouldn't exchange a rifle for a jar of jam'. He was becoming an expert at distinguishing between field batteries, siege guns and the revered French 75. The winter continued, six days in the trenches, three days out: his poem 'The Aisne (1914–15)' describes his baptism of fire on the chalky Craonne plateau (the Chemin des Dames) and the 'surf of blood along the Aisne'. The Germans held the ridge, which was repeatedly assaulted by the French with great loss, but they 'helped to hold the lines along the Aisne'. He mourned for the ruined villages, the looted châteaux, the pitiful abandoned personal possessions of the owners – family photographs and postcards – but was thrilled to discover a 'beautiful library . . . [with] finely bound, immaculate sets of Rousseau, Voltaire, Corneille and Racine'.

The spring passed, and by 18 June he had become fatalistic and philosophical about his chances of survival. 'You must not be anxious about my not coming back. The chances are about ten to one that I will. But if I should not, you must be proud like a Spartan mother, and feel that it is your contribution to the triumph of the cause whose righteousness you feel so keenly,' he lectured his mother. He was still convinced, like Brooke, of the righteousness of the cause and the beauty of death to a good soldier.

In July, 1915, Seeger had welcome leave in Paris, followed by several weeks of rest for the battalion. Then he was plunged into the 25 September Battle of Champagne, which he described in vivid detail. The main objective, to take the town of Vouziers, failed, but Seeger felt satisfaction in getting out of the trenches and to meet 'the enemy face to face and to see German arrogance turned into suppliance'. His admiration for and loyalty to the French soldier and his disdain for the German increased.

Like Graves, Seeger was erroneously rumoured to have been killed. 'I am *navré* to think of your having suffered so,' he wrote to his mother. But in February he was in hospital 'with sickness' (bronchitis), followed by two months' convalescent leave in Biarritz and Paris. In April he retrieved the *Juvenilia* manuscript from the Belgian printer, re-reading it with interest and pleasure and decided to add his subsequent poems to the collection. He returned to the front until May, 1916, billeted in the grounds of Bellenglise château.

He delighted in sneaking off on solitary scouting excursions, bringing back scraps of German newspapers and leaving his visiting card on the German wire. 'It was very thrilling work,' he exulted, as he longed for the Croix de Guerre.

He was flattered to be asked by the Committee of American Residents to write an 'Ode in Memory of the American Volunteers Fallen For France', to be declaimed in Paris on 30 May, 1916 (Decoration Day – an annual holiday to honour American war dead). Amazingly, he completed the hundred-line ode in two days. But to his great disappointment the promised leave did not materialize and he could not travel to Paris. The great fight for survival and the protection of *la Patrie* had begun in Verdun, where the French endured what must have been the worst conditions of all theatres of the Great War. Seeger longed to be in the thick of the fighting.

In the spring of 1916 Seeger wrote the poem reproduced here, the best-known American poem of the war. Its fatalism is prophetic and it is reproduced in most First World War poetry anthologies.

Seeger made his rendezvous with death on the Somme. On 28 June he wrote, 'We go up to the attack tomorrow [postponed because of the weather]. This will probably be the biggest thing yet. We are to have the honour of marching in the first wave.' In fact the *Régiment du Marche* of the tough Moroccan Division went into reserve trenches and did not move up to the front line until 3 July. On 4 July, American Independence

Day, Alan's section, on the right of the line, was ordered to take the village of Belloy-en-Santerre. A friend described watching the tall American running forward with bayonet fixed on his newly-issued Chauchaut automatic rifle. His group was enfiladed by fire from six machine guns concealed in a hollow. Alan was hit several times and fell. Others recall him cheering them on as successive waves swept over the first wounded, and singing in English, 'Accent of ours were in the fierce mêlée.' The village was taken and the next morning the Légionnaires returned for their wounded. But Alan Seeger was already dead.

When the fighting was over there was no trace of his temporary grave and he was posted as missing. As a memorial his grieving parents paid for a bell in the rebuilt church of Belloy after the war. Its peal represented the voice of Alan Seeger still singing over the land he grew to love and for which he paid the ultimate sacrifice. His sister, who lived in Biarritz, arranged for a church bell to toll for him there too, at the other end of France. In 1940 Belloy church was again badly damaged, but a new bell still sings today in his memory. The village children are taught some lines of their *'poète americain'*, and there is a plaque to him on the *mairie* attached to their school.

Seeger was posthumously awarded the Croix de Guerre for which he had so longed, and the Médaille Militaire. In the Place des Etats-Unis in Paris there is a statue in memory of the American volunteers who died *'pour la France'*, modelled on Alan Seeger, and some of his verses are inscribed on the memorial. In the 1920s the French concentrated their burials into large national military cemeteries; in one such, at Lihons, as well as rows of named graves marked with concrete crosses, are two large mass graves (*ossuaires*). It was not until 1982 that the French Ministère des Anciens Combattants revealed the fact that Légionnaire Alan Seeger, who had 'that rare privilege of dying well', lay in Ossuaire No 1.

Ivor Gurney

PRIVATE, GLOUCESTER REGIMENT

FIRST TIME IN

After the dread tales and red yarns of the Line
Anything might have come to us; but the divine
Afterglow brought us up to a Welsh colony
Hiding in sandbag ditches, whispering consolatory
Soft foreign things. Then we were taken in
To low huts candle-lit, shaded close by slitten
Oilsheets, and there the boys gave us kind welcome,
So that we looked out as from the edge of home.
Sang us Welsh things, and changed all former notions
To human hopeful things. And the next day's guns
Nor any line-pangs ever quite could blot out
That strangely beautiful entry to war's rout;
Candles they gave us, precious and shared over-
    rations—
Ulysses found little more in his wanderings without
    doubt.
'David of the White Rock', the 'Slumber Song' so soft,
    and that
Beautiful tune to which roguish words by Welsh pit
    boys
Are sung — but never more beautiful than there under
    the guns' noise.

PRIVATE IVOR GURNEY

The strange, appealing, talented soul that was Ivor Gurney teetered for many years on the tightrope separating genius and madness before slipping irrevocably into the abyss and ending his sad days in a mental hospital.

How gifted he was: music was his first love and to many he was a greater musician even than poet, and how lonely, always seeking the warmth of friendship but set apart by his oddness. The two great themes running through his poetry are his love for his comrades and his love of his native land around Gloucester.

Gurney was born on 28 August, 1890, the son of a tailor of Gloucester. His musicality emerged early and in 1900 he joined the cathedral choir and attended King's School. Already he had intellectually outgrown his simple working family but in 1906, encouraged by his godfather, the Reverend Alfred Cheesman, Ivor was articled to the cathedral organist, Dr Brewer. Herbert Howells and Ivor Novello were fellow pupils. It was one of Gurney's happiest times, when he made close friends with William Harvey, also to become a soldier poet. Together, kindred spirits, they roamed the Gloucestershire countryside, rowed the Severn River and climbed the Cotswold hills, until the landscape was indelibly imprinted on their minds – a private room into which they could retreat at times of particular stress.

In 1911 Gurney left the comforting womb of Gloucester to take up a scholarship at the Royal College of Music under Sir Charles Stanford. He soon developed a reputation for outstanding musical ability but complete 'unteachability'. There was some quality about the vulnerable Gurney that attracted protection and patronage: first Cheesman; then, at the RCM, Marion Scott, editor of the college magazine, music historian and author, encouraged his composition and writing and preserved them for posterity. At their first meeting she noted his 'latent force' and the multi-hued eyes that Erasmus equated with genius. Next an entire family, the Chapmans, took him under their friendly wing. Gurney met them when he took the post of organist at Christ Church, High Wycombe, where Mr Chapman was churchwarden, and they became his surrogate family. The parents he nicknamed 'Le Comte and La Comtesse', the children found him an amusing and stimulating companion for music-making, playing cricket (at which Ivor was good), ping-pong and generally having fun.

In 1914 intimations of the mental instability that was to manifest itself so tragically later in his life caused him to return to the balm of Gloucestershire, wracked with self-doubt and self-hate. Yet he was capable of composing fine pieces (the 'Eliza' song cycle, setting Elizabethan lyrics to music, and instrumental pieces were published) and writing poetry.

When war broke out Gurney enlisted, out of patriotism and a feeling that the disciplined life of a soldier might stabilize him. He was rejected at first because of poor eyesight, but by February, 1915, the army was lowering the standard of its physical requirements and he was accepted into B Company of the 2nd/5th Gloucestershire Regiment. The battalion trained in Northampton, Chelmsford and Epping Forest. In September Gurney naturally gravitated to the regimental band, but later called it 'a washout'. He wrote regularly to William Harvey (and was delighted at Harvey's DCM and his beautiful poem, 'In Flanders', which he later set to music) and to the Chapman family. In 1986 these letters were published under the title *Stars in a Dark Night*, Gurney's own phrase for the joy the family's letters gave him. Even at this stage Gurney was worrying about his mental health and openly discussed his 'neurasthenia' and the state of his mind with Mr Chapman.

At the beginning of 1916 the Glosters moved for active service training on Salisbury Plain and on 25 May they arrived at Le Havre. The keen but inept soldier's experience of war at first hand inspired poetic lines of intense and original beauty, with some of the most evocative pastoral descriptions and expressions of comradely love written in that war. His unique combination of talents – for music as well as for words – was responsible for the lyrical quality of his verses, the true voice of the private soldier in the trenches.

Gurney's military itinerary can be traced not only from battalion diaries, but also from his regular correspondence. From May to October, 1916, the battalion was in the Laventie-Fauquissart sector. They were in trenches with the Welch Regiment at Riez Bailleul and this meeting entranced Ivor. He was stimulated by the lively Welsh minds (they discussed 'Omar Khayamm [sic], Borrow, Burns, Wordsworth and Oscar Wilde etc. etc.') and lilting voices. He called it 'the most amazing experience, it may be, in my life', and said, 'these few days . . . with my Cymric friends are of the happiest for years'. The magical experience is crystallized in the delightful poem reproduced here, 'First Time In'.

In July two of his new friends, Privates Skellern and Hall, were killed. In their memory he wrote 'To Certain Comrades (FS and JH)'. 'Laventie' was a successful demotic poem which captures the atmosphere of the trenches in 1916 – all First World War army life is there. In August he set John Masefield's 'By a Bierside' to music, a staggering achievement when one considers the circumstances under which he was working, with no access to any musical instrument.

From May to October the Glosters moved from billet to billet – Richebourg, Neuve Chapelle, Robecq and 'at rest' in Gonnehem. During this period Gurney sent many manuscripts, both poetry and music, to Marion Scott. Moving down to the Somme sector near Albert in October they took part in the offensive round Grandcourt, Aveluy and Ovillers. Here he wrote the powerful and disturbing 'Ballad of the Three Spectres'. The third spectre gave as its dire prophecy, 'He'll stay untouched till the War's last dawning/Then live one hour of agony'. Later, to the confused post-war Gurney the conflagration appeared to be continuing, even to his own end, and the prophecy must have seemed to him to have come to pass.

The routine of 'Stand To 5.30. Stand Down, clean rifles 6.0. Breakfast 7.30. Work 8.30–12.30. Dinner 1. Tea 4.30. Stand to 5–5.30. Stand Down. Then Ration fatigue. Listening Post. Sentry. Wiring Party' (the last sometimes all night) depressed him; the 'cheerier spirits' of his comrades kept him sane. He wrote to Marion Scott that the 'insensate fury' of the guns was 'a horrid sensation'. His RSM told their CO of Gurney, 'a good man, sir, quite all right . . . but he's a musician and doesn't seem able to get himself clean,' and chuckled to Ivor, 'Ah, Gurney, I am afraid we shall never make a soldier of you'. Ivor dubbed him a 'brick' and wrote a triolet for him. 'He backed me up once; I shall never forget it.'

1917 started with training at Varennes and in February the battalion moved south to the Ablaincourt sector. In March, moving to Caulaincourt, Ivor wrote 'Severn Meadows' in a ruined mausoleum, the only one of his own poems he set to music, and put together for Marion Scott the poems which made up the anthology *Severn and Somme*.

During an attack on Good Friday, 6 April, Ivor was wounded in the arm at Bihécourt and spent six weeks at Hospital No 55 1 BD at Rouen but, 'as the beastly bullet hit absolutely nothing at all profitable' (as he wrote to Marion Scott), he was sent straight back to duty as a machine gunner on the Arras front. There he wrote a series of rondels on the real-ities of his day-to-day life: 'Letters', 'Shortage' ('no jam, no bread, no butter'), 'Paean' (to the joy of 'Half a Loaf Per Man today'), 'Strafe (1)' on lice and 'Strafe (2)' on 'crumps'.

In July Sidgwick & Jackson agreed to publish *Severn and Somme*, Ivor's settings of Masefield's 'By a Bierside' and Harvey's 'In Flanders' were performed at the RCM and preparations for Third Ypres (Passchendaele) began. Gurney was convinced that his friends in London must have heard the deafening bombardment. He was 'rattled' by the shelling but excited at seeing a German plane shot down. In September came an incident at Saint Julian which Gurney described as 'being gassed'. There is little hard evidence of any serious gassing; one theory is that Gurney and some friends sheltered in an abandoned dug-out in which there were still traces of gas from a previous attack, hence the mildness of his symptoms. But it gave Gurney the 'Blighty' one he longed for. Escaping active service for the remainder of the war for such a slight disability may well have produced feelings of guilt which contributed to Ivor's mental instability for the rest of his life.

He was sent to Bangour War Hospital near Edinburgh, where he fell in love with his nurse, Annie Drummond. It was not his first love affair: in 1914 he had felt enamoured of the eldest Chapman daughter, but had gracefully ended the relationship when told she was too young to become engaged. There is little doubt that Gurney's sexual feelings were ambivalent. His war poems contain many sensual physical descriptions of his fellow soldiers. 'To His Love', for example, has strong homo-erotic undertones and is usually assumed to have been written when Ivor heard that his close childhood friend, William Harvey, was posted missing and presumed killed in August, 1916. The assumption seems tenable if based only on the first half of the poem, which accurately describes the haunts and pastimes they enjoyed together as boys. But the final version of the poem was sent to Marion Scott with a letter dated as late as 20 January, 1918, long after it was known that Harvey was alive and a POW in Germany. Even at the time the news first came, Gurney obviously saw no body. The harrowing description of the awful 'red wet Thing' that had once been a friend is therefore either entirely imaginary or a quite separate experience involving a different dead friend. The deaths of comrades affected him deeply.

Whatever his sexual inclinations, Annie Drummond's ultimate rejection of him the following May sent him into utter despair. She appears to have been a kindly, pretty and intelligent woman and their relationship gave him a joy he had never before experienced. After he left Bangour in November, Ivor spent a few days with the Chapmans and a few days in his adored Gloucester. Then he was sent to Seaton Delaval in Northumberland (a 'Hell of a Hole') on a signals course. The bright news was that *Severn and Somme* had favourable reviews and by 9 November had already sold out.

Ivor was hospitalized again in February, 1918, with stomach trouble and, after his discharge, trained at Brancepeth Castle. During this period he was aware that his 'neurasthenia' was returning, feeling guilty that he was in 'Blighty' while his Gloster pals were still under fire on the Western Front. On 28 March he wrote to Marion that he had communed with the spirit of Beethoven. He recognized that this might qualify as 'A Ticket . . . for insanity'. His condition deteriorated: reduced by Annie Drummond's rejection to absolute breakdown, he was admitted to Lord Derby's War Hospital at Warrington in May. On 19 June he contemplated suicide. 'I know you would rather know me dead than mad,' he wrote despairingly to Marion after having funked throwing himself into the canal. Gurney's war, and his tenuous hold on mental stability, were over. In October he was discharged with 'delayed shell-shock'.

After the war Gurney returned to the RCM, which had held his scholarship open, and studied under Vaughan Williams. The second collection of his poems, *War Embers*, was published in 1919. It was a prolific period for Gurney, both musically and poetically, and it is hard to believe that a poem like 'The Silent One' was written by a man who would soon be certified insane. It describes a soldier with the 'infinite lovely chatter of Bucks accent' who dies on the accursed wire. The indomitable, irreverent spirit of the British private soldier comes over in the delightful lines:

> . . . the politest voice – a finicking accent, said:
> 'Do you think you might crawl through there: there's a hole.'
> Darkness, shot at: I smiled, as politely replied –
> 'I'm afraid not, Sir.'

But by 1922 his mental state had so deteriorated that he was committed to Barnwood House mental asylum in Gloucester. His terrible anguish is described in the poem 'To God' as 'Gone out of every bright thing from my mind'. He was then moved to Stone House, Dartford in Kent where, relieved only by visits from his friends like Marion Scott and Edward Thomas's wife, Helen, he ended his tragically bleak days. He continued writing and his works, both poetic and musical, continued to be published, mainly through the efforts of the musician Gerald Finzi. Gurney, however, was not capable of enjoying the limited success he achieved in his lifetime, even though Marion Scott found him 'so heartbreakingly sane in his insanity'. He died of tuberculosis on 26 December, 1937, and was buried in the churchyard at Twigworth, where his godfather was rector.

Early critics were patronizingly dismissive of his talent. Blunden, in the introduction to his 1954 edition of Gurney's poems, called him 'gnarled' and 'uneven'. But after Michael Hurd's 1978 biography, the publication of Gurney's letters, a Channel 4 film, *Stars in a Dark Night*, with all its imperfections, his centenary in 1990 and commemorative plaque in Gloucester cathedral, there has been a resurgence of interest in, and appreciation of, this undoubted genius.

John William Streets

SERGEANT, 12TH YORK AND LANCASTER REGIMENT

A SOLDIERS' CEMETERY

Behind that long and lonely trenched line
To which men come and go, where brave men die,
There is a yet unmarked and unknown shrine,
A broken plot, a soldiers' cemetery.
There lie the flower of youth, the men who scorn'd
To live (so died) when languished Liberty:
Across their graves flowerless and unadorned
Still scream the shells of each artillery.
When war shall cease: this lonely unknown spot
Of many a pilgrimage will be the end,
And flowers will shine in this now barren plot
And fame upon it through the years descend:
But many a heart upon each simple cross
Will hang the grief, the memory of its loss.

SERGEANT JOHN WILLIAM STREETS

'I am not a dilettante but rather a moralist and will not have Art for Art's sake but rather Art as an interpreter of life. I love art (painting and sculpture) – I painted in my youth. I am passionately fond of music.'

This sophisticated statement was not made by an ex-public schoolboy with an Oxbridge degree, nor by someone brought up on a gracious country estate or in a smart London house. The author's parents were not able to send him to Europe to broaden his mind, nor provide an artistic, musical and literary environment to foster his obvious intellectual capabilities. It was written by a Derbyshire miner who was born in a tiny terraced house where he slept in a bed with his five brothers and who left school at the age of thirteen.

John, born on 24 March, 1886, was the eldest of the Streets's twelve children, but soon had to share the limited space of 16 Portland Street, Whitwell, with an ever-increasing brood. The first-born of a large family has little time to be a child before taking on responsibilities for the younger ones, and although Will, as he was known, showed exceptional brightness he turned down the opportunity to go to grammar school to help support them. He went to St Lawrence's Public Elementary School and also attended Sunday school at the Wesleyan chapel in Welbeck Street, where he particularly enjoyed singing in the choir. Cricket was his other favourite form of relaxation.

At the age of fourteen Streets went to work in the local Whitwell coal mine and spent fourteen years at the coal face. The dangerous, grimy, claustrophobic life must have been particularly abhorrent to a lad who instinctively loved Derbyshire's open spaces, hedgerows, woodlands, flowers and birdsong. Will first tried to encapsulate this love in paintings, and sketch-books from around 1907 show delicate studies of horses, leaves and flowers. His meticulously-written notebooks from this same period show the range of his interests and his experiments with various literary forms. There are essays on the Balkan Wars, a scene from a play set in classical Roman times, isolated phrases and lines: 'a cry from the depths of dumb despair'; 'as fickle as a fair unconquered maid'. His vocabulary was expanding as he tested ideas and concepts.

Encouraged by his mentor, Will continued his education at home by correspondence course after a gruelling shift underground, determinedly working in the eye-straining light of a paraffin lamp to the noisy background of his young siblings. The better to understand the classics, Will taught himself Latin and Greek, and was thrilled on 2 July, 1913, to 'satisfactorily complete' his course in Conversational French, Part 8, from the International Correspondence School with the exemplary mark of 97 per cent. He also became a teacher at his Sunday school and learned to play the piano and the organ with great accomplishment. So versatile were his talents that Will really didn't know which was his preferred medium – poetry or art.

In 1912 he sent a long poem about his coal-mining experience, 'Truth, an Allegory', to *Poetry Review*. The publication's 'adjudicator', Herbert Trench, was impressed by the realism with which it dramatically described the frustration of an intellect trapped in a literally inescapable pit. It seemed as if poetry were almost choosing itself as his true *métier*.

On 4 August, 1914, he was shocked by the outbreak of war. John Mills was a soul-mate who shared his delight in the countryside and understood his ambition to break free through education; writing in the introduction to Streets's collected poems (*The Undying Splendour*, May, 1917), he described the effect of the news on the 29-year-old artist/poet. It 'sheared away any doubt that remained, destroyed a certain anaemic tinge in his make-up, crystallized his thoughts and gave, in lines like those in the sonnet "Gallipoli", the fine spirit and real feelings that had been germinating within him and striving after expression for years.' Mills quoted the line, 'O Liberty, at thy command, we challenge death' as explaining 'in essence the reason that led one who hated war to go from that quiet North Derbyshire village to make one of the millions who are fighting for us and our Allies.'

He enlisted in the 12th (Service) Battalion of the York and Lancaster Regiment, one of that extraordinary phenomenon, a Pals' battalion. When war was declared, in the contagious patriotic frenzy to save 'Poor Little Belgium' from the rapacious invading Hun, men flocked in their sacrificial thousands to the recruiting stations, took the King's shilling and enlisted in groups: cricket and football teams, employees of local firms, the entire manhood of fighting age of streets, villages and communities – hence the name 'Pals'. Streets' battalion was known as the Sheffield City Battalion or the Sheffield Pals. It was officially formed on 10 September, 1914, but recruiting actually began on 2 September and by 11 September 900 men, all at least five feet six inches tall and with thirty-five-and-a-half-inch chests, had been accepted. It was conceived as an élite battalion of university students, public schoolboys and professional men; many of the early recruits met these criteria, supplemented by men from the Penistone railway and nearby mines.

On 6 September, 1914, Will wrote the first of many letters home to his family (usually addressed to his mother). 'I have just completed my first day as a soldier', he reported with pride. The Sheffield Pals drilled at Bramall Lane football ground and on 9 November were proficient enough to be inspected by General Plumer, GOC Northern Command. On 5 December, 1914, they moved to Redmires Camp in atrocious weather conditions, several of the men dying of pneumonia.

Streets recorded his reaction to Brooke's newly published *Sonnets* on 20 April, 1915. He was particularly impressed with 'The Dead', and there is little doubt that his poem 'To a Dead Poet' was written on hearing the news of Brooke's death. 'I, too, have loved with you our mother Earth', he explains, ending with the hope that he will show 'brave serenity . . ./ When out with Death into the night I go.'

On 12 May, 1915, Streets moved to Penkridge Bank Camp, Rugeley. He was happy in these surroundings, more like the beautiful dales around his home: 'It seems like a vast moorland', he wrote to the family, 'two minutes walk and we are knee-deep in heather, which contrasted sharply with the night manoeuvres a week earlier, when the night was cold and foggy; not a smile flitted across our faces as we marched (or rather ambled) against the north wind and the fog.' But life in Rugeley was not always so pleasant and included a nineteen-mile route march in full kit. Then on 30 July they moved to Ripon for weapon training. Foreign service was drawing closer and on 25 October Will wrote a moving and sensitive letter to his mother, preparing her for his possible death:

Now mother, I am going to be frank. I hate to be cruel, but one has to be so sometimes, in order to be kind. In the first place our family is one in a thousand – twelve children and yet all living today. We all know the struggle you and father have had to bring us up, yet you accomplished it in a rare and supreme manner. You were just beginning to receive the benefits of your labours when this cruel war came and clouded again the beauty of your days . . . . Your letters show that you are not yet facing the real possibility that this war may bring – I must encourage you both to face it. As you will never regret, four of your sons have volunteered. For what? Not because they looked to the army for their career (I hate it from the bottom of my soul). Rather because they wished to save civilization from being destroyed by one of the most sinister fates, a fate which has sent thousands of innocent victims to the grave in order to strike terror into humanity, a fate which has murdered Miss Cavell in cold blood . . . . That is why we volunteered to fight, we who hate war as we hate our bitterest enemy.

Throughout this training period Streets was writing poetry. His first group of thirteen sonnets, with the collective title 'The Undying Splendour', chart in traditional and patriotic tones the epic story of 'A race of Saxon

112

freemen' who lived 'in England fair', whose navy is 'a wonder of the world', which has a tradition of humanity, liberty and greatness, whose youth's name is engraved 'upon the scroll of Fame', whose lovers are fecund, whose adventurous youth settles down as industrious family men, but whose horizon is swept by 'A flaming meteor . . ./Signal of bloody strife, presage of war'. When the 'lawless hosts' invade 'peaceful Belgium', 'The workmen fled his offspring and his wife;/And lion Youth fearless and rampant came/To follow Freedom's flag into the strife . . ./And go to death, calmly, triumphantly' and in a spirit of sacrifice.

Gallipoli inspired a poem of the same name which was particularly admired. The poems have a nobility and sincerity which shine through their rather stilted style. In November, 1915, Streets wrote a long poem, 'Hymn to Life: Hurdcott Camp', in which his strong religious faith helps him to contemplate death undaunted while exulting in life. This theme recurs in 'Love of Life'.

On 25/26 September the battalion moved to Salisbury Plain and on 16 November to Larkhill, where they were issued with SMLE rifles. 'The weather is bitterly cold. We have no coal in camp and we are having a trying time in the mud. Our clothes and equipment are plastered with the horrid stuff. Oh, yes! We are having larks down here at Lark Hill.' On 20 November, 1915, the day of that letter, the battalion received orders to move to France, but on 30 November the orders were cancelled. In early December they sailed from Devonport to Alexandria in Egypt on the 14,000-ton *Hector* as part of 31st Division, arriving on 1 January, 1916. Will suffered badly from *mal-de-mer* on the voyage.

The division's task was to defend the Suez Canal, and they became part of a huge labour force to complete its defences. It was hard work; some days they were digging trenches for eight hours. On 10 January Will reported sick for the first time in his army life, but was soon back to normal after the MO's dosing of 'number nine'.

On 10 March, 1916, the 12th Battalion embarked for France on HMT *Briton*, a Union Castle liner also used as a troopship in the Boer War, landing on 15 March at Marseilles. On 18 March, 1916, they arrived at Pont Rémy near Amiens after a fifty-three-hour train journey, marching the final eight miles to their camp at Huppy (near Abbeville). Only two days later they had a ten-mile route march, fired their weapons, which were checked by an armourer, and underwent gas warfare training. The weather deteriorated and further route marches in the slush and snow ruined their boots. On 27 March Will reported:

> went into the trenches with the 48th Division, 8th Battalion, Worcestershire Regiment. A hellish experience . . . . There are moments in the trenches when you sit down and think that you are in some quarry or cutting. A blue sky above, larks are singing and

a blackbird is cackling; suddenly a great bird appears – an aeroplane – and there is a rat-a-tat of machine guns, the boom of artillery and the pit-pat of rifles and you realize that you are at war, part of a great game . . . . Mother, it is a jingle with death.

On 28 March they marched to Beauquesne and on 2 April moved to Colincamps, where the surrounding countryside 'bristled' with every calibre and type of gun in preparation for the Somme offensive. The next day they were issued with rubber gas capes and steel helmets, and battled up the line to their trenches in sticky mud. Will vividly described his first night watch – 'a veritable death trap' – and going out on wiring parties, where he managed to keep his nerve despite the suspense and agony. 'If I get through I shall win through some day as a poet,' he vowed. The battalion was rotated in and out of trenches before the village of Serre, a continually active sector, thereby gaining twelve weeks of front-line experience before the attack on 1 July. The trench system behind the Copses, named after the Four Apostles, was originally held by the French and was under sustained artillery fire, resulting in many casualties.

In these circumstances Streets managed to continue writing poetry of an exceptionally high calibre. There were tender love poems, like 'To . . .' and 'Remembrance', a poem in which the themes of love and a recognition of the closeness of death merge. The charming poem 'Shelley in the Trenches', written on 2 May, 1916, shows some of his poetic influences. It is interesting that Streets, with little formal education, uses classical language and chivalric themes as if he had been nurtured in the public school ethos, while classically-educated poets like Sassoon and Frankau describe flesh-and-blood soldiers in demotic language. Streets's description of 'A Soldier's Funeral' contrasts sharply with accounts by poets like Gurney and Studdert Kennedy of pals dying and being buried. The nearer to death Streets got, as he moved into the danger zone of trench life, the more realism creeps in: titles like 'April Evening: France, 1916' and 'The Hedge', written in May, celebrating 'Nature' amidst the 'unceasing fight', give way to 'A Soldiers' Cemetery' and 'The Wayside Cross', a narrative poem describing a delirious wounded soldier who finally expires.

Throughout the poems runs Streets's fear that he was destined to die. He was anxious to preserve them and sent them off as they were written. Galloway Kyle, editor of *Poetry Review*, writing in the preface to *The Undying Splendour*, describes how they would arrive from the trenches written in pencil on scraps of paper stained with mud and sent off unpolished lest the death that lurked by day and night all round should suddenly strike. Kyle thought highly of them, feeling they showed 'a rare spirituality and an unequalled intensity of expression'. Streets's last batch of sonnets, read at a meeting of the Poetry Society, profoundly impressed the audience, who were thrilled by their dignity, beauty and application to the occasion. Streets's accompanying letter explained:

> They were inspired while I was in the trenches, where I have been so busy I have had little time to polish them. I have tried to picture some thoughts that pass through a man's brain when he dies. I may not see the end of the poems, but I hope to live to do so. We soldiers have our views of life to express, though the boom of death is in our ears.

Streets also sent poems to George Goodchild, who was compiling a book, *Made in the Trenches*, to raise funds for the Star and Garter home for totally disabled soldiers and sailors. Goodchild wanted it to be 'not so much a work of great literary or artistic merit, but a really representative idea of the life and thought of the Army as a whole. In particular I am delighted to be able to include the very fine poems of Corporal [he had not yet been promoted] Streets.' Other contributions included work by the artists Bert Thomas and Bruce Bairnsfather, and a variety of prose and poems, mostly of *The Wipers Times* brand of humour. Streets's poetry stands out for its quality.

On 13 May, 1916, Will wrote in his diary, 'I am a proud and lonely soul . . . a lonely fellow who lost love,' who only had one friend (probably a reference to John Mills), who was '30 years of age, muscular but lithe and supple' and stood '6 feet tall'. Women loved him, and he loved women. 'I am sane because I love poetry. I am mad because I write it.' Entries such as these and his letters show how he felt distanced from his family and background in his desperate search for poetic achievement. The quality of his letters is far removed from the normal 'in the pink' type of communication of the majority of his class. His last, unfinished, letter (dated 6 June 1916) is a perfect example of his poetic vision, keen sense of observation, love of nature and thoughtful personality:

> The village where we are staying in spite of its ruins is sweet. Its gardens and orchards now in full bloom tumble down to the minstrel brooks that trespass the flowery meadows. The birds hold carnival and the nightingale sings from deepening sunset until dawn . . .
>
> I am afraid even the English people fail to understand completely the English Tommy. His leviathan laughter in the face of grave peril and death seems to suggest a callous view of Life. On the contrary, in it often there lurks his noblest scorn; scorn for his own life and happiness when by yielding it he can benefit posterity . . . . . Yes, Tommy in spite of his faults which are legion is a splendid fellow.

He needs not any praise for what he does is natural and free . . . .
Where there is freedom of action there is freedom of spirit.

Sadly Streets was not to live to enjoy the success he achieved in the literary world. His battalion took part in the great Somme assault of 1 July, 1916, moving into assembly trenches behind John Copse (Streets wrote a poem about nearby 'Matthew Copse'). The Sheffield Pals advanced in waves, arms at the port at walking pace, after an artillery barrage which their officers had guaranteed would pulverize the enemy wire and slaughter him in his trenches. But the German dug-outs were deep, the wire remained undamaged, and the slowness of the British advance enabled the German machine gunners to mount and fire their weapons the minute the barrage lifted. The premature blowing of the Hawthorn mine at 7.20am gave the Germans in this sector ten minutes' warning of the attack and time to man their front line to await the British advance at 7.30am. The Sheffield Pals were quickly reduced to half their strength.

Streets was wounded soon after the attack began; going back to get his wound tended, he went to the assistance of a more seriously wounded man and disappeared. One of his brothers sent Adcock, author of *For Remembrance*, Will's 'worn, red-covered pocket-book'. Adcock wrote:

> There are jottings in it of stray ideas or phrases that occurred to him for stories or for verses and on certain of its pages, or on loose leaves folded in between them, are various poems, two or three of which have not been included in his published volume. They all bear marks of haste, are in pencil and often difficult to read, and show little signs of revision. Two of these unpublished poems are characteristic of the high idealism and the spirit of mystical exaltation in which he entered upon the war. All his beliefs were opposed to it, and nothing but the martyrdom of Belgium and a burning love of his own country and of the peace and liberty that must be saved from the menace of the Hun, could ever have made a soldier of him. One of them was called 'The Vigil', the other 'The Fallen'.

Six of Streets's poems were published by Erskine Macdonald in *Soldier Poets* in September, 1916. It went into six editions. Macdonald also published Streets's slim collected works, *The Undying Splendour*, in May, 1917. The book contains tributes from his officers, showing he was a respected and well-liked man. His major wrote, 'If his verses are as good as his reputation as a soldier, you may rest assured that the book will be a great success.' His captain added, 'It is given to few men to win the confidence of their comrades as completely as did Sergt. Streets . . . . Steady-eyed and rather stolid, he gave an impression of coolness even under extreme tension. The only time we ever saw him shaken was when he lost several of his section, with whom he had lived and trained for over eighteen months.' Streets's body had not then been found, and there was some faint hope that he might have been a prisoner of war. His captain wrote, however, 'We knew that Streets was not the man easily to surrender.' His body was eventually identified and buried in Euston Road Cemetery, Colincamps.

William Noel Hodgson M.C.

LIEUTENANT, 9TH DEVONS

BEFORE ACTION

By all the glories of the day
  And the cool evening's benison,
By that last sunset touch that lay
  Upon the hills when day was done,
By beauty lavishly outpoured
  And blessings carelessly received,
By all the days that I have lived
  Make me a soldier, Lord.

By all of all man's hopes and fears,
  And all the wonders poets sing,
The laughter of unclouded years,
  And every sad and lovely thing;
By the romantic ages stored
  With high endeavour that was his,
By all his mad catastrophes
  Make me a man, O Lord.

I, that on my familiar hill
  Saw with uncomprehending eyes
A hundred of thy sunsets spill
  Their fresh and sanguine sacrifice,
Ere the sun swings his noonday sword
  Must say good-bye to all of this;—
By all delights that I shall miss,
  Help me to die, O Lord.

published June 29th, 1916

LIEUTENANT WILLIAM NOEL HODGSON, MC

> My dear Babe,
> So our game of tennis will have to wait for a bit – never mind, the result was worth the delay . . . . The total loss is heavy. Martin, Hodgson, Holcroft, Rayner, Riddell, Adamson, Hirst, Shephard have all gone to their long home, Pridham, Butland, Dines & others are wounded. Nearly all the casualties were just by the magpies' nest. I buried all I could collect in our front-line trench.

The Reverend Crosse, chaplain to the 8th and 9th Devons, was snatching a quiet moment to write to one of his officers wounded in the first hours of fighting on the Somme. Meanwhile, far away in Devon, the casualties of an earlier battle shared an odd little act of remembrance for one of the dead men on his list. Led by a lieutenant, they left their military hospital and climbed to the top of the nearest hill. They were remembering Noel Hodgson, bombing officer of the 9th Devons, in a way he would have appreciated and enjoyed. When so many were dying, it was an unusually personal tribute.

Hodgson's loyalty to the Devonshire Regiment had never weakened his love of the north. He was proud of a family connection with Cumberland stretching back for centuries, though he was born in Gloucestershire on 3 January, 1893. When he was four his family moved to Berwick-on-Tweed, where his father became vicar of Holy Trinity Church, serving the town and the local garrison of King's Own Scottish Borderers. It was a very military setting; even the vicarage was on the town's defensive wall, with a thirteen-gun saluting battery right outside the front door.

The youngest of four children, Noel enjoyed a secure and uneventful childhood. His father was a gentle man who knew how to encourage his children without pushing them; all were bright and would become prolific writers, but Noel was his particular favourite. The Reverend Henry Hodgson hoped his son would follow him into the church, as he had followed his own father and grandfather. From their mother the children gained glimpses of a wider world. Penelope Hodgson came from a family with a long naval tradition, had a sharper wit than her husband and viewed life with a more critical eye; the vicarage could be a lively place and its children were never short of laughter. From this background Noel derived a very deep faith, owing as much to the natural world as it did to the church, an awareness of history, and a sense of fun.

In 1905 Noel went as a boarder to Durham School, armed with a twenty pound scholarship. He was extremely happy there and did well, both academically and on the sports field. It was a small school with less than a hundred pupils, which gave any boy who tried a chance to shine. It also had a proud sense of its own long history, and the most spectacular setting, perched high above the River Wear looking towards the castle and cathedral. For a boy like Noel a better environment could hardly have been found, and he relished it all.

Poetry seems rather out of place in that hearty, muscular world. All public schoolboys were steeped in the classics, learning to analyse Latin and Greek verse and produce competent translations, but creativity was not on the curriculum. But by 1909 Hodgson was certainly experimenting with writing. He toyed with some glum little lyrics on love and death; as years passed love became far more interesting to him. He tried historical epics and showed a neat touch with humour and parody, but by the time he left school the landscape, particularly the hills, had become his favourite theme. Two of his closest friends, Nowell Oxland and Robert Parr, also wrote poetry; a letter to the school magazine in Hodgson's final term complained that:

> there are at least three poets in the school at present, perhaps more. I know that two of them have spent considerable time and trouble over the composition of attempts which the authorities never even desired to see.

In 1911 Noel won an exhibition to Christ Church, Oxford, but university must have seemed like an extention of school. Oxland, Parr and two of his other Durham friends were also there; they clung together and sent regular letters to the school, though within their colleges they found new friends and opportunities. Hodgson played rugby, hockey and cricket for Christ Church, and had some writing published in the *Oxford Magazine*. He gained a first in Classical moderations in 1913. He also joined the OTC; while his school had no military tradition, the idea of war was in the air and most young men wanted to prepare themselves. The summer camp of June, 1914, was a hot, lazy affair, following which Noel went to stay with friends for a few days before making his way to the Lake District. On 2 August letters began to go out from Oxford summoning OTC members back to be interviewed for the services.

It has become accepted fact, passed from anthology to anthology, that Hodgson was so influenced by Brooke's 1914 sonnets that he rushed to enlist after reading them. Nothing could be further from the truth. As an OTC member he was called up months before Brooke's sonnets were even written; he saw the war as a duty and went in a mood of profound sadness. 'Roma Fuit', written that summer and published in *New Witness* on 6 August, shows his feelings. In the silence of the northern hills he reflects that this place too was once a battlefield, and the dead of both armies, Roman and Pict, lie forgotten under the grass. The poem's Latin title means 'Rome is no more' and its message is understated but obvious. On 22 August he took a farewell walk in the Cumbrian hills, past Wastwater and over the Sty Head Pass to the top of the Gable. He described the route in detail in a letter to his sister, and she repeated the walk in his memory every year until the mid-1920s. The next day he returned to Oxford, where the Dean of Christ Church was busy turning undergraduates into officers. He was sent to the newly formed 9th Battalion, Devonshire Regiment, and arrived at Rushmoor on 16 September.

The next eight months were spent in training at various camps in southern England. The 9th Devons were an odd mixture of men from Wales, Birmingham and London, with only a few genuine west country men among them; Hodgson's first platoon were native Welsh speakers. Quiet and easy-going, he fitted in well, earning the nickname 'Smiler', and the outdoor life appealed to him, but he was still restless. His poems show an acute awareness of all that might have been. On leave in May he visited Durham and wrote several poems about the school; another, 'Splendide Fallax', describes a soldier leaving the girl he loves for certain death. The imagery is powerful: the soldier's 'hair was like the corn' and the poem ends, 'But no more comes her lover,/ And hark! they mow the corn.' It may or may not have been his own experience, but it shows what was in his mind. At the end of July, 1915 the 9th Devons sailed from Southampton on an Isle of Man paddle steamer, which docked at Le Havre after a ten-hour crossing.

A few more weeks of training followed before the battalion had its first experience of the trenches, near Festubert. Noel was in good spirits and wrote regularly to his sister describing his experiences. A cousin and several Durham Old Boys had already appeared in the casualty lists, but the first loss which really shook him was Oxland's death far away in Gallipoli. Noel found his friend's name in the paper one Saturday, after a particularly exhausting spell of trench duty, and it took him back to holidays spent hill-walking together. He made a little funeral pyre that evening with some moss from the Gable, and wrote 'In Memory of Nowell Oxland', which was never published, though it is one of his best poems.

The 9th Devons were preparing for their first battle, and on the morning of 25 September, 1915, they moved forward in support of the 8th Devons at Loos. Uncut wire and drifting gas added to the confusion of a badly-planned day; finding the trenches congested, the 9th were forced to advance in the open and lost their battalion commander and most of their experienced officers. By 10am the battalion had dwindled to scattered groups of survivors, unsupported and unable to move forward. Hodgson was among them, with three other young officers and about a hundred men. Despite heavy rain they dug new trenches for themselves around the guns the 8th Devons had captured; at midnight the Germans counter-attacked, but they held their position and remained through the next day until relief finally came.

Within days they were back in the trenches, and the ordeal continued for the next two months, though the battalion was well below strength. Noel was acting adjutant for several weeks, and had the unpleasant duty of collecting evidence for a man on trial for his life. He was mentioned in despatches and awarded the Military Cross for his actions at Loos, though the award was not announced until January, 1916.

In December the Devons moved south, and Christmas saw Noel as mess president, bombing officer, scout officer, officer in charge of athletics and OC Headquarters Company. He wrote home describing the celebrations:

When I went round dinners I was greeted with 'For he's a jolly good fellow' played on cornets and lustily sung, and one gentleman in a voice husky with beer and emotion assured me that if ever I wanted a man to follow me into a tight place, 11132 Private Harry Gay was the man in question. We did jolly well too − I personally assisted at the concealment of four turkeys and five plum puddings in forty-five hours.

Despite these extra duties, Hodgson was delighted to find a new outlet for his writing. *New Witness*, which had been publishing his poems for some time, expressed an interest in prose descriptions of trench life, and from February onwards the paper carried his writing almost every week. Hodgson's trench prose is vivid, honest, effective, and sometimes funny. He tried to show the reality behind official language and drew heavily on his own experience, though he changed all names and published under the pseudonym Edward Melbourne.

The 9th Devons spent the first few weeks of 1916 out of the line, but by February they were back in trenches near Fricourt. Noel was in hospital early in March, probably as result of illness rather than injury, and in his letters the strain of war was beginning to tell. Another schoolfriend had died of pneumonia contracted in the trenches. 'Not even "killed in action,"' Noel wrote in the last of his *New Witness* sketches, 'but dead in a hospital among strangers.' He was depressed and tired, and his one happiness was the news that his sister was expecting a baby. 'Good luck to you and your 1936 soldier,' he wrote. 'I hope he's luckier than his Uncle Bill, and doesn't get involved in silly squabbles of European potentates.'

Hodgson had home leave that spring, probably in April when the Devons had their first experience of the Mansel Copse trenches which would be their front line in the Somme offensive. As summer drew nearer, preparations began in earnest. The Devons held the high ground opposite the German-held village of Mametz, also on high ground, with a road and a railway line in the valley between. Both front lines crossed the road at right-angles, so the advance would follow the valley in full view of machine-gun positions in the German third line. None of the Devons was confident that their bombardment would destroy those machine guns; some believed they would be cut down as they left their trenches.

Fortunately the last few weeks before the attack were very busy, with little time to think. Noel was thrilled to hear that his sister had produced a baby girl and wanted him to be godfather. He was amused by a letter from his old headmaster asking him to play in a cricket match on 29 June. 'Think of it,' he wrote to a friend, 'white flannels, drinks and delightful smooth-haired children with brown faces; what an irony.' Also on 29 June, two days before the battle, 'Before Action' was published in *New Witness*; the popular story of Hodgson writing the poem two days before his death is based on a misunderstanding. When the Reverend Hodgson dated his son's poems in *Verse and Prose in Peace and War* he gave dates of publication in *New Witness*. Later anthologists asssumed that these were dates of writing, and the poignancy of the line 'Help me to die, O Lord' being written so close to the poet's death gave rise to the legend.

The Devons rested in the Bois des Tailles, three miles behind the line, that day and the next. The evening before the battle they had a sing-song around a fire of old boxes and marched away at 10.30pm. From their assembly trench they watched the bombardment of Mametz and waited. They went over the top at 7.27 the next morning, and just hours later Hodgson was dead. He and his bombers fell victim, as they expected, to the German machine guns. Noel was hit in the neck and leg, and the Reverend Crosse found his batman dead beside him with a bandage in his hand. They were not alone: 144 of the 9th Devons died that day, and 40 of the 8th. The chaplain buried those who could be found in their old front-line trench. Proud that they had achieved their objective, he put up a sign, 'The Devonshires held this trench. The Devonshires hold it still.'

As the war drew to an end, Hodgson was one of the best-known of the soldier poets, but new voices were coming to the fore, and their poetry had a hard, political edge. Hodgson's poems were never angry, only filled with an aching sadness for all that his generation stood to lose in a cause which, at the beginning, seemed so right. That sadness, and a sense of the long perspective of history, are his contribution. In a poem written in the spring of 1916, which may even be his last, he made one wish for himself, for Nowell Oxland and his other friends, and for all those fated to die far from home: that 'we shall see the hills again'.

Leslie Coulson

SERGEANT, LONDON REGIMENT ROYAL FUSILIERS

THE RAINBOW

I watch the white dawn gleam,
  To the thunder of hidden guns.
I hear the hot shells scream
Through skies as sweet as a dream
  Where the silver dawn-break runs.
And stabbing of light
  Scorches the virginal white.
But I feel in my being the old, high, sanctified thrill,
And I thank the gods that the dawn is beautiful still.

From death that hurtles by
  I crouch in a trench day-long,
But up to a cloudless sky
From the ground where our dead men lie
  A brown lark soars in song.
Through the tortured air,
  Rent by the shrapnel's flare,
Over the troubleless dead he carols his fill,
And I thank the gods that the birds are beautiful still.

Where the parapet is low
  And level with the eye
Poppies and cornflowers glow
And the corn sways to and fro
  In a pattern against the sky.
The gold stalks hide
  Bodies of men who died
Charging at dawn through the dew to be killed or to kill.
I thank the gods that the flowers are beautiful still.

When night falls dark we creep
  In silence to our dead.
We dig a few feet deep
And leave them there to sleep —
  But blood at night is red,
Yea, even at night,
  And a dead man's face is white.
And I dry my hands, that are also trained to kill,
And I look at the stars — for the stars are beautiful still.

France, August 8th 1916

SERGEANT LESLIE COULSON

A few miles from Albert, in open farmland to the north of the Somme valley, Grove Town is one of many cemeteries forming a lasting reminder of the battles of 1916. Then, the place was an administration area for army support services, including a casualty clearing station, and Sergeant Coulson of the 12th London Regiment was carried there in October, 1916, badly wounded and beyond help. He died within hours. Today there is nothing to distinguish Leslie Coulson's grave from well over a thousand others of men who never left Grove Town, but in the cemetery register he is distinguished as a well-known journalist and poet. The *Sunday Times* called him 'one of the most brilliant of our younger writers'.

Coulson was born on 19 July, 1889, in a small street off the Kilburn High Road on the edge of the most built-up part of London, the second son of Frederick, an outfitter's warehouseman, and his wife. They shared their house with another family and a single lady lodger. Commercial life did not satisfy Frederick, who wanted to be a writer and was already selling verses and stories. In 1894, when Leslie was five, Frederick felt confident enough to abandon other work and chase the dream; within a year he had secured a position on the literary staff of the *Sunday Chronicle*, and his first book of verse was published in 1899. He was a success and passed on his enthusiasm for writing to both his sons.

Leslie was not a strong boy and was often ill. Surrounded by buildings and people, he grew up longing for the open air and spent all his free time walking in the countryside. He developed a great affection for the rural landscapes of southern England, which he explored on long weekend rambles and holidays. His father's introduction to *From an Outpost*, the posthumous collection of Leslie's poems, leaves the impression of a sensitive, rather sweet character, dreaming in the fields, but this was only one side of Coulson. Ambitious to make his name in journalism, his eyes were set on Fleet Street. An intelligent young man with a mind of his own, he opted to learn the trade by working on provincial newspapers. It seems likely that he spent some time with the *Manchester Guardian*; certainly the staff of the paper knew him well. He worked his way back to London, gaining a reputation and a good deal of respect on the way, and sold some of his reports to Reuters. His father was still a columnist on the *Sunday Chronicle* and his brother wrote for the *Sketch* and the *Daily Dispatch*;

Leslie outdid them both by becoming assistant editor of *The Morning Post*, one of the most popular newspapers of the day.

He found London an unsympathetic place, with its grime, noise and concentration on material things. Nor was he really content with journalism alone; he tried his hand at short stories and plays, and poured out his frustration with city life in a series of poems. There is a hint of menace in some of his work – even an otherwise lyrical description of nightfall in the country ends with the rise of a sinister mist, and 'God keep you safe tonight'. The feeling is at its strongest in 'Premonition', with its 'shadow of fate' falling between young lovers.

Coulson's unease may have been personal, but there was a general tension in the years leading up to 1914 and many people predicted the catastrophe long before it came. When war did begin his brother went to Belgium as a journalist, but Leslie's response was altogether different. *The Morning Post* was a fiercely patriotic newspaper and he felt honour-bound to follow the line he was helping to promote. He enlisted as a private in September, 1914, dismissing advice to apply for a commission with the often-quoted remark: 'No, I will do the thing fairly. I will take my place in the ranks.' He was confident that, however bad things seemed, they would come right in the end, 'and all the blood that war has ever strewn is but a passing stain.'

He joined the 2/2nd London Regiment, affectionately known as the 'Two-and-Twopennies' because so many of them came from the big London stores. They began their training in Vincent Square but were soon moved to Epsom Downs, billeted in the stables and jockeys' quarters at Tattenham Corner. They trained on the Downs with makeshift equipment. On 15 December they moved to Tonbridge to prepare for foreign service, and all ranks enjoyed a forty-eight-hour leave before the battalion boarded the ship *Neuralia* in Southampton. On Christmas Eve they set sail in a convoy bound for Malta. Coulson never saw England again.

The first part of the voyage was ruined not only by heavy rain and rough seas, but the Christmas puddings had been loaded on to the wrong ship. Later the weather became so warm that the men were allowed to sleep on deck and glimpse exciting views of the African coast to starboard. They sighted Gozo at dawn on 31 December, and a few hours later sailed into the Grand Harbour at Valletta. After two days on board the 2/2nd Londons marched to St Andrew's Barracks, near the eastern shore of the island, which would be their home for several months. They would garrison Malta, the base of the Mediterranean Fleet, releasing more experienced troops for the Western Front.

Their training continued, with leisure time devoted to football, swimming and boating. An outbreak of mumps in mid-January confined them to barracks for seven weeks; this may have been the illness which put Coulson in hospital in Valletta. The poem 'A Soldier in Hospital' captures his feeling of unreality, cut off from any hint of war and even from the daily life of the island. Illness apart, though, he was in his element. He was promoted corporal now, and this poem and others found their way into *The Garrison Goat*, a fortnightly paper which Coulson edited with the MO. It was immensely popular, with a circulation of five thousand, and made a healthy profit which they gave to the Red Cross.

With the coming of summer life changed on Malta. The landscape became barren and dusty and the heat was unbearable, even though the men were issued with light drill uniforms. An influx of casualties from Gallipoli overwhelmed all available accommodation, and the 2/2nd Londons were moved from their barracks into tented camps. Most of their time was spent keeping order in the streets and working on dockyard fatigues, loading and unloading the hospital ships. It must have been unnerving to see the results of the fighting they had not yet experienced; Coulson's poem 'The Ebb' compares the sea lapping on the quayside at night to 'a failing of breath', with 'something of death' in it.

His battalion left Malta, bound for Gallipoli, on the night of 26 August, 1915, and, after a few weeks' rest in Cairo, set sail for war. On 8 October their ship *Simla*, travelling without lights, reached Lemnos in a raging thunderstorm and remained in harbour for four days. Once at sea again, the men were ordered to throw their Malta sunhelmets overboard. The scene stayed in the mind: the long line of discarded helmets bobbing up and down in the ship's wake, with the sunset behind them. They landed at Cape Helles at 9pm that night, 13 October, and were attached to the 2nd Brigade of the Royal Naval Division. The next morning they came under shell-fire for the first time.

Gradually companies of the 2/2nd were introduced to the trenches under the experienced eye of the RND. They followed a pattern of seven days in the line and seven days out, but there were no true rest areas because every camp was in range of enemy shells. It was autumn too; thunderstorms and torrential rain flooded trenches and mule tracks alike, making movement difficult. Even the camps flooded, and it was never possible to find dry clothes; soon illness became a more powerful enemy than the Turks. The 2/2nd began their first tour of duty as a whole battalion on 24 November, and two days later a violent storm turned the trenches into fast-moving rivers. The men were obliged to scramble on to their parapets or be swept away. There was no shelter; the next day the wind shifted and the rain turned to sleet. In intense cold the water froze round their feet and oil solidified in their rifle bolts. For three days a blizzard raged and men were only kept alive by movement and the regular rum issue. It was a miserable time, made worse by an increase in enemy activity.

The decision to evacuate Gallipoli was being made even as the 2/2nd landed on the peninsula. Suvla and Anzac Bay were cleared by 20

December, then troops were withdrawn from Helles. The Londons left in separate groups, beginning on 1 January, and Coulson, who had come through with only a slight wound, was among the last to leave. He was probably in a party attached to the Royal Engineers for fatigue duties on 'W' Beach and taken off during the night of 8–9 January, 1916. At Lemnos the survivors of the battalion were reunited, and after a week of rest they sailed back to Alexandria and Beni Salama Camp near Cairo. There they were able to recover and replace damaged uniforms and equipment, and it was an especial pleasure to find large quantities of mail waiting from home. The men were allowed frequent leave; on 18 February Coulson was on the beach near Sidi Bishr and wrote a powerful poem, 'The Call of the Sea', in which the sea at first appears peaceful and friendly and then becomes a terrifying image of the war itself, with its insatiable demand for more lives.

He spent two further months in Egypt, attached to the defensive forces in the Nile valley, but there was a pressing need for the 2/2nd Londons on the Western Front. Other battalions of the London Regiment were calling for experienced reinforcements, and on 17 April the entire brigade set sail for Marseilles and entrained there for Rouen. Their journey took just over a week, and on arrival the brigade was broken up. Parties of men from the 2/2nd Londons were sent to various units; Leslie Coulson, promoted to sergeant and recommended for a commission, became a member of the 12th Londons, the 'Rangers'. They were in the Hébuterne sector, just north of the area which would soon become the Somme battlefield.

Coulson had been away from England for nearly eighteen months, in places which bore no resemblance to the landscapes he loved. The Somme country is very like parts of southern England, with rolling green hills, little woods and farms. The wild flowers are the same; it felt like home. On the eve of the Somme battle, Leslie wrote to his parents: 'If I should fall do not grieve for me. I shall be one with the wind and the sun and the flowers.' On 1 July the Rangers took part in a diversionary attack on Gommecourt, designed to distract the Germans from the main advance to the south. They reached their objective quickly but became stranded in enemy lines, and by evening had been driven back with appalling losses.

They remained in the Hébuterne area for almost two months; 'The Rainbow' was written during this time, showing Coulson could still respond positively to the natural world although his hope was waning. The devastation of the countryside affected him as deeply as injuries to men; he stopped believing that the earth could heal itself and became angry, not with the enemy but with the whole idea of war. In 'Judgement' he directs his anger against God. The experience of war pushed many men into journalism, recording what they had seen for newspapers and magazines. Strangely Coulson, the professional journalist, seems to have fallen silent after Malta, and his later impressions only survive in the letters and poems he sent to his parents.

Early in September the Rangers moved south and made a successful but costly attack on the northern corner of Leuze Wood. They remained in the area for the rest of the month. In October they took over front-line trenches east of Lesboeufs, with orders to advance against a German position known as Dewdrop Trench. At 1.45pm on 7 October the two leading waves, with Coulson among them, came out of their trench and were immediately subject to very heavy and accurate machine-gun fire. Most of the men were down before they had covered fifty yards, and the third and fourth waves suffered a similar fate; one platoon disappeared completely. Leslie Coulson was shot in the chest and died the next day in the Grove Town CCS. Two poems were found on his body and sent to his parents. 'From the Somme' speaks of the tragedy which finally overwhelmed and silenced him, and 'Who Made the Law?', his most familiar poem, is bursting with rage and incomprehension:

> Who made the Law that men should die in meadows?
> Who spake the word that blood should splash in lanes?
> Who gave it forth that gardens should be boneyards?
> Who spread the hills with flesh, and blood, and brains?

To mark his son's grave, Frederick chose the closing words of Manoah's elegy for his dead son Samson from Milton's *Samson Agonistes*: '. . . nothing but well and fair, and what may quiet us in a death so noble.' It was a sentiment Leslie Coulson would no longer have shared.

 Edmund Blunden M.C.

LIEUTENANT, ROYAL SUSSEX REGIMENT

TWO VOICES

'There's something in the air,' he said
 In the farm parlour cool and bare;
Plain words, which in his hearers bred
 A tumult, yet in silence there
All waited; wryly gay, he left the phrase,
Ordered the march, and bade us go our ways.

 'We're going South, man'; as he spoke
 The howitzer with huge ping-bang
Racked the light hut; as thus he broke
 The death-news, bright the skylarks sang;
He took his riding-crop and humming went
Among the apple-trees all bloom and scent.

Now far withdraws the roaring night
 Which wrecked our flower after the first
Of those two voices; misty light
 Shrouds Thiepval Wood and all its worst;
But still 'There's something in the air' I hear,
And still 'We're going South, man,' deadly near.

LIEUTENANT EDMUND CHARLES BLUNDEN, MC

Of the three great prose accounts of the Great War, Edmund Blunden's *Undertones of War*, published in 1928, is somewhat overshadowed by the literary pyrotechnics and flamboyance of Sassoon and Graves. Blunden's is a deliberately lower-key work: the very word 'undertones' tells the reader this.

In the revised edition of June, 1930, the blurb counters the sensational success of Graves's highly-embroidered account. 'No "revelations" need be anticipated. Panic, brothels, bayonet-fighting. . . were not common.' These are exactly the elements that Graves deliberately included to make his book a popular best-seller. Blunden promised 'further acquaintance with war's ways and a British battalion that quietly, humorously and honourably lived and died in Flanders'. He delivered it with understated, consummate, poetic mastery.

In a backlash against Graves's imaginative sensationalism (rapturously received when published) the 1930 edition of 'Undertones' was admired for its decency and truthfulness. Even the first edition in 1928 sold out almost immediately it appeared in the shops. The reviewers gave rave notices. 'This book will be a classic' (Arnold Bennett); 'A prose poem' (J.C. Squire); 'A great triumph – he shows war as it is really is' (H.C. Nevinson); 'I wish I had a fat literary prize in my gift. It would go by the next post to Edmund Blunden' (J.B. Priestley). The *Daily Mail* critic wrote that of all war books it was 'the noblest and manliest, the most understanding and compassionate'.

It is not surprising that Blunden's account of the war should be gentle and kindly. He was sensitive and essentially pacifist by nature, but also a man of unexpected contradictions, which led to him being branded as a Nazi sympathizer in the late 1930s. In the oft-quoted last line of *Undertones* Blunden describes himself as 'a harmless young shepherd in a soldier's coat'. This is a somewhat disingenuous description of a highly intelligent, intellectual, successful writer and personality, but the 'shepherd' element is genuine in his deep and abiding love of the countryside, and he called his 1922 collection of poems *The Shepherd*, sub-titled 'Poems of Peace and War'. The memory of the war was never to be erased from his mind and Sassoon maintained (Silkin, *Out of Battle*) that of all the war poets Blunden remained the most obsessed by it.

Writing in 1930, Blunden said, 'the emotional shock that so bewildering a change of prospect meant to those who enlisted for three years or the duration of the war awoke deeper utterance than men ordinarily need or permit themselves to attempt.' That emotional shock was bound to leave a permanent scar. In the same essay Blunden perceptively wrote, 'The main mystery of the Old Front Line was that it created a kind of concord between the combatants, but a discord between them and those who, not being there, kept up the War.'

During his happy, mostly rural, childhood thoughts of war could not have been further from Blunden's mind. He was born in London, in Tottenham Court Road, on 1 November, 1896. His father, Charles, was from country stock and at the time of Edmund's birth was headmaster of a Church of England primary school. His mother was from a distinguished family with aristocratic connections, especially with the Verney family.

In 1900 the Blundens moved to the village of Yalding in Kent, where Edmund began a life-long love affair with the surrounding countryside – a continuing thread through his more bucolic poems and prose works. He enjoyed everything about it: the shops with their enticing odours and wares, the kindly country folk, the River Medway and the joys of fishing in its tributaries, the hop gardens, the church and singing in the choir. The Blunden family grew; by 1904 there were five more children, and they moved from the small school-house to a large farmhouse outside the village. It was a traditional, middle-class Edwardian family with an authoritarian father and a motherly mother. Edmund's early memories of her are remarkably similar to Edward Thomas's of his mother: 'How lovely she was as she took off her bodice and washed her white shoulders' (Webb).

By 1910 three more children had been born and the family found it hard to make ends meet (the bailiffs even took away the furniture). Blunden's mother worked locally as a teacher, but his father had to work as a supply teacher in London and moved the family to two dingy cottages in Twyford Bridge. Edmund hated it. In 1913, however, they moved back to the country in Framfield.

Edmund's education continued throughout these disturbing moves. He started at elementary school and in 1907 went to Cleave's Grammar School. There he was intellectually extended and, above all, enjoyed playing cricket and watching county matches. The game was to remain a passion throughout his life. Recognizing Edmund's potential, his teacher arranged for him to take the entrance exam for Christ's Hospital in Horsham. He passed and took up his place in September, 1909, at the age of twelve.

Christ's Hospital was an extraordinary school. It had the quality and reputation of a public school but was endowed to help bright boys whose parents could not afford fees. Founded in 1552 by Edward VI, its list of famous old boys was impressive, including Samuel Coleridge, Charles Lamb and Leigh Hunt. After his initial homesickness Edmund was swept up in its rich life, so steeped in history and tradition: its emphasis on calligraphy (which he particularly loved) and its uniform of long blue coat and yellow stockings. In 1924 he wrote *Christ's Hospital, A Retrospect*, a loving tribute to his school and favourite masters.

The affection with which Edmund looked back at his schooldays may have been due to a rather selective memory. For instance, he remembered his headmaster for the encouragement he gave, his preservation of all that was best from Christ's Hospital's past, and creating a tranquil environment for Edmund to flower in, while other 'Old Blues' recall 'a sanctimonious sadist' (Webb) worthy of the nickname 'The Butcher'. Another great influence was his housemaster, who helped Edmund with his study of Classics, new to him before he arrived at the school. In his turn Edmund was remembered as 'the really perfect boy' by his history master, apart from his propensity for writing poems (Webb).

Blunden was a likeable, popular boy, slightly frail-looking but nevertheless attractive physically. He had very quick movements and a sharp face with a beak-like nose, which led to inevitable comparisons and nicknames connected with birds ('the beaky bard' – Graves) and rabbits (his army pet name was 'Bunny'). He was bright, eager to learn, grateful for the opportunity to do so in such delightful surroundings, keen on games, natural history, literature and French. He read voraciously, entranced by the wealth of books in the school library. Edmund's first published poem, 'The First Winter', was in the school magazine of February, 1913. In 1914 he printed at his own expense his first book of forty-four *Poems*, and a book of *Poems Translated from the French*. They were of a fairly juvenile calibre, but the seeds of his future ability could clearly be seen.

In 1914 old friends were enlisting and being killed. Service in the school OTC was by then compulsory and Edmund remembered being inspected by General Sir John French, commander of the BEF. Boys studying for university were encouraged to complete their courses; Edmund won a scholarship to Oxford, but in August, 1915, he bicycled to the headquarters of the Royal Sussex Regiment in Chichester to enlist.

Two weeks later he was commissioned a second lieutenant in the 11th Battalion and trained at Weymouth and Shoreham. In December he went to Cork, where he found plenty of time to write poetry and produced three little books which his younger brother published for him. The third volume, *The Harbingers*, reproduced the seven poems of the first two. After the war Sassoon made Blunden send it to Edward Marsh who, recognizing its immaturity, still felt it gave 'great hopes of your later attempts.' In June, 1916, he had another collection, *Pastorals*, published. By then he was in France.

The first words of *Undertones of War* are, 'I was not anxious to go.' His mother saw him off at the station and soon he was in the 'thirsty, savage, interminable training camp', the Bull Ring at Etaples ('Eatapples or Heeltaps', as he described it in soldiers' nomenclature). He experienced violent death during his first morning's training, when a magnificent Highland sergeant-major instructor blew off part of his head, killing himself and some other students, while demonstrating a device called a Hales rifle-grenade. The effect on the sensitive boy was profound.

The battalion was soon off to Le Touret, where they held the line between Béthune and La Bassée, moving between Festubert, Hinges, Cuinchy, Richebourg Saint Vaast, Cambrin and Givenchy, not far from the old Neuve Chapelle and Loos battlefields. Their aim was to divert the Germans from the Somme, where the 'Great Push' was planned for July, 1916. Life got hotter and hotter as the weeks passed, but Blunden still made time to read – Masefield, Shelley, John Clare and scavenged copies of Tennyson, Horace, and Caesar's *De Bello Gallico* found in ruined local houses, presumably left by previous literate British occupants. He wrote evocative verses, such as 'A House in Festubert' describing a ruined building 'With blind eyes meeting the mist and moon'.

Blunden's military progress can be followed with precision in *Undertones of War*. The day-to-day life of a raw subaltern, whose 'notion of modern warfare was infinitesimal', is sympathetically recorded and provides an enduring record of life in the lines – boredom, alarms, nervousness, humour, the tedium of army proformas, special soldiers' slang and nicknames, silk postcards in the Festubert windows, copies of *La Vie Parisienne*, lethal concoctions in the *estaminets* (like 'Rhum Fantaisie') and gas courses (difficult for an asthma sufferer like Blunden). Just as vivid are the word pictures of the disastrous mine blown under the Sussex Regiment at Cuinchy (the crater still exists today) and Blunden's distress at a man mourning over his mortally wounded brother, one of sixty casualties.

These images are reinforced by poems, which are especially effective in the Somme and Ypres Salient sections. When the battalion was ordered from Givenchy rumours of 'going south' spread like wildfire. 'Two Voices', reproduced here, gives an authentic feeling of immediacy and apprehension.

On the Somme, having escaped the first costly battles of July, the Sussex found themselves in August in the valley of the Ancre. In the poignant 'The Ancre at Hamel: Afterwards' Blunden recalls the sad sound of the flowing river; other poems describe the chalk cliffs and dug-outs called 'Kentish Caves' where Blunden established his ammunition dump. It was a dangerous and dreadful place and 'death soon arrived there'. In 'Escape', a dramatic and realistic poem, Blunden describes hearing from his colonel of 'four officers. . . / Lying dead at Mesnil./ One shell pitched clean amongst 'em at the foot/ Of Jacob's Ladder. They're all Sussex men.' The reader shares his horror and apprehension that he will have to go to identify them, and then the blessed relief: 'No, not you, Bunny, you've just come down./ I've something else for you.'

Between the beginning of September and the final, successful assault on Saint Pierre Divion, Beaucourt and Beaumont on 11–13 November, 1916, the Sussex were subjected to the worst possible forms of trench warfare. They made frequent attacks on heavily-defended German positions before Thiepval Wood. Edmund was terrified, cold, wet, sleepless, bombarded by relentless and vicious barrages, appalled at the damage to nature and villages as well as to the men he loved. Nevertheless he fulfilled his duties with devotion and zeal, and when he was called to make a reconnaissance of newly-captured positions which had to be supplied with men and wiring materials, he carried out the hazardous assignment so well that he was awarded the Military Cross. He led his runner past the Thiepval Crucifix, the Schwaben Redoubt, and into a murderous hail of shell-fire. His fellow officers, watching the flashing, exploding hillside, never expected to see Bunny again. But the intrepid pair returned, 'zig-zagging down the slope', noticing 'the Ancre silvering in the Beaucourt lights', to report that it would be 'certain disaster' to send out the wiring party.

The news of the battalion's move from the dreaded Ancre area was greeted with 'songs and with amazement' as they marched away through Albert. But they were heading towards the infamous Ypres Salient. At first Blunden was thrilled to see 'life in her rural petty beauties' and the little-damaged town of Poperinghe behind the lines, with its comforts and delights. His cup of joy almost overflowed when he got ten days' home leave and was able to visit his beloved Yalding and the family and female companionship he missed so much. He returned to Flanders in time to celebrate Christmas with the battalion in Elverdinghe.

In January, 1917, they moved to trenches in 'an Arcadian environment' by Potijze château, which 'boasted a handsome cheval-glass and a harmonium, but not a satisfactory roof'. Blunden then had a spell as brigade intelligence officer based at headquarters in the old ramparts near the Lille Gate in Ypres. He missed his Sussex chums, and his daily round with his observer-corporal was fraught with danger. Spring passed and the brigade returned to the line north of Ypres.

Soon preparations for Third Ypres (Passchendaele) began. 'From Poperinghe forward the place was like a circus ground on the eve of a benefit,' commented Blunden. There were miles of new roads and railways, gunners registering their targets, much aerial activity – enemy and allied – and recce patrols into no-man's-land. As the battle opened on 31 July Blunden found time to read a poem by Sassoon in the *Cambridge Magazine* and wondered how he could 'pass one or two technical imperfections. . . in his fine verse'. The battle is described in Blunden's epic

140

poem, 'Third Ypres': an horrific episode is viewed through a poet's eye and described in poetic form, where the incongruity of 'the red lilac' looking through a window contrasts with the searing image of forty men reduced to splashing arms and legs. Blunden has no time for grief, but he is furious at the impotence of the Allied guns to cut the 'snarling wire'. When he emerges, the only survivor of four, from a pulverized pillbox, his sanity is saved by the sight of 'a score of field-mice nimble,/ And tame and curious'. The sights, sounds and smells of these two terrifying nights would remain with him for the rest of his life.

Other poems from the Ypres sector appear gentler. 'Vlamertinghe: Passing the Château, July 1917' starts with a quotation from Keats' 'Ode to a Grecian Urn' and has a distinctly Georgian flavour, shattered by the demotic final couplet. Even the innocent-sounding 'Concert Party: Busseboom' (a rest camp with baths and a delousing station in a small village below Poperinghe), with its laughter and dance, jest and rhythm, is starkly contrasted with 'the maniac blast/ Of barrage' under which 'men in the tunnels below Larch Wood/ Were kicking men to death'. The 'harmless young shepherd' was capable of feeling and realism that at times emulated Wilfred Owen.

After the opening phase of Passchendaele, in which the Royal Sussex sustained fearful casualties, Blunden was granted another three weeks' home leave. The balm of Yalding was just what he required to recover from the shock of 'the most wicked twenty-four hours I have been through'. But the chasm between civilians still thirsty for the last drop of blood and survivors from those who had spilt it was unbreachable and uncomfortable; he was almost glad to be back in Ypres on 31 August. After attending a signalling course, where he missed the battalion, he returned to it in the Kemmel–Meteren area. His CO recommended Blunden for a captaincy, but the general deemed him too young. He was given the job of 'tunnel major', overseeing the limited but coveted underground accommodation in Hedge Street tunnels. Life continued, unpleasant but comparatively quiet, through Christmas of 1917. Another signallers' course came and went.

The next battalion move was in early 1918 to Mont Saint Quentin, in trenches south of Gouzeaucourt. Rumours were of the arrival of the Americans and an impending battle, which started on 21 March. Blunden was in charge of the signallers and observers, and on the night of the attack the whole battalion was ordered to put out wire in no-man's-land. This they successfully did, despite being the target of murderous machine-gun fire. Several intensive days and sleepless nights followed, and Edmund received with mixed feelings the news of a posting to a training centre in England. He was not happy in his present job, unusually for him not getting on with his superiors, but he hated to leave the men with whom he had gone through such ordeals. He summed up his feelings of betrayal in 'Gouzeaucourt: The Deceitful Calm', 'There it was, my dears, that I departed,/ Scarce a greater traitor ever!' It was the end of his active service: his asthma was exacerbated by exposure to gas and he was exhausted.

The rest of Blunden's war was spent at Stowlangtoft in Suffolk. It was not a happy environment and Edmund desperately tried to rejoin his battalion – in vain. One compensation was meeting an eighteen-year-old barmaid, Mary Daines, whose 'background read like a Hardy novel' (Webb). Attracted by her simple country manner and 'to save her from dangerous people advantaged by the war', the unhappy and lonely young officer married the blacksmith's daughter on 1 June, 1918.

The Armistice passed almost unnoticed in Stowlangtoft, but shortly afterwards, despite Mary's pregnancy, Edmund was sent to rejoin his battalion in the Arras sector. He wished to exert the privileges due to him as winner of an Oxford scholarship to obtain early demobilization, but his marriage was considered a bar to him taking up that scholarship. He wrote an anguished and angry letter to 'the withered "Pooh-Bahs" at Oxford', but to no immediate avail. In mid-February he accepted demobilization (he had considered continuing with the army of occupation on the Rhine) and returned to his simple little wife and uncertainty about the university place he longed for, finally going up to Queen's College in October, 1919, to read English.

His career as a war poet and author continued, however. Besides *Undertones of War*, perhaps his greatest memorial to the war and to his battalion, poetry collections, from *Poems 1914–30* to *Eleven Poems*, published as late as 1965, continued to dwell on the theme which stayed with him vividly and painfully throughout his prolific literary life. He married twice more, became a great scholar and professor in Hong Kong, Japan and Oxford, and a biographer and acknowledged master poet of the English language.

Blunden's final tangible link with the war was his rather unwilling appointment as 'literary adviser' to the Imperial War Graves Commission in 1936 to succeed Rudyard Kipling on the latter's death. In the introduction to Philip Longworth's history of the Commission, *The Unending Vigil*, Blunden recalls wartime cemeteries and burials, marked with simple wooden crosses, describes the history of 'the disposal of the dead after battle' and pays tribute to the dedicated inspiration of Sir Fabian Ware, the Commission's instigator, and the workers who carried out his design. Finally Blunden answers the question he himself poses, 'Why spend money on the dead?', thus: 'a war cemetery, with all its inscriptions for youths in the main dead ere their prime, is the chief sermon against war. . . . Life is commonly regarded as a marvellous gift – the giving back is the equal marvel, and the war cemeteries are in a sense the poetry of that high action.'

Blunden kept in touch with several of his fellow war poets: Sassoon was a lifelong friend and with Graves he had a half-affectionate, half-irritated relationship. He promoted the poetry of Ivor Gurney and Wilfred Owen. He regularly attended battalion reunions and revisited his old battlefields, sometimes in his capacity as an officer of the Imperial War Graves Commission. When he heard that the rebuilding of Ypres was almost complete he wrote: 'I/ Am in the soil and sap and in the beeks and conduits/ My blood is flowing, and my sigh of consummation is the wind in the rampart trees.'

At Blunden's funeral, after his death on 20 January, 1974 at the age of seventy-seven, his old battalion runner dropped a wreath of Flanders poppies on his coffin.

Alan Patrick Herbert

SUB-LIEUTENANT, R.N.V.R.

A LOST LEADER
(OR, THOUGHTS ON TREK)

The men are marching like the best;
  The waggons wind across the lea;
At ten to two we have a rest,
  We have a rest at ten to three;
  I ride ahead upon my gee
And try to look serene and gay;
  The whole battalion follows me,
And I believe I've lost the way.

Full many a high-class thoroughfare
  My erring map does not disclose,
While roads that are not really there
  The same elaborately shows;
  And whether this is one of those
It needs a clever man to say;
  I am not clever, I suppose,
And I believe I've lost the way.

The soldiers sing about their beer;
  The wretched road goes on and on;
There ought to be a turning here,
  But if there was the thing has gone;
  Like some depressed automaton
I ask at each estaminet;
  They say, 'Tout droit,' and I say 'Bon,'
But I believe I've lost the way.

I dare not tell the trustful men;
  They think me wonderful and wise;
But where will be the legend when
  They get a shock of such a size?
  And what about our brave Allies?
They wanted us to fight today;
  We were to be a big surprise —
And I believe I've lost the way.

SUB-LIEUTENANT ALAN PATRICK HERBERT

The Royal Naval Division was one of the most interesting and unusual units of the First World War. Winston Churchill, First Lord of the Admiralty at the outbreak of war and ever the non-conformist, always had a soft spot for this individual organization and did everything to smooth its remarkably speedy formation. It was officially formed on 3 September, 1914 from Royal Naval and Royal Marine Brigades. The Naval Brigades consisted of surplus naval reservists, supplemented later in the war by some surplus Kitchener recruits. The eight battalions were named after famous admirals. The new division seemed an ideal use for the surplus sailors in the naval reserve and Lord Kitchener, the Secretary for War, was delighted to include it in his military forces.

The RND was determined not to lose its naval identity and insisted on keeping naval terms and customs. They flew the White Ensign over their land-based camps, marked the passage of time by bells, requested 'leave to go ashore' and if they failed to return on time they were reported 'adrift'. Instead of sergeants and corporals they had petty officers and leading seamen. The symbol of the anchor was omnipresent – on flags, badges and even on their limbers. When ill they attended 'sick bay', field kitchens were known as 'galleys' and the King's health was drunk sitting down in the 'wardroom'. They were allowed to grow beards and referred to 'port' and 'starboard' instead of left and right. As Winston Churchill succinctly put it in his introduction to Douglas Jerrold's history of the RND, 'It need scarcely be said that these manifestations inspired in a certain type of military mind feelings of the liveliest alarm.' To the staff-trained product of 1914 with a go-by-the-book mentality, conformity was next to godliness.

It seems that wherever there was a scrap, there would be the RND. Their first action was the defence of Ostend; then came the enthusiastic but unsuccessful defence of Antwerp against the advancing German tide on 4 October, 1914. In 1915, it was off to Gallipoli (the brainchild of their patron, Winston Churchill) and another gallant failure, ending with the evacuation in January, 1916. Their losses were extremely heavy – from sickness as well as in battle - and the division had to undergo a major reorganization.

In May, 1916, they arrived in the Souchez section near Vimy, going into the fighting line on 17 July. On 19 July they were officially taken over by the army and became the 63rd (Royal Naval) Division. The next great battle, indelibly and emotionally linked to them, was the Ancre in November, 1916, followed by Gavrelle, part of the Battles of Arras. The divisional artillery acquitted itself with honour, but the Royal Marine Light Infantry was decimated. In October they moved to the Ypres Salient to take part in Passchendaele and in December, 1917, were at Cambrai. In March the division fought at Les Boeufs, High Wood and Courcelette, eventually finding themselves again on the Ancre. They took part in the final Advance to Victory, ending the war near Mons at 11am on 11 November, 1918.

It was a distinguished war record, and much of their success was due to the calibre of men the RND attracted. Many famous names served with it, including Rupert Brooke; his friend the brilliant scholar and poet Patrick Shaw-Stewart; Denis Browne, the talented musician; Charles Lister, son of Lord Ribblesdale; Bernard Freyberg, VC, who became Governor-General of New Zealand; Arthur Asquith, a poet and the Prime Minister's son; Vere Harmsworth, son of Lord Rothermere, the newspaper proprietor; Cecil A. Tooke, the artist; and, of course, A.P. Herbert, the *Punch* humorist, dramatist and Independent MP.

Herbert was born on 24 September, 1890. Despite his prominent nose, which often led to the mistaken belief that he was Jewish, Herbert's parents were a 'full-blooded Irish' father and an English mother from the distinguished Selwyn family. The former was Catholic, the latter Protestant and it was the Protestant influence that predominated in the family (Pound). Alan seemed to have little interest in his roots and only visited Ireland twice in his life. He and his two younger brothers were born in Leatherhead, in a graceful but shabby house with a large garden ideal for family games. It was a happy childhood, marred by an accident which permanently damaged Alan's spine and curtailed by his mother's early death from consumption when he was eight. Herbert was sent to prep school, where he was perfectly content, studied well and enjoyed playing the piano and games. The maternal role at home was supplied by a nanny.

Alan then went to Winchester, where he was a keen Classics scholar, active in the Debating Society, won prized King's Medals for English Speech and English Verse and developed a penchant for rhymes with a humorous slant. He even had the temerity to submit some of his verses to *Punch*. Although he didn't publish these puerile poems, the editor took the trouble to write constructive criticism in the margins before returning them.

Robert Nichols, probably, with Brooke, the most popular war poet during and shortly after the Great War, but now universally dismissed as negligible, was his contemporary, and attempted serious poetry while Herbert was composing light verse. Herbert admired Nichols' works, but

Nichols did not include a poem by Herbert in his *Anthology of War Poetry*. Herbert was Captain of Houses, one of the divisions of Winchester's tough form of football, and badly damaged his knees and ankles playing the game. At the end of the Christmas term, 1909, he left the school with an exhibition to New College, Oxford.

By this time the family had moved to Kensington. Herbert spent the months between leaving school and going up to Oxford bicycling around London, roller skating, attending political meetings (he was impressed by Winston Churchill), going to the pictures, socializing with Old Wykehamists' sisters and suffering excessive adolescent mood changes and emotions. In April he went to Newport, Isle of Wight, to study Classics; while he enjoyed exploring the picturesque island, he got rather bored with a surfeit of Homer and Thucydides. In June his first selection of poems, *Poor Poems and Rotten Rhymes*, was published by Winchester College's printers and reviewed in *The Wykehamist* by Gilbert Talbot.

Herbert passed his remaining holiday by reading and going to the theatre. His verses were published for the first time in *Punch* on 24 August, 1910. He arrived at Oxford on 13 October, a contemporary of Gilbert Talbot, Duff Cooper, Harold Macmillan, Robin Barrington-Ward (future editor of *The Times*), Sir Henry Newbolt's son Francis ('Cherry'), and Cyril 'Cis' Asquith, the Prime Minister's youngest son. Their companionship, and that of his many other friends, Herbert valued above all the other benefits of university life. He joined several clubs, debated at the Union and obtained 'a very good First' in jurisprudence. Destined for a career in the law, he first spent a year at the Oxford House Mission in Bethnal Green, acting as head cook and bottlewasher.

Herbert was staying at the home of the poet Sir Henry Newbolt when war was declared. Drake-like, the great patriot hardly interrupted his game of bowls to pass on the telephoned news (Pound). On 5 September Herbert enlisted in the Royal Naval Volunteer Reserve as an ordinary seaman. His youngest brother was training to become a submarine officer and Alan vaguely thought that he might meet up with him if he joined a naval organization. Alan continued to attend the Oxford Mission, taking his new love, Gwen Quilter, with him, and she was persuaded to take over the running of the Women's Club there. Herbert sat the exam for the All Souls' Prize Fellowship that autumn, but blew his chances by writing his answers in 'frivolous', even 'bawdy', verse according to a fellow candidate (Pound). His promotion to acting leading seaman was taken more seriously and he assiduously practised Morse and semaphore. In December Alan and Gwen became engaged and were married in January, 1915, in the church of St James the Great in Bethnal Green by the head of the Mission.

The RND trained at Crystal Palace and Blandford prior to embarkation. The bulk of the division sailed for the Dardanelles on 1 March, but

Hawke and Benbow Battalions had been so depleted at Antwerp that they had to stay behind to reorganize. On 10 March Herbert was commissioned as a temporary sub-lieutenant in Hawke, commanding the 11th Platoon in C Company. The battalion sailed from Avonmouth on 10 May, calling at Malta en route, and anchored in the harbour of Mudros on 17 May, 1915.

There are many famous accounts of the Gallipoli campaign, but perhaps the most human and moving is in Herbert's *The Secret Battle*. It is an extraordinary book. Today we might describe it as faction, for it tells a true and tragic story but alters names and some facts. In his introduction, Winston Churchill wrote, 'The tale is founded on fact. Nevertheless, as the writer has been careful to make clear, it is not an authentic account. All the facts on which it rests happened. . . but they did not all happen to the same man.' The story of the main protagonist, whom Herbert calls Harry Penrose, is based on that of Sub-Lieutenant Edwin Dyett of Nelson Battalion, RND, one of only three officers (and 343 men) to be executed during the First World War – he was shot on 5 January, 1917. In 1918 his case was taken up by Horatio Bottomley's magazine, *John Bull*, and was the subject of a discussion in the House of Commons. Judge Babington examines the case in some detail in his book *For the Sake of Example*, 1983. One has the strong impression that both Babington and Herbert believe Dyett's execution to have been a miscarriage of justice. Herbert wrote the story in 1919 not only because of his anger at Dyett's harsh treatment, but to exorcize his pain from his war experiences. It has even been suggested that Herbert refused to act as 'Prisoner's Friend' to Dyett at his Court Martial (perhaps fearing his own lack of ability to plead the case strongly enough) and that *The Secret Battle* was written in an attempt to expiate the guilt he felt at Dyett's subsquent conviction and execution. Extensive researches at the PRO have failed to prove this theory conclusively.

From embarkation at Plymouth to the landings at Cape Helles on the night of 28–29 May, 1915, to the Somme in 1916, *The Secret Battle* tells Herbert's own story too, in a sympathetic, realistic manner. Together with his poems, it gives a sometimes humorous, sometimes sad, sometimes horrifying picture of a subaltern or sub-Lieutenant's war.

At Gallipoli Herbert continued to write poetry. He was particularly amused by the accents and antics of the Tynesiders, 'stout miners all', brought in to swell Hawke's depleted ranks. He struck up a close friendship with Lieutenant William Kerr and wrote of the two of them together, looking across the Trojan plains (all Classical scholars were aware that they were fighting in an area steeped in ancient history and lore) and sitting talking 'of happy things'. He soon earned a reputation as a wag, a flaunter of regulations, in a division that encouraged non-conformity, and gained kudos from his contributions to *Punch*. The magazine even published his name in 'Mr Punch's Roll of Honour' in September, 1915, as having been wounded; he actually had severe enteritis and was invalided home in August 1915.

After a period of convalescence, he was passed as fit for light duty and given a job with Admiralty Intelligence reporting on the Method of Agriculture in Egypt! After the failure of the Gallipoli landings, when the RND returned to the Western Front, Herbert rejoined Hawke Battalion, becoming assistant adjutant in July, 1916. On 17 September a new Divisional Commander, Major-General Shute, arrived and began an abortive attempt to impose army discipline on the unruly division. The adjutant found Herbert an energetic ally in his efforts to oust the unpopular commander. When Shute objected to Lieutenant Codner's beard it became the focus of their crusade to preserve RND traditions. Herbert wrote in *Punch*: 'Now Brigadier-General Blank's Brigade was tidy and neat and trim,/ And the sight of a beard on his parade was/ A bit too much for him.' Codner refused to shave 'his face all fringed with fur', his mark that he belonged 'to the King's Navee', and the row continued even after Shute moved on.

Although Jerrold's RND history attempts to adopt a dry historian's attitude, he and Herbert were kindred spirits. They shared an irreverent sense of humour, loving to 'stir things up' and carouse together. As adjutant he put his assistant, Herbert, in charge of communicating with brigade, tickled pink at Herbert's tone 'of mingled authority and irresponsibility'. With promotion came a horse, not an animal with which Herbert had a great affinity. Leading a column of men was the inspiration for the poem reproduced here – a favourite on battlefield tours when a retired officer guide hesitates with his map-reading. As with much of Herbert's poetry, it is improved by being read aloud. But Herbert was more than a writer of light, amusing verse. The effects of the terrible Battle of the Ancre brought forth lines of beauty, deep sorrow and sensitivity.

After the lack of progress in the 1 July, 1916, attack north of the River Ancre, a major assault was planned for November to bring the British line forward to align with the front south of the river. The hated General Shute set the RND digging assembly trenches on the slopes leading down to the Ancre valley. 'A wise decision,' commented Jerrold, 'but one that involved a risk,' for when the final attack orders came the men had reached 'their limit of endurance'. It was a complicated battle plan: the divisional objective was Beaucourt, and Hawke Battalion, with the 1st RM, Hood and Howe, was to advance in four waves, in time with a 'creeping barrage'. The attack began at 5.45am in the dark and under a thick mist. At first all seemed to be going well, then Hawke came under murderous machine-gun fire from a hitherto unidentified strongpoint and nearly all the officers and men became casualties.

On either flank of the strongpoint a few men got through, including, on the left, Vere Harmsworth, who 'led a fine attack' with some of his men on the German second line, during which he was mortally wounded. On the right two officers and a score or so men pressed on, about a dozen joining Freyberg's Hood Battalion in front of Beaucourt. Hawke Battalion 'virtually ceased to exist', sustaining nearly 400 casualties in the first half hour from their strength of 435. Being Assistant Adjutant, Herbert was left out of the battle and so survived unscathed – physically, that is.

Stand today on the top of the Ulster Tower that overlooks the Valley of the Ancre, the site of this slaughter, and the beautiful Ancre CWGC Cemetery where several of the victims lie, and say aloud Herbert's 'Beaucourt Revisited'. You will feel his grief tangibly. The poem was written when Herbert returned to the Ancre, then held by 'new men', in the spring of 1917. The poem, a verse of which appears below, first appeared in the RND magazine, *The Mudhook*.

> And here the lads went over and there was Harmsworth shot,
> And here was William lying – but the new men knew them not.
> And I said, 'There is still the river and still the stiff, stark trees;
> To treasure here our story, but there are only these;'
> But under the white wood crosses the dead men answered low,
> 'The new men know not Beaucourt, but we are here – we know.'

Under what are now white headstones, not crosses, in the Ancre cemetery, still lies 'Harmsworth' – Lt the Hon Vere Harmsworth, on whose grave is an unusual bronze wreath placed by the Hungarian scouts, because Harmsworth's father, Lord Rothermere, in his paper, *The Daily Mail*, maintained that Hungary should have had territory returned after the war. 'William', surname Ker, a great friend of Herbert who, said Jerrold, was 'a personality of rare promise and rarer charm', may well also lie there under an 'Unknown' headstone. He is actually commemorated on the Thiepval Memorial.

'The Tide' is almost a sequel to 'Beaucourt Revisited'. It describes the spring of 1918, when the Germans retook Beaucourt and took Hamel. Herbert, and the RND in general, felt strongly about 12th Division's failure to hold it. Jerrold movingly wrote: 'For all, during many months, and for many, always, the valley of the Ancre remained in the background of their thoughts.' After the battle the division was withdrawn for two months' rest and major reorganization. In 'After the Battle', Herbert commented:

> We only want to take our wounds away
> To some warm village where the tumult ends,
> And drowsing in the sunshine many a day,
> Forget our aches, forget that we had friends.

The reorganization introduced another batch of army officers, causing discontent on top of the division's painful emotional wounds. They moved back to the Somme area in January, 1917, Herbert rejoining his battalion after leave as adjutant, when he 'revitalized Battalion headquarters' with his humour, resiliance and nonconformity (Jerrold).

On 1–2 February Hawke and other RND battalions attacked northeast of Beaucourt, close by where they had suffered such heavy casualties in November, 1916. They acquitted themselves with dogged bravery and many DSOs and DCMs were won. In March the division was withdrawn for 'rest', the usual round of working parties, but on 9 April was again in the thick of offensive action and on 23 April a major attack was launched on the village of Gavrelle. During their move to the first objective, Hawke suffered heavy losses. 'Among those wounded,' reported Jerrold flatly, 'was the adjutant, Lieutenant A. P. Herbert, RNVR, whose wit was already famous outside the Naval Division.'

He was seriously wounded in the left buttock, surely the butt of many ribald jokes. It was a 'Blighty' one, and Herbert had a lengthy period of convalescence, during which he started *The Secret Battle* and contributed regularly to *Punch*. The magazine allowed him to join the élite who signed their work with their initials only, beginning the use of 'A.P.H.' which remained his signature thereafter. He missed the companionship of the battalion – the collection *The Bomber Gypsy* is dedicated 'To my wife and to all the wives who have waited and wondered but especially to the wives of the RND.' The poem which gives it its name tries to explain the strength of the bond between men who have fought together. Herbert wrote to Gwen of 'The fellowship that laughs at fear'.

In a poem published on 10 April, 1918, during the dark days of the Great Retreat when backs were to the wall, A.P.H. dreamed of better days in 'The Windmill', subtitled 'A Song of Victory'. In October, 1918, he sailed from Liverpool to Alexandria as assistant commodore to a convoy. He had no sea-going experience other than the voyage to and from Gallipoli and was dismayed when the commodore went sick in the great 'flu epidemic'. One of the ships in the convoy was sunk by an enemy submarine, women and children going down with her. They also encountered fearful storms; Port Said, even though he found it 'A dirty, uninteresting place', provided a welcome break from the terrors of the sea. They sailed on to Tunisia, where he visited the archaelogical site at Carthage.

When the Armistice was declared on 11 November, 1918, A.P.H. was in Tlemcen, 'the only Englishman for at least 80 miles', having gone there alone by train. Nightmares of the war continued to haunt him and were to stay with him throughout his long, varied and successful career as humorist, barrister, novelist, dramatist and Independent MP. He expressed them in 'The War Dream':

> I wish I did not dream of France,
> And spend my nights in mortal dread.

In later years he was annoyed by fashionable interpretations of the war, like Joan Littlewood's acclaimed Theatre Workshop production of *O What a Lovely War!*, and commented:

> I, at least was not there because of Kitchener's pointing finger, and I don't think the recruiting ditties had then begun (those ditties. . . which seem so funny to the audiences today seemed funny to us at the time – and later we howled at them with affectionate derision before we went up into the line). No, I was calmly persuaded that we had gone to war for a just cause, and that I ought to be in it. . . How I dislike these anaemic belittlers of our past.

He died in 1971, ironically on Armistice Day, 11 November.

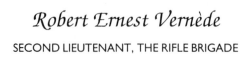

Robert Ernest Vernède

SECOND LIEUTENANT, THE RIFLE BRIGADE

THE LITTLE SERGEANT
(Sergeant — , The Rifle Brigade)

He was one of the Bugler lads
  Born in the Army and bred also.
And they gave him the stripes that had been his dad's
  For knowing what soldiers ought to know.
And then you'd see him swanky and small
  Drilling grown men of twice his span,
Dressing them down and telling 'em all
  That the British Army teaches a man.

Lef—right—lef — how he'd make them run —
  All for their good as he let them see. . .
'It's the way the Army has always done,
  Don't argy the point.' he'd say, 'with me.'
Sometimes they groused, but mostly they laughed —
  For there wasn't a job but he bore the brunt,
And when the time came, there was never a draft
  Smarter than his when he went to the Front.

Somewhere in France on a night of drench. . .
  When their guns had pounded the line to hell
The Germans rushed what had been a trench
  And the Sergeant's men and the Sergeant fell.
Light in some Boche I'm sure he'd let
  Before they could count him as reached full-stop:
And if there was breath in him, then I'll bet
  He told 'em why England would come out top.

Swanky and small and full of guts—
  I wonder, now that he's out of the fight,
Down what dark alleys his small ghost struts
  Giving his men 'Lef—right—lef—right'.
There where the darkening shadows fall
  I think I can hear him chanting slow—
'The British Army's the best of all,
  Don't argy the point — I ought to know.'

France, August 1916

SECOND LIEUTENANT
ROBERT ERNEST VERNEDE

Imagine a tall, dark, oval-faced, striking-looking man with the lithe, graceful movements of a leopard; an energetic sportsman with a natural manner but an interesting, biting wit, a sharp intellect and an air of distinction. He is obsessed with looking youthful and is often taken for fifteen or so years younger than his age of forty. A film star, perhaps?

This attractive person is Robert Vernède, who, despite his foreign-sounding name, was born in London on 4 June, 1875. The Vernède family had been driven from France in the Huguenot persecutions of 1685 and, while proud of their French ancestry, were completely anglicized.

Robert attended St Paul's School, with its strong classical tradition, where he met and made a lifelong friend of the poet and author G. K. Chesterton. In the introduction to Vernède's *War Poems*, Chesterton paints a word picture of a mature, direct character, at ease with himself and his personal philosophy, who loved life, his country and the country-side. These impressions are confirmed by another close friend, Frederick Salter, who was at school with Robert from the age of nine, and also his contemporary at Oxford. He stressed Vernède's lack of pretension, inquiring mind, calmness, ability to inspire affection and loyalty, and the fact that he was a person who would remain quiet and apparently reserved in company until he had something pertinent to say, when he could become an animated and fascinating conversationalist.

Another character witness was Vernède's wife, who adds another dimension – his voice: 'low and soft and peculiarly pleasant'. She loved him for 'his writing, his physical grace, his tender heart, his good taste, his good humour'. What emerges is a complete, rounded personality.

Four years after graduating from St John's, Oxford, with a degree in Classics, Robert married Carol Fry. It was a very happy marriage and the young couple settled in the Hertfordshire countryside at Standon, their garden being a particular joy to them. They had no money and Vernède set out to earn a living as an author. In 1905 his novel *The Pursuit of Mr Faviel* was published, followed in 1906 by *Meriel of the Moors* and in 1908 by *The Judgement of Illingborough*. Tours of Canada and India (notably Bengal) inspired *The Fair Dominion: a Record of Canadian Impressions* and *An Ignorant in India*, both published in 1911. Then came *The June Lady* in 1912 and, published posthumously after the war, *The*

Quietness of Dick, 1919 and *The Port Allington Stories and Others*, 1921.

Although he was productive, acclaim eluded Vernède and earnings were small. Recognition and success seemed just around the corner when his self-confessed humdrum life was shattered by the outbreak of war. Robert loathed the idea of war and its destructive power, but he saw what Salter describes as 'a clear-cut issue of right and wrong' and a threat to all he held precious. To enlist would mean losing his sole, small source of income, but duty was calling and his attitude was first expressed in a torrent of poetry. It was in high, exhortatory style. 'England to the Sea' warns that 'When they come forth who seek this empire o'er thee,/ And I go forth to meet them – on that day/ God grant to us the old Armada weather'. 'The Call' is equally patriotic: 'Here is the game of games to play. . ./ This day England expects you all.'

On 4 September, 1914, Vernède took the plunge and enlisted in the 19th Royal Fusiliers, a public schools' battalion, as a private soldier, claiming that he didn't know enough about the military to apply for the commission strongly advised by his peers. As his friend Frederick Salter put it, in words that seem amusingly patronizing today, this meant 'subordination. . . to all sorts of stupid duties and persons'. At thirty-nine he was four years above the age limit for enlistment, but refused to lie about his age; he had to try several recruiting stations before he found a recruiting sergeant who of his own volition wrote down 'thirty-five' and accepted him.

The brigade assembled in Hyde Park on 8 September and travelled to Epsom, where he was allocated very 'pleasant' billets and joined by his wife at the end of November – a 'cushy' start to army life. She stayed with him until the battalion was moved into huts on Woodcote Park in March, 1915. On 14 May, his thirteenth wedding anniversary, Robert and his great friend Frederick were gazetted into the Rifle Brigade and moved to the Isle of Sheppey for training. Once again Carol was able to join him and recounts an anecdote of this period which highlights Robert's delight in being taken for younger than his years. In the mess a fellow subaltern, having discovered Robert's real age, asked the other officers to guess. Twenty-eight and twenty-nine were suggested, then 'one man, feeling himself very clever, said daringly, 'Thirty-five'. The subaltern's joy at being able to say forty was great.'

The jolly days were soon to end. On 18 November, 1915, Vernède wrote to his wife from Folkestone, en route to France. The next day he wrote from a camp 'in the sand dunes', the following day his letter was written on hotel notepaper – 'Grand Place, Etaples' being scored out for the censor's benefit. Robert's one regret was that he was separated from Frederick, who was in another battalion, but he consoled himself with his prowess at 'sokker', a game which he had never played before but in which he was exultant at having 'easily outrun most, if not all, of my platoon'. He found life interesting but was worried that 'the whole thing is too undemocratic, and distinctions of rank demoralize human relations'. Being virtually old enough to have fathered some of his fellow officers gave Vernède a calmer and more reflective view of the war and what it meant.

From 7 January, 1916, when the battalion first went into the trenches, Vernède saw almost continuous active service, first at Hooge in the Ypres Salient. There he came under heavy bombardment, at one stage running right into the 'Boche barrage'. His natural reaction was to look for shelter, but he showed a typical junior officer's faith in the wisdom of his sergeant who admonished, 'No, sir, the best thing is to get on,' which, said Vernède, 'accordingly we did'. With refreshing honesty and self-knowledge he added, 'I wish I felt really fit to lead these sort of men. I haven't had enough of it to feel really useful.' It was a characteristically mature observation that could not have been made by many of his youthful and enthusiastic fellow subalterns. He had quickly developed a genuine love and respect for his NCOs and men. In a letter to his wife Vernède described with sympathy how 'a sergeant from another regiment – suffering from nerves – dashed in, having abandoned his digging party, of which he felt sure none remained. . . . I gave him a kola nut and sent him off.'

There were periods of rest in Vlamertinghe, a spell in reserve trenches near Ploegsteert Wood, and in August the battalion moved to Carnoy on the Somme. There he wrote 'The Little Sergeant', reproduced here. It has sincere feeling and affection, a celebration of the down-to-earth guts and humour of the British Tommy. Another poem written in August in praise of 'The Sergeant' starts, 'The sergeant 'as 'is uses' – mainly to offer practical tips for survival, such as:

> Shells, though you can't believe it,
> Aren't always aimed at you,
> But snipers if they see your 'ead
> Will put a bullet through.

Letters to his wife do not disguise the horror of war. The 'false and breezy representation of a battle' which appeared in the newspapers disgusted him. He described horrifying incidents like having to wait 'in a trench choked with our dead and Boche wounded and dying for two days and then do another attack'.

On 1 September, 1916, Vernède, leading his company as his captain was sick, was wounded in the thigh during an attack on Delville Wood. It was a hideously costly action for the battalion – all the officers in his own company were casualties – and although Vernède was pleased with his own 'Blighty' one he mourned the loss of three valued platoon sergeants, two of them killed, in 'At Delville':

> . . .one of them called out as he died –
> 'I've been so ambitious, boys'. . .
> And I thought to myself, Ambitious!
> Did he mean that he longed for power?
> But I knew that he'd never thought of himself
> Save in his dying hour.

After a period in Somerville Hospital at Oxford, Vernède convalesced at home, had a term of light duty at Sheppey, and was back on the Somme at Maricourt by 7 January, 1917. He resisted all efforts to make him take a safe War Office job, wanting to return to the men he loved, and was therefore bitterly disappointed to return to a different (service) battalion of the Rifle Brigade. Although by now he was an experienced junior officer, the battalion had its full complement of officers so Vernède had to take the lowest-of-the-low position of 'newest-joined subaltern'. His captain noted that he bore the humiliation with 'unselfish loyalty'.

On 22 January, 1917, his friend Frederick Salter was seriously wounded, and Vernède wrote 'To F.G.S. "Seriously wounded"' as a reaction. At the end of the year he polished lines he had first penned in the Ypres Salient, and called the poem 'Before the Assault'. It is a powerful and passionate prayer for peace, not for his own generation but their children. He was still, even after experiencing the beastliness of war, convinced of the righteousness of the Allied cause; that there was no alternative but to fight on to the bitter end of German abomination.

After fifteen years of marriage Robert and Carol were still very much in love. In the love song 'To C.H.V.' he asks what he should bring her when he came back from the war. Finally he decides:

> What if I bring you nothing, sweet,
> Nor maybe come home at all?
> Ah, but you'll know, Brave Heart, you'll know
> Two things I'll have kept to send:
> Mine honour for which you bade me go
> And my love – my love to the end.

On Easter Day, 8 April, 1917, he wrote to Carol, 'I think it will be summer soon, and perhaps the war will end this year and I shall see my Pretty One again'. The next day Vernède was hit in the stomach by a concealed machine gun whilst leading his platoon in an advance on Havrincourt Wood. He was carried by the men who loved him to an aid station, but died (on the same day as Edward Thomas, who had been at the same school and university) on the journey to the next medical point. They buried him in the French cemetery at Lechelle, with a cross surrounded by the bulbs from a bowl of daffodils that had given Vernède pleasure when they bloomed in the mess. After the Armistice, his body was reburied in Lebuquière Communal Cemetery Extension.

Robert's *Letters to His Wife* and *War Poems and Other Verses* were both quickly published in 1917. The former was edited by his wife Carol, and the latter had an introduction by Edmund Gosse (later Sir Edmund) the influential man of letters: it was a great accolade. These volumes give a vivid picture of a graceful and dedicated man, whose maturity gave him an unusual perspective on the war that took his life.

Gilbert Frankau

CAPTAIN, ROYAL FIELD ARTILLERY

HEADQUARTERS

A league and a league from the trenches – from the traversed maze
    of the lines,
Where daylong the sniper watches and daylong the bullet whines,
And the cratered earth is in travail with mines and with
    countermines—

Here, where haply some woman dreamed (are those her roses that
    bloom
In the garden beyond the windows of my littered working-room?),
We have decked the map for our masters as a bride is decked for the
    groom.

Fair, on each lettered numbered square – cross-road and mound and
    wire,
Loophole, redoubt and emplacement – lie the targets their mouths
    desire;
Gay with purples and browns and blues have we traced them their
    arcs of fire.

And ever the type-keys chatter; and ever our keen wires bring
Word from the watchers a-crouch below, word from the watchers a-
    wing:
And ever we hear the distant growl of our hid guns thundering;

Hear it hardly, and turn again to our maps where the trench lines
    crawl,
Red on the grey and each with a sign for the ranging shrapnel's
    fall—
Snakes that our masters shall scotch at dawn, as is written here on
    the wall.

For the weeks of our waiting draw to a close. . . There is scarcely a
    leaf astir
In the garden beyond my windows, where the twilight shadows blur
The blaze of some woman's roses. . . 'Bombardment orders, Sir.'

CAPTAIN GILBERT FRANKAU

In the foreword to his autobiography, *Self Portrait*, Gilbert Frankau bemoaned the fact that 'to me, my own character is still unclear'. The picture that emerges from his attempts at self-assessment is of a flamboyant, sometimes endearing, at times opinionated and irritatingly bumptious, perpetual Peter Pan with a sometimes inventive, sometimes fifth-form sense of humour and imagination. He was a bon viveur who loved women; a born story-teller with a prodigious and varied literary output, but who worked hard to make a success of the business he inherited from his father.

Frankau was born on 21 April, 1884, son of Arthur, a workaholic wholesale cigar merchant and Julia, better known as the novelist Frank Danby. He had a privileged childhood: a smart London house, a solicitous nanny followed by a 'kindly, competent, virtuous' governess, a Latin tutor 'of no mean repute' and aristocratic friends. Gilbert's prep school was St Michael's, Westgate-on-Sea. His literary mother, he said, 'dinned into me. . . that I must "win a classical scholarship at Eton".' He complied, and also won a scholarship to Harrow.

Gilbert went to Eton in January, 1898, after spending a term in Versailles to improve his French. His housemaster was a brilliant Latin scholar and his house 'carried off every scholastic and athletic triumph'. At school Frankau behaved like any normally mischievous, typical product of his age. When he felt in the mood, however, he found his schoolwork relatively easy. His mother had a Balliol scholarship in mind for him, but he was more interested in 'sport, love, and winning of my "Boats"' (his rowing colours). 'Pansies' were one of Frankau's pet hates, at school and in later life; he boasted that he managed never to come in contact with the Eton 'practisers of amatory unorthodoxy'. His great enthusiasm, once he discovered his facility for writing verses and stories and his pleasure in doing so, was the founding of the *X Magazine*. The third edition, with its 'bits of spicy gossip about various masters', was condemned as having 'the very worst features of yellow journalism . . . Let it cease'.

In 1901 he was inordinately thrilled to have his first book of satiric verse, *Eton Echoes*, published, yet was positive that he did not want to continue his education. To please his mother he dashed off the four-hour Oxford entrance exam in forty minutes and passed, but insisted on leaving school to go into the family business. Gilbert's confidence for a seventeen-year-old was impressive. He later wrote that he was thankful that from an early age, far from having an inferiority complex, he had the 'virtues' of exhibitionism, independence and ambition – and a vivid imagination, all fostered by his exceptional parents. Gilbert respected and loved his father, 'the perfect epitome of the Christian gentleman, utterly honest, universally kind and . . . completely fearless. . . . Unlike most children of the period, I had never been afraid of my father.' As for his mother, Gilbert seemed to treat her more like a slightly irresponsible sister. When his father died Gilbert acted as escort and holiday companion to Julia, as he always called his less than grief-prostrated mother. She played poker and bridge with panache, stayed at the dinner table with the gentlemen for coffee and liqueurs at the 'racy' dinner parties she threw, and energetically travelled abroad. Gilbert's younger brothers and sister seem inconsequential, and there is little doubt that to Julia her first-born was very special.

In July, 1901, Gilbert went to Hamburg to learn German, then holidayed in Italy – where his amorous adventures inspired a steamy, and for those days unpublishable, story, 'Seamew and Pantheress'. He spent Christmas, 1903, in Paris, learning the cigar business between love affairs, parties, visits to the music hall and travel. Gilbert was in Berlin when he was called home in time to see his father die of 'some form of galloping consumption' in November, 1904. Gilbert assumed the mantle of head of the family for a year before he 'fell seriously in love with a "nice girl".'

In December, 1905, he married Dorothea (Dolly) Drummond-Black at the fashionable St Margaret's in Westminster. In hindsight Gilbert frankly admitted that he was probably more in love with love than with Dolly; he had no desire for children, nor any intention to change his lifestyle. The honeymoon, in New York and then the mecca of cigars, Havana, doubled as a business trip, marred for Gilbert by Dolly becoming pregnant.

Back in London he adopted an attitude of 'resentful neutrality' towards the impending baby. He was 'more depressed that I had ever felt in my whole young life' when the hapless Dolly only managed to produce a girl, and doubly depressed when Dolly was careless enough to become pregnant again. He continued a more or less bachelor existence, gambling (a bounced cheque at a club landing him in court in 1908), being baled out by the indulgent Julia, travelling to Havana on business. Another daughter, Pamela (the well-known novelist), was born on 3 January, 1908. 'Officially she is non-existent – as I forgot to register her birth,' is his only comment about her arrival in his autobiography.

In 1909 the family moved to Chislehurst, Gilbert returning home somewhat unwillingly after his day at the office, the relations between possessive mother-in-law and unfortunate daughter-in-law deteriorating fast. Gilbert found solace in the glittering array of actresses and personalities, like Horatio Bottomley, whom he met through Julia. His literary acquaintances included Sir Hugh Walpole and the notorious Frank Harris, who asked Gilbert (who righteously declined) to write pornographic stories for him to publish, as well as lesser-known novelists. His own literary life was arid: the combination of an unhappy marriage and business worries silenced his muse. Financially things, deteriorated rapidly.

He was forced to sell the Chislehurst house and move to a modest one in Harrow. He finally managed to write – a 'novel in verse' called 'The Nut Errant'. (A 'nut' was a fashionable man about town.) The novel was published (with, of course, Julia's unfailing help) under the title *One of Us*. It went well and a sequel, *More of Us*, followed.

Business went from bad to worse and Gilbert decided he had to break into the export market. In December, 1912, he embarked on an extended business trip to Australasia, South America and the West Indies. He was away for fourteen months, during which time he wrote a prose novel, *The Woman of the Horizon*, and a long, dramatic poem, 'Tid' apa'. He fell in and out of love at least twice on his journeys and arrived back at Tilbury in January, 1914, on the brink of pulling off a lucrative contract. But his excitement at his homecoming was marred by Julia's deteriorating health. She had diabetes and, like his father, consumption.

It soon became inevitable that there would be war with Germany. Julia, assured by the influential friends that it would be a short one, commanded, 'You'll all have to go. I must see my three sons in khaki.'

Frankau showed his usual lack of false modesty when he quoted St John Greer Ervine writing in a book review in the *Daily Express* as never being quite certain whether Frankau or Mr Lloyd George 'won the Great War'. Ervine was probably referring to Gilbert's contribution to morale with his humorous verses and stories rather than to his military prowess. He was commissioned into the 9th (Service) Battalion, the East Surrey Regiment on 6 October, 1914, as a temporary lieutenant. At thirty he was considerably older than most of the men who were enlisting at this time. His CO was a Territorial officer who had not attested to serve overseas and Gilbert refused to serve under him. 'One of us must go,' he insisted. He transferred to the Royal Field Artillery, was promoted to second lieutenant on 25 March and to lieutenant on 11 August, 1915, serving as adjutant in 107th Brigade, RFA, 24th Division.

After the Loos battle of 25 September, Frankau's CO, 'Sleepy' Coates, called on the dying Julia to assure her of her son's 'sterling military worth and complete physical safety'. When Coates returned to France the brigade was in the village of Acquin, and Frankau actually stayed in the house where Rudyard Kipling's son John was billeted before he went missing with the Irish Guards on 27 September, 1915. Gilbert plucked up courage to write to his hero Kipling about his son, thereby starting a correspondence.

Gilbert got home leave in December, 1915. He showed Julia the 'soldier poems' he had written at the front and had a bristling meeting with H. G. Wells, who ridiculed him for wearing spurs. The evening was particularly memorable to Gilbert as he also met the future second Mrs Frankau at the party.

In 1916 the brigade moved to the Ypres sector and Gilbert was in his dugout by the Ypres Canal when Coates, returning from another leave, delivered a letter from Julia's solicitor announcing her death. Although she left him an envelope containing £500, he was in a parlous financial situation. Bankruptcy loomed.

Gilbert was by now contributing poems to the magazine *Land and Water* and writing regularly for that extraordinary wartime journal, the *Wipers Times*. It was started by a Sherwood Forester who discovered 'an old printing house [complete with press] just off the Square at Wipers'. The famous magazine was full of schoolboy humour that especially appealed to the young subalterns, many of whom were fresh from school: puns, 'satire', in-jokes about senior officers and politicians, thinly-disguised pseudonyms – Herlock Shomes, Belory Helloc (or Hilarious Bolux as Frankau called him), pseudo ads for 'new patent tip duck boards', Sapper Bros Ltd, Consulting Engineers, and Dead Cow Farm Cinema.

The journal was printed in a casemate in the old Vauban ramparts of the town and changed its name as the editorial team moved: the *New Church Times* (Neuve Chapelle), the *Kemmel Times*, the *Somme Times* and finally, when the censor intervened, simply the *BEF Times*. They were all produced in the most appalling and dangerous conditions, between shelling and other vicissitudes of war. Gilbert was a leading light in their production and his help was gratefully acknowledged by the editor in the bound copy of the complete magazine in 1918.

His contributions were often pastiches in the style of well-known poets, like James Elroy Flecker – 'Eve, Blanche and Phrynette', for example: 'This is the song of the pretty prattler; who signs herself "Eve" in each Thursday's "Tatler".' He commented on current news: 'Wails to the Mail' bemoans the fact that 'married men of the latest armies will receive 104 pounds per annum in addition to the usual separation allowance', while 'others SAID NOTHING, GOT NOTHING, BUT WENT.'

But Frankau had his serious side. Seeing friends killed and wounded had made him virulently anti-German and he wrote indignantly to the *Daily Mail* complaining about the 'official' prayer intoned by the chaplain: 'And we pray that our enemies may be healed of their bodily hurts.' Frankau maintained that he would never willingly attend church parade again. He was also furious about the story (which he himself used in a novel) of a Belgian girl being raped by 'more than a dozen drunken Hun infantrymen while their officers looked on'. It irritated him that 'people with less prejudiced minds than my own may suggest that such behaviour is possible in all warring armies'. Frankau felt that 'poor bloody Tommy' and his officers and NCOs were such gentlemen that 'it would have been utterly impossible' in the British army.

Frankau pulled no punches when he was riled. 'The Other Side', sub-titled 'Being a letter from Major Average of the Royal Field Artillery in Flanders acknowledging a presentation copy of a book of war-verse written by a former subaltern of his battery – now in England', is scathing about the poetry, which he considers,

> The same old tripe we've read a thousand times. . .
> . . .all the eye-wash stuff
> That seems to please the idiots at home. . .
> 'Heroes who laugh while Fritz is strafing them.'
> (I don't remember that you found it fun,
> The day they shelled us out of Blauwport Farm!)

Frankau felt he should be writing about:

> Mud, cold, fatigue, sweat, nerve-strain, sleepnessness,
> And men's excreta viscid in the rain,
> And stiff-legged horses lying by the road,
> Their bloated bellies shimmering green with flies. . .

He painted a vivid picture of the attack on the Bois de Bernafay, when the poet staggered in to tell Frankau about a gunner's death, "His head – split open – when his brains oozed out,/ They looked like bloody sweet-breads in the muck.'/ And you're the chap who writes this clap-trap verse!' It is among the most starkly realistic and harrowing poetry of the war. Although its message is virulently anti-war – 'A dirty, loathsome, servile, murder-job' – Frankau still believed in the rightness of the cause, that the war would have to be fought to its conclusion and that it really would be 'the war to end all wars'.

The subject matter of the poem reproduced here is unusually technical for a First World War poem, showing the map-reading skill of the gunner in laying down his bombardment to accurate effect. Perhaps Frankau's most popular war-time poem, however, is the epic ballad 'How Rifleman Brown came to Valhalla', with its rollicking rhythms and demotic power. Rifleman Joe Brown comes unmarked, with unbloody bayonet, and unsullied rifle to the lower hall of Valhalla to prove his right of entry to the battered, maimed 'killer-men' inhabitants. He is scorned and rejected, until a man with a hideous head wound tells the saga of Joe Brown who stood in a forward sap straining to detect the first signs of poisonous gas approaching and waited there long enough to bang the warning gong, thereby saving his comrades but virtually committing suicide. He was unanimously passed and qualified for 'the Endless Smoke and the beer of the free Canteen'. Despite its doggerel form and gore the poem shows a sympathetic and hearty respect for Tommy Atkins and has an extraordinarily moving effect.

'The Deserter' shows less empathy. The unfortunate, contrite deserter is led out 'To die his death of disgrace'. As the muzzles of the firing squad flamed, 'the shameless soul of a nameless man/ Went up in the cordite-smoke'. Had Frankau been sent back to the front after being diagnosed as suffering from shell shock, he might have had more sympathy.

On the Somme in July, 1916, Frankau clashed angrily with his erstwhile favourite CO, Coates, who was generous enough to ignore the spat and recommended Frankau for anti-aircraft training. Gilbert then pulled all the influential strings he could reach at home to get himself transferred to the Italian front, where there was a cushy job going for someone with his skills – fluent Italian and commercial knowledge. He cheekily demanded to see the brigade general, to whom he passionately put his case, and was ordered home to take up the Italian job in September.

He was promoted temporary captain and 'wore the green tabs and hatband of the Intelligence Corps with his artillery badges', was seconded to the Foreign Office and detailed to take films to Rome. He was to work on propaganda and also a hush-hush job: 'The Official Secrets Act. . . will slightly handicap this part of my story,' he mysteriously hints in his autobiography. It all made him feel very self-important and pleased with himself.

Unfortunately he began to show a delayed reaction to an incident he described as 'a certain shell which had decapitated the infantryman at my side, knocking me flat, and embedding three tiny pieces of grit behind my left ear'. He was conscious of behaving outrageously to his superiors, replying to the propaganda director's comment, 'Well, we seem to have saved your life for you, Frankau,' with the words, 'You can flatter yourself that you've rendered a supreme service to English literature.'

Settled in the Grand Hotel, Rome, his task was to combat German propaganda and persuade the Italians that the British effort in France and Flanders was strong and committed. The films he brought were meant to demonstrate this, but the Italians weren't impressed and Gilbert rushed back to London where he 'looted every scrap of official film [he] could find', collected an etching of a tank in action and assembled stirring, martial music like 'The British Grenadiers' and 'Tipperary'. He took this persuasive cache to Milan.

Aided by an Italian film-maker, he scrambled the British film snippets into a masterpiece, *The Battle of the Tanks*, introduced by 'Capitano

Gilbert Frankau, Sotto Maggiore Inglese'. They sold all twelve copies and it was, according to Frankau, rapturously and emotionally received. To his further joy Rudyard Kipling arrived in Rome when the city was plastered with advertisements for the film and crowds queued to see it.

Gilbert's cup of joy nearly overflowed when he met Kipling, whom he regarded 'as something more than a man', and whose entire poetic output he claimed to know by heart. Sitting by Kipling at a showing of the film, he noted the master didn't flicker at Gilbert's liberties with fact and merely asked, 'How did you come to think of that fiction?' Finally he chuckled. 'Superb. But you will be slain for this, my friend.' He was. But Gilbert's confident cheek and his explanatory report on the making of the film and the reasons behind it gained him a temporary reprieve at the Foreign Office.

Frankau then moved to the Italian army headquarters at Udine, where he strutted flamboyantly before visiting VIPs and royalty and diced with military death by disregarding regulations. All through his time in Italy, for instance, he had managed to keep his own personal RFA driver, for whom he had fiddled a pass when leaving the Somme, even taking him back to Britain on his trip to obtain film. By August, 1917, his frenzied existence and the delayed shell-shock were taking their toll. He had lost weight dramatically: on joining up he weighed 148 pounds, now he was only ninety-seven pounds (just under seven stone). And finally he was sacked.

He was interviewed by John Buchan (author of the patriotic *The Thirty-Nine Steps*), who had been appointed Director of Information. Frankau vaguely remembers Buchan promising to make up three months' salary he was owed and pronouncing that he should be returned to the army. Furious, Gilbert stormed the Military Secretary at the War Office, which resulted in him being demoted to lieutenant in the Artillery. His apoplectic reaction was predictable and friends advised him to see a doctor. He avoided the RAMC and went to see the future Lord Horder, a personal friend and an expert on shell-shock and neurasthenia. Horder pronounced him the worst case he had seen, recommended three months' home leave and refused a fee.

Frankau was in dire financial straits: he was forced to sell his furniture and persuaded Chatto and Windus to give him an advance on his next novel. Then came a stunning blow. His typist's maid threw notebooks containing 150,000 words of his new novel into the fire. To sublimate his rage he worked on poems, some started in the trenches of Ypres, and managed to sell them. The *Tatler* offered him a twenty-six-week commission at eight guineas a week. Verse poured out of him, even while he was hospitalized for shell-shock in Reading and then formally invalided out with a lieutenant's gratuity in February, 1918. 'The Reason', published in the *Daily Mail* on 2 November, 1918, shows Frankau's continuing hatred of the enemy. His brother had been killed with the Rifle Brigade leading his platoon in an attack in 1917 and Gilbert felt bitter:

> You ask me why I loathe these German beasts
> So much that I have dedicated self–
> Brains, heart and soul – to one black creed of hate.

He embarked on a frenzy of writing, beginning with *Peter Jackson, Cigar Merchant*, subtitled 'A Romance of Love, War and Business', published in 1919. Peter Jackson had first appeared in *The Woman of the Horizon* and he used the character to tell his story of the Great War. *The Guns*, Frankau's first collection of war poems, had appeared in 1916, followed by *The City of Fear* in 1917. Vera Brittain was particularly impressed by a description of a church destroyed by enemy shells. It was written, she wrote rather loftily in her diary, 'by a certain Captain Gilbert Frankau, who had not then begun to dissipate his rather exciting talents upon the romances of cigar merchants.' 'The Other Side' appeared in 1918, '*The Judgement of Valhalla*' in 1918 and *Collected Poems* in 1923.

The Armistice made little difference to him and his writing programme. In February, 1919, he wrote a poem to his sister, 'The Answer', angry that 'the simple men inspired to godlike deeds/ By love of country' were now branded as 'Northcliffians, Jingoes, Kiplingites'. Those who prate of '"peace", "the brotherhood of man" and "reconciliation of the world"' were 'dirty hounds'. His nerves never recovered from his shell shock and his grandson remembers birthday teas at the Cavalry Club when Gilbert's hands shook so much that conversation was impossible over the loud rattling of cup against saucer.

His prodigious literary output and colourful lifestyle continued: two divorces and two more wives, more novels (some of which were filmed in Hollywood), more poems and short stories. He flirted with far-right politics in the 1920s, impressed by the pomp of Mussolini's fascism, but failed to win a parliamentary seat. In 1939 this extraordinary man was commissioned in the RAFVR and promoted to squadron leader in April, 1940.

Frankau's daughter, Pamela, describes how he 'took his Jewish blood more light-heartedly than I took my half-share', and he converted to Catholicism five months before his death. But one faith he always kept was his remembrance of his fallen comrades. The final words of his autobiography, written just as the Second World War broke out, were, 'This time, if this thing must be, let all who survive see to it that no puling politician betray our victorious dead.' Gilbert Frankau, who died on 4 November, 1952, at the age of sixty-eight, never did.

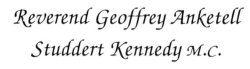

Reverend Geoffrey Anketell
Studdert Kennedy M.C.

"Woodbine Willie"

TEMPORARY CHAPLAIN TO THE FORCES

HIS MATE

There's a broken, battered village
Somewhere up behind the line,
There's a dug-out and a bunk there
That I used to say were mine.

I remember how I reached them,
Dripping wet and all forlorn,
In the dim and dreary twilight
Of a weeping summer morn.

All that week I'd buried brothers,
In one bitter battle slain,
In one grave I laid two hundred.
God! What sorrow and what rain!

And that night I'd been in trenches,
Seeking out the sodden dead,
And just dropping them in shell-holes,
With a service swiftly said.

For the bullets rattled round me,
But I couldn't leave them there,
Water-soaked in flooded shell-holes,
Reft of common Christian prayer.

So I crawled round on my belly,
And I listened to the roar
Of the guns that hammered Thiepval,
Like big breakers on the shore.

Then there spoke a dripping sergeant,
When the time was growing late,
'Would you please to bury this one,
''Cause 'e used to be my mate?'

So we groped our way in darkness
To a body lying there,
Just a blacker lump of blackness,
With a red blotch on his hair.

Though we turned him gently over,
Yet I still can here the thud,
As the body fell face forward,
And then settled in the mud.

We went down upon our faces,
And I said the service through,
From 'I am the Resurrection'
To the last, the great 'adieu'.

We stood up to give the Blessing,
And commend him to the Lord,
When a sudden light shot soaring
Silver swift and like a sword.

At a stroke it slew the darkness
Flashed its glory on the mud,
And I saw the sergeant staring
At a crimson clot of blood.

There are many kinds of sorrow
In this world of Love and Hate,
But there is no sterner sorrow
Than a soldier's for his mate.

THE REVEREND GEOFFREY ANKETELL STUDDERT KENNEDY, MC
'WOODBINE WILLIE'

Woodbine Willie is rarely included in anthologies of poets of the First World War, despite the fact that from personal experience in the trenches he wrote verse full of rhythm and passion, the very essence of poetry.

Few authorities accept Studdert Kennedy's work as 'poetry' and it is interesting to ask why that is so. Too often, it seems, the place of a poet or writer in the hierarchical structure of critical acclaim is more a measure of the sophistication of their output than their ability readily to communicate ideas and feelings.

Yet Studdert Kennedy wrote poetry that crystallized the hopes, fears and experiences of the men in the trenches in a way that those men understood. He wrote in dialect, using simple rhymes, he wrote from personal experience because he had been there, and he wrote in order to communicate. He was not concerned so much with the intellectual merit of the words he used, but more with their ability to communicate the ideas that lay behind them – and not only was his 'versifying' unlikely to find favour with the 'poets' simply because it was versifying, but his ideas were often unpopular with the Establishment too.

Although born in Leeds in 1883, Studdert Kennedy grew up to speak in a strong Irish brogue. He came from a line of clergymen – his father was vicar of St Mary's Quarry Hill, a poor parish in the city. Geoffrey was the seventh son of a lively family where debate and discussion were part of everyday life. He was teased unmercifully for his capacity to become completely absorbed in any book he picked up. His brother said 'he had a mentality like a vacuum cleaner'. He was intelligent, generous, good-natured and incorrigibly scruffy in his dress – appearances simply didn't matter to him, and he would give clothes away without a second thought. From an early age his 'Irishness' showed in his facility with words – he had the gift of the gab.

That Geoffrey would go into the priesthood was probably never questioned. It was after all a family tradition. Yet he was not conventional in his approach to belief and its promulgation, and the urge to question accepted wisdom and express one's own beliefs and way of worship also came from within his family.

He entered Trinity College, Dublin, at the age of fourteen – extraordinarily young – then suspended his course and settled at Leeds Grammar School, returning to Trinity to take exams. He left Leeds at Christmas, 1901, and finished his Dublin course working from home. He gained a First in Classics and Divinity in December, 1902, at the age of nineteen and graduated in 1904. After graduation he taught for a couple of years, attended a theological college for nine months and in 1908 was ordained deacon, joining a Rugby parish church as curate. In 1912 he left Rugby to assist his father as curate in Leeds until his father's death in 1914. All the while he was exercising his gift of communication. Emotional by nature, he said what he thought, pouring out his feelings in a torrent of inspirational words that carried him along on a tide of his own oratory. He visited pubs and sang the songs of the working people, he stood on boxes at street corners and he wrote poetry – or, as he called it, 'verse'.

On St Mark's Day, 1914, he married Emily Catlow in St Mary's in Leeds, and they moved to St Paul's, Worcester, that summer. When war broke out he made no secret of his belief that every able-bodied man should volunteer, but was unable to leave St Paul's until the bishop gave him permission and found a suitable replacement. His ministry to soldiers began almost immediately, however, as Worcester became a training centre for the new army. At the end of November, 1915, the bishop recommended him as Chaplain to the Forces and he was appointed on 21 December. He was in France by Christmas Day, leaving his wife at home with their baby son. It was a happy marriage and he missed her.

After a week in France he was posted to Rouen, where he hoped for hospital work but found no vacancies. Instead he was sent to Lady Mabelle Egerton's canteen at the Rive Gauche Siding, which served hundreds of soldiers every day. He was an immediate success with the men with his unique blend of Irish songs, honest, uncompromising Christianity and gifts of cigarettes. No priest they had ever seen before so sprinkled his texts with swear words or poured such a healing balm, alternated with excitement and conviction, over them. Soon the men were flocking to hear him and he developed a deep love for them. Watching the troop trains depart for the front often moved him to tears, although he would try to hide his emotion. He spent four months at Rouen, and during Lent, 1916, gave six addresses which were published in the spring of 1918 as *Rough Talks of a Padre*.

In 1916 the Church of England reversed the order that forbade their padres to visit the front line, so Studdert Kennedy was able to be under fire with the men he loved. In June, 1916, he joined the 137th Brigade of the 46th (North Midland) Division, who were involved in the diversionary attack on Gommecourt on the opening day of the Somme offensive. 'His Mate', the poem reproduced here, describes a scene he must have witnessed time and again that summer: on one day the division sustained 2,455 casualties – and that was regarded as 'light'. He was withdrawn from the front at the end of October, a decision which made him so angry that he took his protest directly to the Deputy Chaplain General, but to no avail.

In 1917 Studdert Kennedy was with the 17th Brigade of 24th Division at Messines. *Rough Rhymes of a Padre* was dedicated to the two divisions and the men with whom he had served. On 16 August, 1917, the *London Gazette* published the citation for his award of the MC, for conspicuous gallantry in seeking out and attending to British and enemy wounded under heavy fire and for 'his cheerfulness and endurance'. In 1918, with 42nd Division, he took part in the final offensive that broke the Hindenburg Line and spent some time at three army infantry schools.

Studdert Kennedy brought comfort, humour, understanding and deep love to the men who formed his flock. And he brought Woodbine cigarettes. How the ordinary soldier felt about this turbulent priest is best summed up by the apocryphal story of the time when a fellow officer was looking for him in the trenches. 'Have you seen Captain Kennedy?' he asked a sentry. 'No sir.' 'Well have you seen the chaplain then?' 'No sir.' 'What about the padre?' 'No sir.' Exasperated, the officer tried again. 'Have you seen Woodbine Willie?' 'Oh yes sir. He's just gone by.'

Besides his tendency to use swear words for effect, another trait of Woodbine Willie's that upset the hierarchy was his habit of voicing aloud his doubts about God. His belief, which had been almost automatic since birth, was severely tested by the inhuman sights in the trenches. 'Suppose it is not true, and Jesus never lived' begins 'If Jesus Never Lived'. Studdert Kennedy argued aloud his own doubts and hesitations, sharing them with his audience, building a case against convention and then, in a living language, bringing himself and his audience closer to God. On one occasion in 1918, General Plumer didn't wait to hear Studdert Kennedy's planned counter-arguments and not only walked out from the sermon but had Geoffrey removed from the Second Army.

He was demobilized at the end of March, 1919, and took up an appointment as one of the King's Chaplains. He returned to St Paul's in Worcester and his parish work, but he was in demand all over the country; recognizing the value of his popularity and communication skills, the Church allowed him a travelling ministry. Technically he was Rector of St Edmund, King and Martyr in the City of London, but Worcester remained the home base for his happy family life. He and Emily had two more sons, and Studdert Kennedy was devoted to all three children.

He wrote six books, including a novel, *I Pronounce Them*, which dealt with marriage, divorce, contraception and abortion – avant-garde themes that brought him few friends in the Establishment. His collected poetry, *The Unutterable Beauty*, was published in 1927. Of the 105 poems, only twenty are in dialect. Many are simple verses, Kiplingesque in their rhythms. In'Dead and Buried' he criticizes the terms of the Treaty of Versailles. Speaking on behalf of the Tommies who were 'crucified in Cambrai and again outside Bapaume' or 'scourged for miles along the Albert Road. . . driven, pierced and bleeding,' he proudly claims, 'Yet my heart was still unbroken', until 'The statesmen brake my legs and made my shroud. . . mid the many-fountained Garden of Versailles.'

Despite the enthusiasm and effectiveness of his ministry, despite the books that he wrote and the speaking tours of Britain and America, Studdert Kennedy was (apart from his early post-war appointment as King's Chaplain) never accepted either into the literary establishment or the company of the great and the good. His preferred milieu was that of the working man. Studdert Kennedy was Woodbine Willie, champion of the people, and would not be accepted as a 'poet'. But then he would not have cared.

When he died in 1929, worn out by a combination of the asthma that had plagued him all of his life and the frantic pace of his preaching, the two-mile route of the cortège from Worcester Cathedral to the cemetery was lined by crowds of ordinary people every step of the way, and his coffin was showered with packets of Woodbines.

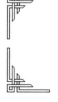

Francis Ledwidge

LANCE CORPORAL, INNISKILLING FUSILIERS

SOLILOQUY

When I was young I had a care
Lest I should cheat me of my share
Of that which makes it sweet to strive,
For life, and dying still survive
A name in sunshine written higher
Than lark or poet dare aspire.

But I grew weary doing well,
Besides, 'twas sweeter in that hell,
Down with the loud banditti people
Who robbed the orchards, climbed the steeple
For jackdaws' eggs and made the cock
Crow ere 'twas daylight on the clock.
I was so very bad the neighbours
Spoke of me at their daily labours.

And now I'm drinking wine in France,
The helpless child of circumstance.
Tomorrow will be loud with war,
How will I be accounted for?

It is too late now to retrieve
A fallen dream, too late to grieve
A name unmade, but not too late
To thank the gods for what is great;
A keen-edged sword, a soldier's heart,
Is greater than a poet's art.
And greater than a poet's fame
A little grave that has no name.

LANCE-CORPORAL FRANCIS LEDWIDGE

In his introduction to *For Remembrance*, Adcock described Francis Ledwidge as 'a scavenger on the roads of Ireland'. Whether the 'scavenger' tag was justified or not, Ledwidge's heart certainly remained on those Irish roads throughout his life, be he in Gallipoli, Salonika, Egypt, France or Belgium.

Ledwidge was born in the shadow of Tara Hill on 19 August, 1887, and grew up surrounded by hills, meadows and rivers of outstanding beauty which became indelibly painted on his mind's eye. Like other nature-loving poets he retreated inwards to this soothing countryside when surrounded by the horror of war, yet his work rarely reflected that horror.

His background and upbringing could not have been more different from that of the public-school poets. He was the eighth child (of nine) of an evicted tenant farmer who died when Francis was only nine. He left school at twelve and was then self-educated. He worked in domestic service, on the fields, as an 'overseer of roads' in the Slane area and, for a while, in a coppermine. There, appalled at the working conditions, he organized a strike and was dismissed, returning to work on the roads.

The young Ledwidge was romantic, fuelled on stirring tales of the *Mabinogion* and other Celtic sagas; folklore and the little people; Keats and Yeats. He also had a reputation as a tearaway, but with a strong social and political conscience. He served on the Navan District Council, was secretary to the local Farmer's Union and County Insurance Commissioner.

All the while he was writing poetry, and managed to get some verses published in the *Drogheda Independent*. In June, 1912, he also sent his poems to Lord Dunsany, an inspired move. Dunsany was a dramatist and storyteller with a fertile imagination who explored what he called 'the mysterious kingdom where geography ends and fairyland begins'. In the simple Irish country boy he found a kindred, imaginative spirit and immediately recognized the presence of a pearl in the craggy oyster shell. He encouraged his protégé, 'astonished by the brilliance of that eye that had looked at the fields of Meath and seen there all the simple birds and flowers with a vividness that made those pages like a magnifying glass, through which one looked at familiar things seen thus for the first time.'

180

Dunsany worked with Ledwidge on a collection of his poems, entitled *Songs of the Fields*, and began to introduce him to a literary world. Ledwidge was gaining in confidence. 'I look forward to fortune and fame,' he wrote to his patron.

But the First World War was threatening and the politically-aware Ledwidge was faced with a dilemma. He was an Irish Nationalist and had helped organize the local Slane Corps of the Irish Volunteers. The Volunteers were themselves split over the question as to whether they should fight with the hated British in the war. Perhaps influenced by Dunsany (who also served with them), Ledwidge joined the 5th Battalion, Royal Inniskilling Fusiliers in October, 1914. His decision was not universally welcomed by his Nationalist comrades, but Ledwidge explained, 'I joined the British Army because she stood between Ireland and an enemy common to our civilization.' The war took him far from his beloved Ireland and he longed for it perpetually. 'I am always homesick,' he later wrote to the poetess Katherine Tynan. 'I hear the roads calling and the hills and the rivers wondering where I am.'

Ledwidge's obvious intelligence led to his early promotion to lance-corporal, and his letters to Dunsany and friends in Slane record his army career. In July, 1915, his battalion sailed to Gallipoli, landing on 6 August at Suvla Bay. Just nine days later they attacked Kiretch Tepe in an advance described by one of the officers as taking place under 'the din of the guns and the bursting shells, the incessant and voluminous roar of rifle fire and the whole orchestra of bullets and ricochets and shell splinters that streamed past us.' They sustained fearful casualties. But Francis soon developed a respect for his Turkish opponents. 'They fought us a clean fight, and we must admit they are brave soldiers,' he wrote to Dunsany. 'In my admiration for them I have read the Koran.'

After the fierce battles of mid-August, 1915, his letter had echoes of Wilfrid Gibson's 'The Question', which starts, 'I wonder if the old cow died or not'. During the 'hell' of the battle, Ledwidge commented, 'Once I found myself wondering if a cow that I knew to have a disease called "timber-tongue" had really died. . . . It was a horrible and a great day. I would not have missed it for worlds.' The depleted 10th Irish Division was evacuated in September and sent to Salonika on the Graeco-Serbian border.

That autumn *Songs of the Fields* was published, and was well received. Edward Marsh, working on the second volume of *Georgian Poetry*, proposed to drop five of the contributors to his first anthology as being too senior; in their place he included Ralph Hodgson and, on the strong recommendation of Dunsany, Ledwidge. James Stephens, another Georgian poet, was helping with the anthology and felt that Ledwidge 'must digest his ancestors before we know what he is really like. Meanwhile he has a true singing facility, and his promise is, I think, greater than that of any young poet now writing.' To the sophisticated Stephens, Ledwidge appeared 'a lump of a lad . . . panoplied in all those devices, or disguises, which a countryman puts on when he meets the men about town' (*Edward Marsh*, Hassall). Marsh chose three poems: 'The Rainy Day in April', 'The Lost Ones' and 'The Wife of Llew'. The last is a magical poem inspired by the *Mabinogion* of how Math, Lord of Gwynedd, helped his nephew Gwydion create a wife for Llew, Gwydion's protégé, of wild flowers.

The winter of 1915 was bitter – thirty degrees below freezing was recorded – with howling gales. Undeterred, Ledwidge continued to write poetry. Thinking of the May countryside he wrote:

> And when the war is over I shall take
> My lute adown to it and sing again . . .
> But it is lonely now in winter long,
> And, God, to hear the blackbird sing once more!

In more realistic mode he wrote 'When Love and Beauty Wander Away', inspired by fears of the end of the civilized world, and laments that 'a pale fear lies on the cheeks of youth'. Ledwidge was obviously aware of Rupert Brooke's death en route to Gallipoli and his burial on the island of Skyros, for he wrote of 'the lonesome isle which Brooke has made/ A little England full of lovely noons'.

Meanwhile, in December, 1915, the Bulgarians forced the British to retreat. During a punishing six-day march Ledwidge lost several manuscripts. The appalling weather affected his lungs and he was sent to hospital in Cairo with acute bronchitis. He was haunted with nightmares of his harrowing experiences and, for comfort, wrote a poem to his mother. The army chaplain (a Church of England padre who withdrew his interest when he discovered that Francis was a Catholic) and his MO were aware of his ability as a poet, and the latter helped to get him sent home. During a spell in Manchester in April, 1916, when he was devastated by the news of the Easter Uprising in Dublin, Ledwidge went on a 'blinder' and at a court-martial was demoted for insubordination and going AWOL. The next month he returned to Derry and spent seven months in Ebrington Barracks.

At the end of December, 1916, Ledwidge returned to his battalion on the Somme at Picquigny. As always his thoughts were of home and he wrote the lilting '*Ceol Sidhe*' ('Fairy Music'). He began an interesting correspondence with Katherine Tynan – the two poets had much in common: their 'Irishness', their nationalism, their interest in Celtic mythology. Tynan was already an established writer, and he confided to her, 'If I survive the war I have great hopes of writing something that will live.'

The spring of 1917 arrived when Ledwidge was in the Arras sector. He celebrated it with a lyrical song entitled 'Spring'. 'Ascension Thursday, 1917' followed and was sent to Katherine Tynan. His homesickness was becoming unbearable and he was beginning to feel disillusioned about the war. His only joy was the recognition he was beginning to achieve for his work. On 1 July Francis wrote to Edward Marsh, thanking him for including his poems in an anthology 'that will live'. He described the pyrotechnics of a big strafe, maintaining that during it all his soul was 'by the Boyne cutting new meadows under a thousand wings and listening to the cuckoos at Crocknahara'. By then his battalion had moved to barracks in Proven in the Ypres Salient. Ledwidge was still longing for leave to see his mother and his beloved Ireland. In 'Home' he wrote of a robin singing a song 'about the little fields/ That call across the world to me'.

But the great battle of Passchendaele (Third Ypres) was soon to begin. On 31 July the Inniskillings were below the Pilckem Ridge near Boesinghe. His Catholic faith intact despite his despair, Ledwidge attended mass in the morning. That evening, while taking tea during roadmaking one mile north-east of Hellfire Corner, he was killed outright by a seven-inch German mortar. He was twenty-nine. He is buried in Artillery Wood Cemetery, on the Pilckem Ridge, within sight of the spires of Ypres close to another Celtic poet, the 1917 Bard, 'Hedd Wyn' (Ellis Humphrey Evans) killed on the same day.

The lilting poem 'Soliloquy', reproduced here, is typical of his work and philosophy, and makes a fitting epitaph.

Ledwidge was a sad loss to the world of literature. He seemed to have so much potential. Harold Monro was writing to Marsh about the young poet during the first week of August when he broke off, mid-letter. His eye had caught Ledwidge's name in the casualty list in his newspaper. 'Lord! How ugly it is,' he exclaimed. 'The whole world is a kind of corpse factory. It surely wasn't worthwhile to kill him. We wanted to know what he would do. He might have been so much use – real use.'

Lord Dunsany had no doubts as to what he might have done. 'I give my opinion that if Ledwidge had lived, this lover of all the seasons in which the blackbird sings would have surpassed even Burns, and Ireland would have lawfully claimed, as she may even yet, the greatest of peasant singers.' In his poem, 'In Memoriam Francis Ledwidge', the Nobel prize-winning poet, Sheamus Heaney, summed up the essential Ledwidge as 'Literary, sweet-talking, countrified'.

Isaac Rosenberg

PRIVATE, KING'S OWN ROYAL LANCASTER REGIMENT

RETURNING, WE HEAR THE LARKS

Sombre the night is:
And, though we have our lives, we know
What sinister threat lurks there.

Dragging these anguished limbs, we only know
This poison-blasted track opens on our camp —
On a little safe sleep.
But hark! Joy — joy — strange joy.
Lo! Heights of night ringing with unseen larks:
Music showering on our upturned listening faces.

Death could drop from the dark
As easily as song —
But song only dropped,
Like a blind man's dreams on the sand
By dangerous tides;
Like a girl's dark hair, for she dreams no ruin lies there,
Or her kisses where a serpent hides.

Summer, 1917

PRIVATE ISAAC ROSENBERG

Bernard Shaw wrote, 'He who can, does. He who cannot, teaches.' It is to the great benefit of the world of art and literature in the decade 1910–20 that Edward Marsh was an artist/writer manqué who, instead of devoting his considerable creative energy to producing his own works, encouraged a coterie of talented young artists and poets.

The one creative genius whose work straddled the worlds of art and literature, and who also came under Marsh's wing, was the unlikely figure of Isaac Rosenberg. The 'golden boy', Rupert Brooke, was the avuncular Marsh's favourite 'nephew'; Rosenberg, the pale, sickly son of a Jewish immigrant from the poor Bristol and London East End ghettoes, could not have offered a greater contrast.

Rosenberg's father, Barnett, a devout orthodox Jew, emigrated to England to escape military service and the anti-semitism which erupted in the 1880s in his native Lithuania. He settled briefly in Leeds and gained a living as an itinerant pedlar, then moved to the great commercial port of Bristol where he was joined by his wife, Anna, and daughter. There, in the slum district near the old city centre, Isaac was born on 25 November, 1890, the sole survivor of twins. The fragile boy was immediately adored by Anna, who was the anchor of the family – strong, resourceful and naturally intelligent.

By 1897 three other children had been born and the family moved to the East End of London, to Jubilee Street in Stepney. They locked into a warm and strongly supportive Jewish community, where organizations like the Jewish Board of Deputies existed to help newcomers integrate and survive in the harsh poverty that was the lot of most immigrants. Yiddish was the principal language of the parents, but the Rosenberg children soon forced them to communicate in English. The children were instructed in Jewish law and religion, and at thirteen Isaac received his barmitzvah.

The East End at the turn of the century was a joyless environment for an imaginative child to grow up in. The Rosenbergs were poor and Anna had to take in washing and sewing to supplement Barnett's erratic income. Yet Isaac was never ridiculed or discouraged when from an early age he developed an interest in drawing and then in the written word. At the age of seven he attended the St George's-in-the-East Board School and a year later, in November, 1899, moved to the Baker Street Board School. His general education seems to have been perfunctory. A withdrawn and serious child who made few friends, he was often left to his own devices and spent a good deal of time drawing. His obvious ability was recognized and Isaac was sent for extra art and craft classes to the Stepney Green Art School. His love of poetry was also developing. With the confidence-boosting encouragement of the librarian at the Whitechapel library, he discovered Keats and Byron and was inspired to write verses of his own. His earliest surviving poem is 'Ode to David's Harp', written in 1905.

Rosenberg left school in 1904 and the family, acknowledging his artistic bent but unable to afford to send him to art school, apprenticed him to an engraver as being the most artistic occupation they could find. He continued furiously writing poems with a mystic element which celebrated his Jewish origins, and felt that the mundane trade of plate-making was fettering his artistic soul. He found some outlet for his creativity in 'The Whitechapel Group', a collection of aspiring artists and poets whose focal points were the Whitechapel library and art gallery and the Toynbee Hall, which provided cultural, intellectual and leisure activities to deprived East Enders. Rosenberg and his friends were hungry for such stimulus. But even within the group Rosenberg kept himself somewhat apart and was never actively political. He was not a social animal and felt he lacked communication skills. He did, however, make particular friends of the poet Joseph Leftwich, who had a similar background, and the writer John Rodker. They formed a small 'writers' circle' and criticized each others' work.

Rosenberg's poetry in this period reflected his bleak environment and lack of hope of breaking out of it. He was reading Rossetti and Francis Thompson, Coleridge, Edgar Allan Poe and Verlaine, whose ideas he absorbed, but he was experimenting too with his own powerful images. Because his background was so different from the classically-educated public school poets, Rosenberg was not constricted by their traditions of form or vocabulary and produced startlingly original work which sometimes succeeded, sometimes failed in its boldness. Nor did Isaac neglect his painting. He drew the Jewish characters he saw around him, the nearby countryside of Epping Forest, and in 1907 started evening classes at the London County Council School of Photo-engraving and Lithography, where he met the artist Paul Nash. The following year he started classes at the Birkbeck Institute and impressed its head and his tutor.

In 1911 a euphoric Rosenberg left the engraver, but the exhilaration was short-lived and quickly replaced by despairing depression and dilemma: how could he earn money until he qualified as an artist, but how could he qualify until he earned some money? Then one day, while copying a picture in the National Gallery, he met Mrs Herbert Cohen, a sister of the Royal Academician. Impressed by the quality of his work, she introduced him to her painter sister Lily Joseph and her artistic friends the Lowrys. Isaac became particularly friendly with their daughter Ruth, and his excitement at his exposure to a cultured, prosperous family is reflected in the poems he wrote describing their expeditions and the chalk drawing he did of Ruth in 1912. His three lady benefactors showed their faith in Isaac by paying his fees for the Slade School of Art in October, 1911. It was a turbulent period in the development of art, with the vigorous Post-Impressionist and even more avant-garde schools rocking traditional bastions in Paris and Germany – but the Slade continued its rigid teaching of draughtsmanship and life classes. Rosenberg thrived under the demanding régime and soon had work accepted by the new English Art Club.

The Slade was a daunting environment for someone of Rosenberg's background and he was preoccupied with his lack of confidence, money and breeding. Fellow students were an eclectic mix of society lovelies like Diana Manners, for whom it was a type of finishing school, public school products like Paul Nash, and underprivileged but genuinely talented pupils like Isaac. One student he related to was the charismatic Mark Gertler, another Jew from a poor East End background. Another bright figure on the artistic horizon with whom Isaac made friends was David Bomberg, who was attracted to the avant garde Vorticist movement. Yet for the most part Rosenberg remained isolated from his brilliant, confident class-mates. He felt an affinity with Blake; Stanley Spencer and Augustus John were also powerful influences, although he remained strongly attracted by the more neo-classical style of Rossetti and the Pre-Raphaelites.

As well as developing as an artist, Isaac continued to write poetry, encouraged by the established poet, Laurence Binyon, when Rosenberg plucked up the courage to send him some poems. In 1912 his first collection of poems, *Night and Day*, was published. At this stage his work was somewhat derivative; he was still searching for his own characteristic voice and poetic identity.

Unfortunately Rosenberg's relationship with his patron, Mrs Cohen, deteriorated and she reduced his allowance. Thankfully, the Jewish Educational Aid Society paid his Slade fees.

On 10 November, 1913, Gertler introduced Rosenberg to Edward Marsh. Marsh's elegant town house, spectacular art collection and glittering and witty guests made it an overawing experience for the poor Jewish art student. But Marsh's natural charm and genuine interest relaxed him. The chasm between their backgrounds and education, however, made it difficult for Marsh fully to understand and appreciate the powerful and original elements in Rosenberg's poetry. Although Rosenberg maintained that he wished to be known as a 'poet' rather than a 'Jewish poet', he was tempted by his new literary acquaintances (Marsh introduced him to colourful characters and original thinkers like Lascelles

Abercrombie, Gordon Bottomley, T. E. Hulme and Ezra Pound) to return to his Hebrew roots for inspiration and attempt long, difficult works like the inaccessible 'Moses'. Another booklet of his poems was prepared, entitled *Youth*, and he had some poems published in *The Poetry Magazine*.

He left the Slade in March, but although Marsh bought one of his paintings and promised further financial help with the publication of his poems, earning a living became a big problem. The strain of maintaining his dual poetic and artistic output was taking its toll on Rosenberg's poor physique and health. His chest was weak and his doctor recommended a sunnier clime. In June, 1914, he suddenly decided to visit his sister, who had emigrated to South Africa. Marsh smoothed Isaac's passage by accelerating the necessary paperwork at the immigration office and he sailed for Cape Town.

This stay in South Africa was productive: the light was perfect for painting and Rosenberg met new, stimulating and interesting people. War was declared while he was there, provoking the poem 'On Hearing the News of the War'. He felt no compulsion to rush home to enlist and did not arrive back in England until May, 1915, his motivation unclear. He was beginning to get the odd commission for his paintings, he was against the war on principle, and yet he still saw no clear path or direction to his life. Edward Marsh was preoccupied by the death of his favourite protégé, Brooke, although still willing to offer some financial and critical help with the publication of *Youth*, which emerged in June, 1915. Interest was minimal. People's minds were on other things than art and poetry – unless it came directly from the trenches. By October Rosenberg was despairing. 'It seems I am not fit for anything,' he told Marsh.

As suddenly as he had left for South Africa, Isaac impulsively decided to enlist, without even telling his family – one of the last to do so before conscription was brought in, in early 1916. He wanted to join the RAMC, as the idea of killing another human being was abhorrent to him, but because of his poor physique he was only accepted by the Bantam Battalion of the 12th Suffolk Regiment. The Bantams were formed in 1915 when the minimum height requirement was lowered, so acute was the shortage of men. By October, when Rosenberg joined, the minimum chest measurement had also been lowered to thirty-four inches. In January, 1916, he was transferred to the 12th South Lancs, then moved again to the 11th Battalion, the King's Own Royal Lancasters, who were in training for active service.

Like his fellow soldier poet Gurney, Rosenberg had another equal if not stronger talent than poetry, was temperamentally and physically unsuited to the hurly-burly of army life and, although extraordinarily intelligent, remained a private soldier throughout his military service. Unlike Gurney, however, Rosenberg had no easy point of contact with his fellow soldiers.

189

He could not relate to their lack of intellect and unpleasant personal habits – although Isaac's officers and NCOs found him scruffy and slovenly as a soldier. Rosenberg referred to the Bantams as 'a horrible rabble. Falstaff's scarecrows were nothing on these.' He was also, perhaps, over-sensitive and suspicious of anti-semitism in the ranks. A corporal who served with him recalled: 'He was a shy sort of fella, very quiet and seemed to keep to himself. He was writing and paid little attention to me; I wanted to show him friendship because I think he thought he was often shunned because he was Jewish.'

In June, 1916, strengthened by his tough army training, Rosenberg went to France still dubbed 'completely hopeless' as a soldier by his captain. He simply could not understand the rationale behind army regulations and discipline, let alone conform to them. He was completely unco-ordinated and inept at drill or smartening his appearance. His mind was on the completion of his epic poem, 'Moses', extracts from which Marsh included in *Georgian Poetry 1916–1917*. Isaac was extremely gratified by Lascelles Abercrombie's and Gordon Bottomley's generous praise and the latter's constructive criticism.

Rosenberg joined the 40th Division, then near Béthune, appalled by the devastation war had wreaked on the countryside and the rigours of trench life. The division moved to the old Loos area in July and in September Isaac wrote his most famous poem, 'Break of Day in the Trenches'. On the strength of the originality, flashes of pure invention and powerful imagery demonstrated in this poem and in his other masterpiece, 'Dead Man's Dump', Rosenberg is regarded by many critics as having the greatest potential of all the war poets. Yet he was writing in conditions that could not have been less conducive. As a private he lacked even the bare necessities, such as paper, let alone the understanding and mental stimulation of poetry-appreciating peers. His captain, although having no idea that this bumbling private was an artist and a poet with a growing reputation, instinctively tried to give him jobs behind the lines, which probably prolonged his life.

In November the division moved to the Somme. It rained constantly and was bitterly cold. Rosenberg's weak chest began to bother him, as did that other scourge of trench life – lice. His irritation is captured in 'The Immortals':

> I killed and killed with slaughter mad;
> I killed till all my strength was gone.
> And still they rose to torture me.

The carnage angered and anguished him, as so vividly expressed in 'Dead Man's Dump'. The images of the 'quivering-bellied mules' careering round the bend and the wagon wheels grazing the newly-dead boy's face are hard to erase from one's mind. There is no glory in this death, only tragic, useless waste, described with stunning immediacy. The poem was sent to Marsh, who, although being impressed by its power, had some reservations about its form.

By January, when Rosenberg had been at the front for eight months, the cold and wet began to tell on his health, especially on his weak lungs. His family and friends were worried, and asked Marsh if he could pull strings to have him withdrawn. Marsh was able to get Isaac a medical examination, resulting in him being declared 'fit for trench work'. From the forward trenches he wrote, usually on lavatory paper and by the light of a scrounged candle stub, vibrant poetry and letters about the voracious, sucking nature of the mud and the constant punishments he attracted for his sheer absent-mindedness.

On 15 March, 1917, in the wake of the German retreat to the Hindenburg Line, the 40th Division was withdrawn from the front line to the sector north of Arras to help the pioneers make up roads and railways. They had what is euphemistically called 'a quiet summer'. In September Rosenberg had a longed-for home leave. Always strongly attached to his mother, he was overjoyed to see her but otherwise felt the usual soldier's inability to relate to civilian life. Returning to France he was hospitalized at the beginning of October for two months, thereby missing the decimation of the Bantams in Bourlon Wood at the end of the Cambrai Battle. So high were their casualties that they were never reformed. In hospital Rosenberg, who made no attempt to disguise his relief at missing the 'stunt', had more time to read and write. He was determined that the war should not destroy his artistry, although at times he came perilously close to giving up in despair. For a while he was able to write in more congenial surroundings, his last creative period.

Leaving hospital, Rosenberg was sent to Bullecourt. Because of its heavy losses his battalion was amalgamated with the 1st Battalion, the King's Own Royal Lancasters. The change added to his discontent and he chafed to join the Jewish Battalion in Mesopotamia, perceiving service there to be safer and a good deal warmer. But nothing came of it, despite his sister's pleas to Marsh. At the beginning of the German offensive in March, 1918, the battalion was brought up behind the front line in reserve, but the German advance was so rapid that reserve trenches soon became the front line. On 28 March Isaac found time to write to Marsh (probably his last letter), complaining that because of the totally adverse conditions he was unable to write poetry and that his vocabulary was drying up.

Three days later, on the night of 31 March, Rosenberg went out on patrol and was killed in the early hours of 1 April, 1918. Together with nine companions from the 1st Battalion of the KRRC (King's Royal Rifle Corps) he was buried on the battlefield; just who carried out the burials is not known, but a list of the names of those buried was made at the time. The place was named Northumberland Cemetery, Fampoux, but the family were only told that Rosenberg was at 'a place north of Fampoux, east of Arras' and naturally assumed that he had no specific place of burial. In 1926 all the burials at Northumberland Cemetery were removed to Bailleul Road East Cemetery and the unmarked graves of the ten soldiers were discovered. The list allowed a collective but not an individual identification. However, since all the names were known, the War Graves Commission decided that all should be given individual headstones in Bailleul Road with the marking 'Buried near this Spot'. In 1927, at the request of his family, the Commission added a personal message, 'Artist and Poet', to Rosenberg's stone.

Perhaps what makes Rosenberg's poems so arresting, unforgettable and memorable is that dual talent of 'artist and poet'. He applied his painter's eye to the scene he was viewing, and crystallized that vision with a blend of words and images that, when it succeeds, was hardly surpassed in the poetry of the First World War.

Wilfred E. S. Owen M.C.

LIEUTENANT, MANCHESTER REGIMENT

ANTHEM FOR DOOMED YOUTH

What passing-bells for these who die as cattle?
 — Only the monstrous anger of the guns.
 Only the stuttering rifles' rapid rattle
Can patter out their hasty orisons.
No mockeries now for them; no prayers nor bells;
 Nor any voice of mourning save the choirs, —
The shrill, demented choirs of wailing shells;
 And bugles calling for them from sad shires.

What candles may be held to speed them all?
 Not in the hands of boys but in their eyes
Shall shine the holy glimmers of goodbyes.
 The pallor of girls' brows shall be their pall;
Their flowers the tenderness of patient minds,
And each slow dusk a drawing-down of blinds.

Craiglockhart War Hospital, September 1917

LIEUTENANT WILFRED
EDWARD SALTER OWEN, MC

The war poet most in danger of over-exposure must surely be Wilfred Owen, popularly perceived as the greatest of the Great War poets – especially by the younger generation who will, inevitably, have studied him at school. To them he has come to epitomize the 1914–18 poet: daringly realistic and anti-heroic in an otherwise patriotic, dutiful and floral environment; the prophet of disillusion and bitterness and, above all, pity. Owen's preface to *Disabled and Other Poems*, the collection of his work that he was assembling in 1918 which he described to be not about war but about 'the pity of war', is one of the most quoted statements of the whole war.

Undoubtedly Owen as the poet of pity was largely a self-creation. Adrian Caesar in *The Critical Quarterly* wrote a controversial article which quoted Philip Larkin as saying that 'in Owen's poetry there was "a human problem" that even after fifty years we are a long way from understanding', and maintained that Owen's expressed attitude of compassion and realism ignored that 'human problem'. Caesar cites Owen's indifference to the outbreak of war – 'The guns will effect a little useful weeding,' he wrote to his mother – and feels his 'political perceptions are at odds with his private feelings', that in his poems he 'sacrificed authenticity for didactic punch [which] gives the poems an unremitting air of artificiality,' and that he is 'ostensibly detailing suffering in order to provoke a reaction of pity'.

The old brigade of poets (to whom Owen was anathema, the antithesis of all they believed in) considered Owen to be a one-note – suffering – singer. For this reason W. B. Yeats deliberately omitted him from the 1936 *Oxford Book of Modern Verse*. There is a feeling, too, that Owen deliberately used the war as a vehicle for his own poetical advancement. He quoted de Vigny in a letter to his mother, 'If any man despairs of becoming a Poet, let him carry his pack and march in the ranks.' Yet today no anthology or book of poetic criticism is complete without selections from Owen's works.

Owen was not formed in the mould of the ideal poet. He was born on 18 March, 1893, in Oswestry to a lower-middle class father and a mother with pretentions of gentility and artistic snobbery who burned with an almost stifling love and ambition for her oldest son. Always bright and studious, obsessed with poetry from an early age (especially Keats), Owen nevertheless failed to get a scholarship to Reading University. Short and dark, with the piercing eyes that would command attention over the decades from his Celtic face in well-known portraits, a hypochondriac with a weak chest, he was far removed from the tall, athletic, golden, public-school image.

After a period spent assisting the vicar of Dunsden (whom he left under a mysterious cloud with innuendoes of homosexual behaviour), Wilfred took a part-time job teaching English with the Berlitz School in Bordeaux. Here he met the flamboyant French poet, Laurent Tailhade, who exerted a strong influence on him. Already he was experimenting with novel poetic devices: the internal rhymes, half rhymes and pararhymes (what he called his 'Vowel-rhyme stunt') that became his arresting trademark. C. Day Lewis maintained that his 'constant use of the alliterative assonance as an end rhyme' was 'his one innovation'.

After the outbreak of war, in September, 1914, the morbidly curious Owen visited the first French wounded in a hospital at Baignères, illustrating his descriptions of them with extraordinary graphic diagrams of wounds showing 'the actualities of war'. Adrian Caesar felt this showed Owen's 'morbid psychology and its attendant emotional confusions [and] element of voyeurism'. Be that as it may, this objective descriptive gift sprang into creative life when Owen experienced those 'actualities' for himself, and his searing accounts of gassed, maimed, blinded and bewildered men help make his work so original and outstanding.

It was not until June, 1915, however, and after much vacillation, that Owen finally decided he did 'most intensely' want to join the fight. He investigated the Artists' Rifles, an OTC which seemed to him to have the correct literary image to further his ambition to become a poet tempered by the furnace of war. On 20 October, 1915, he was accepted by the battalion and documented his military progress in continuing and frequent letters to his mother. He trained in London, where he was delighted to lodge over the Poetry Bookshop and further his aquaintance with its owner, Harold Monro, who encouraged and offered constructive criticisms of his writing. On 4 June, 1916, he was gazetted second lieutenant in the 5th Battalion of the Manchester Regiment, arriving in France at the end of December.

His overseas career started at the great base camp at Étaples (30 December, 1916), moved on to Halloy near Doullens, to the River Authie (6 January, 1917), and to Beauval, where he heard guns fired in anger for the first time and joined the 2nd Battalion. Their route rook Owen to the area of Beaumont Hamel, where the battalion had suffered heavy losses during the 1916 Ancre offensive that ended the Battle of the Somme. The

Manchesters had withdrawn to Halloy with only 156 officers and men; Owen was one of 527 reinforcements.

He moved forward by bus to Bertrancourt, where he first encountered the curse of the war – mud – and then on foot to a dug-out in no-man's-land, the site of which has now been located near Serre Road No 2 CWGC Cemetery. His letters to his mother at this time did not spare her any of the bleak horror of experiences that were to inspire some of his most vivid poetry, notably 'The Sentry', when a man was blown down the dug-out steps and blinded. Relief came with a transport course in Abbeville, which temporarily saved his sanity. He returned to the battalion at Fresnoy in February, but on 13 March he fell into a cellar in the dark and lay there for about twenty-four hours with concussion, fever and vomiting, which put him out of action for a fortnight.

Returning to the battalion at Savy near Saint Quentin at the beginning of April, he was caught up in a period of intense activity. On 14 April the Manchesters attacked in support of the French near Fayet; going to the start line the battalion was decimated by pounding shells. Back in Savy Wood Owen was blown up by a shell and spent several dazed days in a railway bank, believing in his delirious state that he was surrounded by the dismembered body of a friend. On 21 April the battalion was relieved, but Owen was observed to be behaving abnormally. He was shaky, his memory confused. Diagnosed as neurasthenic (the contemporary euphemism for shell-shock), he was sent back to 13th Casualty Clearing Station, then to Netley Hospital near Southampton and finally, on 26 June, 1917, to Craiglockhart Mental Hospital near Edinburgh.

At Craiglockhart he had a momentous meeting with Siegfried Sassoon, who became a close friend. Sassoon's influence cemented Owen's distinctive, innovative style, most significantly in his most-quoted poem, 'Anthem for Doomed Youth', reproduced here.

The relationship with Sassoon also gave Owen, the stammering, provincial, middle-class technical school product, the confidence to rub shoulders with the upper class and famous literary luminaries. Soon he was talking or corresponding with Robert Graves, Arnold Bennett, H. G. Wells, Robert Ross (Wilde's editor), Charles Scott Moncrieff (Proust's translator), Philip Bainbrigge, Osbert and Sacheverell Sitwell, Robert Nichols, Lady Margaret Sackville, Harold Monro and Edward Blunden. They recognized the touch of genius in this uncut diamond and gave him much praise and encouragement. Owen's most confrontational literary encounter was with Jessie Pope, the blithely insensitive poetess whose jingoistic calls to arms provoked him to write his ironic masterpiece, 'Dulce et Decorum Est'. The great lie, he maintained, was to delude people that it was at all sweet and fitting to die a ghastly death in action.

Discharged and convalesced, his confidence buoyed by his new-found literary acclaim, Owen was declared fit for service and on 31 August, 1918, returned to France. He spent a week in the notorious Bull Ring training camp at Étaples, then rejoined his battalion at Corbie on the Somme as bombing officer. They moved to the Saint Quentin Canal section of the Hindenburg Line, to which the Germans had withdrawn following the failure of the 'Kaiser's Offensive'.

The battalion went into action on 1 October at Joncourt, following the successful crossing of the canal and penetration of the Hindenburg Line forty-eight hours earlier by 137th Brigade of 46th (North Midland) Division. Owen acted decisively and bravely and 'For conspicuous gallantry and devotion to duty in the attack on the Fonsomme Line on 1st/2nd October 1918' was awarded the coveted Military Cross. 'On the company commander becoming a casualty,' the citation in the *London Gazette* continued, 'he assumed command and showed fine leadership and resisted a heavy counter-attack. He personally manipulated a captured enemy machine gun in an isolated position and inflicted considerable losses on the enemy. Throughout he behaved most gallantly.' He had emulated the bravery of his idol, Sassoon, and dispelled the innuendoes of cowardice that lingered from his previous shell-shock.

Owen had, without doubt, become a good officer, liked and trusted by his men. He was concerned that they should understand his poetry and wrote to Sassoon that no man of his should say '*Non compris*' of it. His telling use of army slang and the vernacular is a successful facet of his most realistic works, such as 'The Chances'.

The battalion rested at Hancourt and, on 18 October, moved through Bohain and Busigny to Saint Souplet near Le Cateau. They went forward to the Sambre–Oise Canal, ready to attack. By 2 November they had cleared the west bank at Ors of the last enemy. Wilfred was detailed to lead his company in the dangerous canal crossing, with orders that there should be 'no retirement under any circumstances'. At 5.45am on 4 November, after a five-minute barrage, the Manchesters responded to the shrill note of the start whistle and, despite murderous fire from the strongly-defended German bank, pressed calmly on. Owen, aged twenty-five, was killed in the action and was buried in the tiny CWGC extension to the village cemetery at Ors. Near him lie 2nd Lt James Kirk of the Manchesters and acting Lt Col Marshall, CO of the nearby Lancashires. Both were awarded posthumous VCs for their gallantry and cool leadership during the costly crossing.

Owen was killed just a week before the Armistice and the bells were pealing at the Owen home in Shrewsbury when the inadequate telegram of regret was delivered. In his poem, 'The End', Owen had written the comfortless message:

Shall Life renew these bodies? Of a truth
All death will he annul, all tears assuage? –
Or fill these void veins full again with youth,
And wash, with an immortal water, Age?
When I do ask white Age, he saith not so.

His dedicated, even possessive, mother, her *raison d'etre* snatched from her with his brilliant potential still unfulfilled, inscribed some of these lines on his headstone. But in chopping short the quotation, she totally changed the meaning:

SHALL LIFE RENEW
THESE BODIES?
OF A TRUTH
ALL DEATH WILL HE ANNUL.

The tributes to Owen over the years have been legion. Perhaps the most epic is Britten's dramatic 'War Requiem', first performed in 1962, which uses some of Owen's verses as lyrics. There have been several dramatizations of the extraordinary period when Sassoon and Owen were both patients of Rivers at Craiglockhart, in the theatre and on television, and the actor Peter Florence portrayed Owen in a memorable one-man-show, 'The Pity of War'. In 1991 a plaque was erected in Ors by the Western Front Association and the citizens of the village, and in June, 1993, a striking sculpture by Paul de Monchaux was unveiled outside Shrewsbury Abbey. It is a symbolic representation of the Canal at Ors and First World War trenches and bears the line from 'Strange Meeting', 'I am the enemy you killed, my friend'. It was organized by the Wilfred Owen Association. Most recently, Pat Barker used Owen (and Sassoon) as one of her 'factional', characters, in her award-winning trilogy about the First World War (the third of which, *The Ghost Road*, won the 1995 Booker prize).

Over-exposed, over-rated, or the greatest of the Great War Poets, Owen continues to exert a relentless power and fascination.

Ewart Alan Mackintosh M.C.

LIEUTENANT, SEAFORTH HIGHLANDERS

TO SYLVIA

Two months ago the skies were blue,
The fields were fresh and green,
And green the willow tree stood up,
With the lazy stream between.

Two months ago we sat and watched
The river drifting by —
And now — you're back at your work again
And here in a ditch I lie.

God knows — my dear — I did not want
To rise and leave you so,
But the dead men's hands were beckoning
And I knew that I must go.

The dead men's eyes were watching, lass,
Their lips were asking too,
We faced it out and payed the price —
Are we betrayed by you?

The days are long between, dear lass,
Before we meet again,
Long days of mud and work for me,
For you long care and pain.

But you'll forgive me yet, my dear,
Because of what you know,
I can look my dead friends in the face
As I couldn't two months ago.

October 20th, 1917

LIEUTENANT EWART ALAN MACKINTOSH, MC

Opposite Edinburgh Castle, in Princes Street Gardens, is a memorial to Scotland's effort in the Great War. It shows a Highland soldier, seated but tense and alert, rifle in hand. On a wall behind him is a long column of figures – labourers with staves, miners shouldering their picks, a shepherd with his crook and dog – following a pipe band marching to war. Below them are carved these words by Alan Mackintosh:

> If it be life that waits I shall live forever unconquered
> If death I shall die at last strong in my pride and free.

Mackintosh was in fact English, born about as far from Scotland as you can go without crossing water. His family home was in a smart Regency square in a prosperous part of Brighton, but young Alan was fiercely proud of his Scottish ancestry. He was born on 4 March, 1893, the child of a second marriage; his father came from the Highlands and the family spent many holidays in Scotland.

Alan was eleven when he started to attend the local public school, Brighton College, as a day boy in January, 1905. He showed early promise in English and Classics; the Greek History prize was his for two years running, and his interests turned towards literature, ideas and argument. He joined the debating society in 1908, but never expressed himself forcefully enough to attract the attention of the school magazine. Being a day boy allowed him the space to be different, and he showed no interest in the team games and sports which public schoolboys were expected to enjoy. He appears to have been happy at the school, and later visited it regularly on home leaves while he was serving in France, but moved on with an academic scholarship to St Paul's School in London.

In 1910 young Mackintosh went straight into one of the senior classics forms. He established himself quickly in his chosen sphere and soon became a member of the committee running the school's main magazine. By his last term he was the editor, which gave him the chance to write articles, review books and publish his poems, which already showed considerable skill. He made his mark on the school debating society and joined the Field Society, contributing a lecture on prehistoric Britain. His acting was praised. In the spring of 1912, with his contemporary Victor Gollancz, he entered the Speech Competition; their offering on 'the charm of London' was said to be original but incomprehensible.

Clearly Alan was not overawed by his new surroundings, despite entering the school so late. He was mature, self-possessed and very sure in his ideas. Other boys liked him, but his relationship with authority was not so comfortable. He never worked hard because academic success came easily to him and he preferred to concentrate on the things he really enjoyed. His manner could be flippant, and he may already have been exploring the socialist ideas which he would express as a student. His report on leaving the school was not favourable, though his ability could not be denied.

In October, 1912, Mackintosh went up to Christ Church, Oxford, with a Classical scholarship. The freedom of university life gave him a chance to explore and express his identity as a Scot. He learned to speak Gaelic, which was quite an achievement, and to play the bagpipes. He made friends with other Scottish students and developed a romantic attachment to the stories and legends of the Highlands. He also took time to learn more about poetry; French poetry pleased him and he read all he could find. He wrote poetry too, and much of the work in his first book dates from his Oxford days. He wrote about the pleasure of walking with friends, and produced several rather melancholy poems. Some of his writing suggests that he may have been in love with a girl he could not see very often; 'Sonnet', written in Oxford in 1913, is addressed to a girl he has loved for six months, and in 'To –' the love has become so strong that it eclipses all other interests. By 'The Heartless Voice', written the next year, the love has become frustrating and unsatisfied, and a 1915 poem, 'The Last Meeting', is about a romance that has ended.

By 1915 Mackintosh's student days had also ended. His only published reaction to the start of the war is a poem which looks back nostalgically to childhood as a lost paradise, and forward to death in battle. On the last day of 1914 he received a commission in the 5th Seaforth Highlanders, the Territorial Battalion of Caithness and Sutherland, and joined the 2nd/5th at Golspie on the shore of the Dornoch Firth, in the northern-most part of Scotland. The 5th Seaforths were originally formed by the Duke of Sutherland from the men on his estates and used the Sutherland Crest instead of the normal Seaforth badge. There were men of all ranks in the battalion with the name Sutherland, and a strong emotional bond between officers and men reminiscent of the old clan structure. They referred to themselves as 'the family'. In this atmosphere Mackintosh was in his element, though army discipline was harder for him to accept.

He made new friends, spending off-duty moments in nearby Brora with a recently-widowed woman and her young son and daughter, playing with the children and telling them stories. His poem 'The Waiting Wife' describes a widow's grief and loneliness and, after his battalion had moved south to train in Bedford, he sent a copy of Edward Lear's *Nonsense Songs and Stories* as a present to the children. Alan wrote a poem for them on the flyleaf.

He was at Bedford until the end of July, when his orders came for France, and on 1 August he joined the 1st/5th Seaforths at Authuille. Later this area would become part of the battlefield of the Somme, but in the summer of 1915 it was still a quiet sector, and the sight of local people bringing in their harvest made Mackintosh long for home. He became the battalion bombing officer and was popular with officers and men alike for his good nature and sense of fun. The homesickness which he certainly felt in the early months he kept to himself, expressing it only in poems. The weather was good and the trenches bearable until September, when the 1st/5th moved to La Boisselle and Mackintosh had his first experience of the destructive power of enemy mines. Then he wrote his first poem on a theme which was to dominate the rest of his war poetry: the fear of death and the need to conquer that fear and be free.

By the end of the month the battalion was back in Authuille, where they stayed until the end of December. Mackintosh went home on leave, but all too soon he was back in France. With winter the 1st/5th suffered nights of hard frost followed by days of rain which made the trenches collapse around them. Out of the line, though, there were still compensations; Mackintosh had discovered a talent for writing parodies set to the tunes of popular songs, and these earned him a wide following. To cheer the long, dark evenings the battalion held a concert in the château at Henencourt and he delighted them with a selection of his songs.

Christmas was celebrated in rest billets; the colonel ordered his officers to parade for a ride to Henencourt, which turned out to be more adventurous than Mackintosh might have wished. He was hopeless with horses, and was directed to a small pony which 'looked at me on my approach and burst into a fit of uncontrollable laughter. Sergt. Mackenzie, lengthening the stirrups until they almost touched the ground, wedged my feet, which are popularly supposed to be the largest in France today, into the smallest stirrup irons I have ever seen.' The pony bolted, careered through a solders' football match and beyond, defeating all attempts to stop it until it came to a sudden halt, throwing Mackintosh over its head. He wrote a very funny account of the incident for the *John o' Groats Journal*, which carried regular articles about the battalion's activities.

Early in March the 1st/5th was sent to a new sector north of Arras to take over the trenches of the Labyrinth, made notorious by hand-to-hand fighting between French and Germans. It was a dangerous, awful place where no trench could be dug without uncovering the dead of earlier battles, and the bombing officer was in constant demand to repel attacks and raiding parties. In May Mackintosh was ordered to lead a raid himself; he and a junior subaltern had the task of choosing forty men from over a hundred volunteers and preparing them for action. He was worried. The night before the raid he wrote 'To My Sister', offering as some consolation for his death the thought that he found a pride and exhilaration in fighting, and in rising above the fear of death, which a civilian could never understand. It was another theme to which he would often return.

The raiding party went out on the evening of 16 May, after a short but intense bombardment, and crossed into the German trenches. They did what they were sent to do, but the subaltern and twelve men were wounded, and no simple description can convey the mental and physical stress they all endured. Four men were killed, including one whom Mackintosh carried for many yards and was finally forced to abandon, dead, on the parapet of the enemy trench. For him, and for the others, Mackintosh wrote his most heartbreaking poem, 'In Memoriam; Private David Sutherland', describing the anguish and guilt he felt at their death.

Mackintosh also wrote a moving prose account of the raid first published in *War, the Liberator* in 1918. No other poet described so forcefully the anger and compassion of a front line officer whose men are killed before his eyes. He wrote about real people and real incidents, and this gives his poetry its power. He was awarded an MC for the raid, which was gazetted extremely quickly, only eleven days after the event. He also went home on leave again.

The 1st/5th Seaforths did not share in the main offensive on the Somme but held trenches further north, near Vimy, where Mackintosh wrote the poem quoted on the Edinburgh memorial. Later they moved south and on 21 July were marching towards Fricourt. Mackintosh was in good spirits; the battalion knew the area. Close to Bécourt Château the officers found some whisky they had hidden the year before. On 26 July they moved to reserve positions in Mametz Wood and four days later went into action in an attack on High Wood. They stayed for a week under intense bombardment, digging and extending trenches. By August Mackintosh was back in England, wounded and suffering from the effects of poison gas.

He spent just over a year at home: it took him six months to recover, but the fate of the battalion never left his mind and he felt increasing guilt at being away from it. In September, 1916, a friend was posted missing, and the Seaforths were in action again at Beaumont Hamel in November. He was impressed by the contrast between life at home and the life he remembered in France, and found it hard to communicate with people who had not been at the front. His poem 'Recruiting' begins as a scornful reply to the insensitive call to arms of Jessie Pope and her ilk – 'Fat civilians', 'Girls with feathers, vulgar songs' and 'blasted journalists'. Then an asterisk introduces a second section which gives an honest call to 'Come and learn/ To live and die with honest men'.

Once he had been passed fit he was posted to No 2 Officer Cadet Battalion at Cambridge, to pass on his bombing skills. Here he was happier; he had something to do and the cadets enjoyed his parodies just as much as the Seaforths had. He liked to say that his songs were a deadlier weapon than any bomb or tank. He also fell in love with a Quaker girl, a doctor named Sylvia Marsh. They planned to marry and emigrate to New Zealand, but Mackintosh could never quite push the war from his mind. In April the 1st/5th Seaforths was involved in heavy fighting on the Scarpe; a close friend from Oxford was killed in August and the sense of guilt at being comfortable at home while friends were fighting and dying became more than Mackintosh could bear. He volunteered to return to France and left at the end of September, 1917.

He was posted to the 1st/4th Seaforths and joined them on 3 October, sending home 'To Sylvia' (reproduced here) as part apology and part a plea for understanding. The 4th and 5th Seaforths were preparing for the Battle of Cambrai. At 6.20am on 20 November the British tanks crossed the front line and lumbered forward, squashing the German barbed wire into the ground or dragging it behind them, and the men followed. It was deceptively easy; Ribecourt was taken and the advance pushed on up the slope towards Flesquières, where popular history records it was stopped by a single German artillery officer with a field gun.

Early next morning the advance began again; the Germans had abandoned Flesquières during the night and the troops were able to push on towards Cantaing. The Seaforths took the little village of Fontaine Notre Dame, which formed a salient in the line. Two companies of the 4th Seaforths, Mackintosh among them, held out against a fierce counterattack, but when two whole German divisions came against them they were forced to fall back. Mackintosh was killed in the fighting, and is buried in the military cemetery at Orival Wood.

'Kind and cheerful under all circumstances,' a friend wrote, 'his men loved him and would do anything for him.' The love he felt for them still lives in his poetry.

Vera Brittain

V.A.D. NURSE

THE LAST POST

The stars are shining bright above the camps,
The bugle calls float skyward, faintly clear;
Over the hill the mist-veiled motor lamps
Dwindle and disappear.

The notes of day's goodbye arise and blend
With the low murmurous hum from tree and sod,
And swell into that question at the end
They ask each night of God—

Whether the dead within the burial ground
Will ever overthrow their crosses grey,
And rise triumphant from each lowly mound
To greet the dawning day.

Whether the eyes which battle sealed in sleep
Will open to reveille once again,
And forms, once mangled, into rapture leap,
Forgetful of their pain.

But still the stars above the camp shine on,
Giving no answer for our sorrow's ease,
And one more day with the Last Post has gone,
Dying upon the breeze.

Étaples, 1917

VERA MARY BRITTAIN, VAD

Vera Brittain is not included in this anthology as a mere 'token woman', but earns her place on several counts. Unlike many of the other published women poets of the Great War, she actually served in theatres of war as a VAD. She was literate and educated to an unusual degree for a girl of that period and a highly competent poet. Lastly, the personal losses she sustained during the war – her fiancé Roland Leighton, two other close friends and her beloved younger brother were all killed – showed her its tragic face.

Born on 29 December, 1893, Vera started writing seriously and with enthusiasm in the pre-war years when she lived in the provincial town of Buxton with her bourgeois parents. Her father, a product of his age in being a dyed-in-the-wool anti-feminist, held the traditional view that money should be invested in the education of boys but certainly not of girls, who should be educated just enough to attract a wealthy husband and not too much to frighten him off. So although Vera (known as 'John' to her father, who would have preferred a boy as his first-born) was sent to boarding school at the age of thirteen – St Monica's, of which her mother's eldest sister was co-principal – she was then expected to be content with 'coming out' into sleepy Buxton society until such time as she should make a good match. Her brother Edward was sent to Uppingham, where he made friends with Leighton and Victor Richardson. This only made Vera all the more determined to pursue an academic and scholarly path through her own efforts and ability. Eventually she gained her father's pride and admiration for her achievements, but it was an uphill battle.

She was inspired by Professor (later Sir) John Marriott, whose Oxford University extension lectures on socio-political topics she avidly attended. He encouraged her to write essays and was gratified when Vera won a national competition. She had a heightened awareness for one of her age, sex and background of female suffrage and trades unionism, questioned the validity of the church and traditional religion, and would certainly have considered herself a 'Modern Girl'. Vera was attracted by poetry and started to write, her ally in this medium being her Uncle Will (related to her by marriage), who had himself published several books of verse. She was also ambitious, intolerant and knew – and little cared – that she ruffled feathers and was not universally liked. 'I am beginning to be very keen about writing,' she confided to her diary (published in 1981 as *Chronicle of Youth*).

Heartened by Marriott's confidence in her, Vera single-mindedly pursued her objective of going to Oxford, swotting hard for a scholarship to Somerville. To her delight she was awarded an exhibition for the autumn of 1914. It was a magnificent achievement for a girl virtually studying alone, but Vera always felt that her greater achievement was in persuading her father to let her take it up and go to Somerville. She thoroughly enjoyed the academic stimulation of her first year, corresponding avidly with Roland Leighton, with whom friendship and love were gradually burgeoning.

Unfortunately for Vera her first academic year coincided with the first year of the war, which came 'as an interruption of the most exasperating kind to my personal plans', as she described it in the opening sentence of *Testament of Youth*. She became increasingly uncomfortable in her privileged scholarly ivory tower as the casualty lists – containing the names of friends, acquaintances and distant relatives – lengthened and the news of the sinking of the *Lusitania* and other realities of war bombarded her. She also wanted to be closer to Roland and Edward by being on active nursing service and decided to enrol as a Voluntary Aid Detachment nurse.

On 27 June, 1915, Vera started her training at the Devonshire Hospital in Buxton. In November she moved to the 1st London General Hospital in Camberwell. Vera's diary comments on the events of the war and her reactions to them: the campaign in the Dardanelles: Zeppelin raids on London; trouble in the Balkans; rumours of another big move on the Western Front. She read and quoted liberally from Rupert Brooke and pored over *The Story of an African Farm* that Roland gave her and which became 'their' book. She was delighted when Roland and his exuberant novelist mother compared her with Lyndall, its romantic but determined heroine.

Most of all she waited for Roland to come home on leave. She was agonized by his (or 'His' as she subsequently called him) death on 23 December. Both she and Roland's mother set out to discover every last detail about his last minutes, corresponding with his servant, CO and fellow officers, desperately hoping to find that his death had some purpose. His mother started to write a book about her brilliant son; Vera tried to turn to religion for solace, but remained a sceptic.

Recuperating from German measles, Vera had time to polish a poem called 'May Morning', published in the *Oxford Magazine* and later in her collection of wartime poetry entitled *Verses of a VAD*. It describes her falling in love a year ago and how, this May, her love killed in France, she wonders 'If when the long, long future years creep slow/ And War and tears alike have ceased to reign, I ever shall recapture, once again,/ The mood of that May morning, long ago'. Seventeen years later, writing *Testament*, she answers her own question on behalf of her generation: 'We never have recaptured that mood, and we never shall.'

At the end of June, 1916, it was obvious that the 'Big Push' was imminent. The hospital prepared for a great influx of wounded. Edward Brittain wrote, 'The papers are getting more interesting, but I only have time to say adieu'. On 5 July he was, by an extraordinary coincidence, admitted to Vera's hospital, wounded in an action on 1 July that was to earn him the MC. For the following weeks Vera nursed the wounded of the Somme, including, to her delight, her dear brother.

On 23 September she set sail for Malta on HM Hospital Ship *Britannic*. On the boat she remembered some verses from one of Leighton's poems, 'Roundel': 'I walk alone, although the way is long;/ And with gaunt briars and nettles overgrown;/ Though little feet are frail, in purpose strong I walk alone'. She wrote a poem entitled 'Perhaps. . . To R.A.L.', contemplating that although the sun may shine again one day and she may once again enjoy the seasons and nature in bloom, 'There is one greatest joy I shall not know/ Again, because my heart for loss of You/ Was broken long ago'.

It was an uncomfortable voyage; storms in the Bay of Biscay and the Bay of Naples, and Vera contracted an unpleasant fever when she transferred to the crowded and squalid ship *Galeka* after Mudros, where she thought of Rupert Brooke buried in his 'corner of a foreign field' on nearby Skyros. She was carried off at Valletta on a stretcher, but the warm climate of Malta seemed to soothe her grief from Roland's death and she found it 'a fairy country', despite the fact that life there was dominated by food shortages, chlorinated water and 'maritime disasters' from the many ships sunk around the island's coast. One of them was the *Britannic*, in which Vera had sailed to Malta.

In December she was moved from the eye and malaria ward to become assistant housekeeper in the sisters' quarters – a job she found 'less congenial' than nursing. At 11pm on 23 December, 1916, the anniversary of Roland's death, Vera, who now seemed to regard him as a deity, had a mystical experience, seeing the whole sky lit up. In February she moved to the surgical block and lamented the lack of hygiene prevailing in the hospital. It made unpleasant work even more sordid. Her correspondence with Edward, Geoffrey Thurlow and Victor Richardson were highlights in her life. They discussed literature, exchanged lines of Rupert Brooke, talked of the war and, of course, of Roland. She worried about them during the Battle of Arras, and was alarmed to hear that Victor had been seriously wounded. Not for another four days did she hear from Edward that Victor had been blinded. Both had been awarded an MC. On 23 April came another blow: Geoffrey had been killed in action at Monchy-le-Preux.

On 22 May Vera left Malta on the *Isonzo*, again encountering a fearful storm before landing at Syracuse. From there she entrained to Messina, Rome, Genoa, Turin and finally Paris on 26 May. The next day she arrived at Amiens, thinking how close she was to places where Roland, Geoffrey and Edward had been. From Boulogne she sailed to Folkestone and, after a short visit to her parents, braved a visit to Victor, with the thought of marrying him out of pity. Although he appeared cheerful at first, he suddenly deteriorated and died on 9 June, 1917. Only Edward was left.

Vera applied for service in France, hoping to be near him, but when she arrived at No 24 General Hospital at Etaples she found his battalion had been moved to the Ypres Salient. *Testament* gives a vivid picture of the life of a VAD in this vast, busy base hospital. It was cosmopolitan: she worked in the German Ward, and was surprised to find Portuguese officers in the hospital too. Nothing she had experienced prepared her for the seriousness of the cases she now had to treat: a 'regular baptism of blood and pus'. Many of the wounded were from the battles of Messines and Passchendaele and Vera moved to the surgical hut. Amazingly she found time to write poetry. The poem reproduced here, 'The Last Post', was written, she told her mother, while watching a wounded soldier come round from an operation.

Edward survived Passchendaele, and on 3 November, 1917, Vera received a letter in Latin (to evade the censor's pencil) telling her he was being sent to the Italian front after the Italian collapse at Caporetto. She was disappointed that, after contriving a posting to France to be near him, fate had obviously decided they would not meet. Vera found friendship with a sister she called Mary, to whom she addressed a poem that appeared in *Verses of a VAD*. Soon they were nursing the wounded from the Battle of Cambrai: Vera was deeply distressed by the gas cases, with their burns and eyelids stuck firmly shut, fighting for breath. It was bitterly cold and Christmas seemed particularly bleak to her, but she was brightened by Edward coming home on leave and managing to get leave herself at the same time.

She arrived home with flu and was annoyed that she wasted much of Edward's precious leave being ill. She went to see him off at Waterloo; as a farewell present Edward bought her a bunch of violets, as Roland had done two years earlier. It reminded them of the song 'Sweet Early Violets', a record of which he had bought to take back to Italy. In keeping with its lyrics, she would never see his face again.

Vera and her fellow VADs had to deal with another tide of casualties from the Kaiser's spring offensive. She did a fortnight's stint of fourteen-hour days and described the camp as resembling a Gustave Doré illustration to Dante's *Inferno*. They were terrifying days, when it seemed that the Germans would carry all before them to Amiens and the coast.

Her patients, some of them veterans of the 1916 Somme offensive, were a superstitious bunch and swapped ghost stories of being aware of their old, dead comrades at their shoulders in this most terrible of times. It reminded Vera of Mackintosh's poem, 'Cha Till Maccruimein'. 'Angels of Mons still roaming about,' she sensibly commented to herself.

The personal burden was added to by her father ordering her home because her mother had suffered a breakdown. She felt torn and guilty at asking for leave, and was relieved that it didn't come through until the worst of the danger was over. During her leave, however, the camp at Etaples suffered an appalling air raid; several nursing sisters were killed, others wounded. Vera felt herself a 'deserter'.

As 1 July approached, the second anniversary of Edward's wounding on the Somme, Vera wrote 'To My Brother', with the haunting and much-quoted first line, 'Your battle-wounds are scars upon my heart'. The papers were full of the 'show' on the Asiago Plateau and then came the feared telegram: 'Regret to inform you Captain E. H. Brittain, MC, killed in action Italy June 15th.' The final blow was that when Edward's effects were returned they contained an unopened letter from Vera – one containing her expression of deep sisterly love. It was the bleakest period of all for an extraordinary girl, who had by sheer determination achieved the exceptional success of getting to Oxford, had given up that longed-for education and overcome her genteel and sheltered background to become a first-class nurse in the most dreadful conditions, and had survived her grief at the loss of her fiancé and two dearest friends.

For a while even poetry brought no consolation. She tried to expiate her grief by writing what even she described as a 'wild novel', but sensibly reverted to the medium she loved – poetry. *Verses of a VAD* was well received by *The Times Literary Supplement*, from which she derived some natural satisfaction. Until the end of the war she served in 'St Jude's' (her nickname for St Thomas's) hospital, where she rightly felt her experience was totally wasted, and then at Millbank. The Armistice brought no immediate joy: 'The War was over; a new age was beginning; but the dead were dead and would never return.'

In 1920, in the anthology *Oxford Poetry* (for she returned to Oxford to complete an honours degree in history) Vera wrote 'The Lament of the Demobilised', a bitter poem talking of four wasted years. But those years had taught Vera to hate war, and just as her father's crushing attitude to women made her a life-long feminist, so the horrors of those four years made her a confirmed pacifist. These two deep beliefs formed the plank of her successful life and career as an author, journalist, lecturer and mother. She died on Easter Sunday, 1970.

How might she have reacted had she thought that Roland Leighton (q.v.) no longer wished to marry her?

Wilfrid Wilson Gibson

PRIVATE, ARMY SERVICE CORPS

LAMENT

We who are left, how shall we look again
Happily on the sun or feel the rain,
Without remembering how they who went
Ungrudgingly, and spent
Their all for us, loved too the sun and rain?

A bird among the rain-wet lilac sings —
But we, how shall we turn to little things,
And listen to the birds and winds and streams
Made holy by their dreams,
Nor feel the heart-break in the heart of things?

1917

PRIVATE WILFRID WILSON GIBSON

To some soldiers, one of the worst fates that can befall them is to survive their companions. It leaves them with feelings of guilt that they can never expiate. Not only to have survived one's comrades, but not even to have been allowed to share their danger was, for Wilfrid Gibson, even more difficult to live with. His pain is movingly expressed in 'Lament', the poem reproduced here.

For Gibson never left the British Isles during the First World War. His images of war are so convincing that he is usually described as 'a soldier poet of the trenches' and many commentators believe his vivid descriptions are based on personal experience. But he was an established poet before the war and never went anywhere near a trench; his war poetry is a great feat of imaginative writing based on solid research.

Little documented evidence of Gibson's private life can be found – his family believe that he deliberately destroyed personal papers because he wanted his work to speak for him. This lack of information especially applies to his war service, maybe because he was not particularly proud of it. The slim volumes *Battle, Friends* and *Livelihood*, and the sections 'Chambers', 'Casualties', 'In Khaki' (which includes a rare glimpse of Gibson's personal experience), 'Travels' and 'Home' in his *Collected Poems* contain verses of a quality that caused contemporary critics to use words like 'genius' about their author. Nevertheless they tell a lie.

Wilfrid was born in Hexham in Northumberland on 2 October, 1878, to an educated, middle-class family. His father owned the local pharmacy, which was regarded as such a perfect example of a turn of the century chemist's shop that it was acquired by the Wellcome Foundation in the late 1970s and today a replica façade stands as the centrepiece of the Fourth Floor Gallery in the Science Museum – the fittings are original. He was a keen historian, photographer and writer; he and Wilfrid's elder sister were responsible for the boy's education. So although he came from a literate, comfortably-off family, there was no silver spoon in his mouth, no expensive prep school, public school or university. Yet the drive to compose was so strong that it gave him the courage to embark upon the career of professional, full-time poet.

His early volumes were based on ancient legends, with romantic heroes and heroines – *Urlyn the Harper* and *The Queen's Vigil* – and although they received some attention from an American critic, who thought them 'worth keeping as a curiosity', they were at best experimental. Wilfrid found his true milieu in anthems to the working classes, based on keen observation. He studied the life of factory, mine and farm workers and his first volume of collected poems appeared as early as 1902. By the age of twenty he had been published in *The Spectator* and a collection of pastoral plays followed: *Stonefolds* in 1907, *Daily Bread* in 1910 and *Fires* in 1912. He wrote in direct, colloquial language and became known as 'the poet of the inarticulate poor'. His story lines of unemployment, disablement and poverty were stark, and appealed to the conscience and emotions. Gibson created a new genre of realism, soon adopted by what are popularly seen as the 'second wave' war poets like Sassoon, Owen and Rosenberg, who are considered to have invented it. No wonder Gibson was able to convince people that he was writing from the very trenches.

Emboldened by the success of *Daily Bread* and the acceptance of some poems by the rarified literary magazine *Rhythm*, Wilfrid decided to move to what he perceived to be the hub of contemporary literary life, London, in the summer of 1912. He used the only contacts he had there, Katherine Mansfield and her lover, John Middleton Murry, the editors of *Rhythm*, who became extremely important in Gibson's life. First they decided they must find respectable digs for him. At the last minute their first choice turned out to be 'disreputable', but even as Wilfrid was on the train south they found an alternative. It was a farcical situation, for as the landlord showed the three of them the room, he pointed out the many photographs of his late wife – 'a dipsomaniac, you know'.

Wilfrid was quickly introduced into their avant-garde, intellectual society, and must have been impressed and excited to meet people like Gaudier-Brzeska, Ezra Pound, the philosopher T. E. Hulme and, of course, Edward Marsh. Marsh liked Gibson instantly for what Murry described as his 'singular integrity'.

The most significant meeting of all came on 17 September, 1912, when Marsh introduced Rupert Brooke to Gibson – who, in his capacity as a newcomer to London, was dragged from his lodgings to see a spectacular fire at King's Cross. Afterwards Marsh, Brooke and Gibson went round to Mansfield and Murry's lodgings and a great discussion ensued (Hassall, *Edward Marsh*). There was an immediate affinity between Brooke and Gibson, or 'Wibson' as he affectionately called him. It seemed an unlikely pairing: the glamorous confident Brooke, everybody's darling, and the unsophisticated northerner. But there was a candour, honesty and attractive simplicity about Gibson that made people warm to him.

Two days later came the historic meeting at which the idea of 'Georgian Poetry' was born (see Introduction). Gibson was an automatic choice for inclusion. He had 'arrived'. Gradually, during the compilation of the anthology, the Georgians became a social group, many of the contributors meeting or corresponding with each other through the common denominator of Marsh. Wilfrid's circle enlarged as the months progressed, and his friendship with Brooke deepened. He stayed with him at the Old Vicarage in Grantchester in October, thrilled at seeing the physical process of composition and the sight of Brooke virtually writing poetry to order for Monro.

But Gibson was finding it hard to make ends meet, as his main source of income was writing reviews for the *Glasgow Herald*, for which he was paid half a crown. Marsh, everyone's benefactor, secretly paid him £1 a week as sub-editor of the ailing *Rhythm*. For a while Gibson took rooms in Marsh's own block in Gray's Inn and then, in November, 1912, became the first tenant of the bed-sit over Harold Monro's Poetry Bookshop. Hulme and Owen were future tenants of this historic room. On 29 November Marsh wrote to Brooke (Hassall, *Edward Marsh*) that he had introduced Gibson to Grosse, Hewlett, Newbolt, Sturge Moore, Masefield and de la Mare. 'I wonder if anyone has ever been introduced to so many poets at once.' Another pleasure came with a verbal accolade from Robert Bridges (created Poet Laureate in 1913) who found the Gibson poems destined for *Georgian Poetry* 'very remarkable'. Marsh called Gibson 'the most careful artist of them all'.

In March, 1913, *Georgian Poetry* was well received by the critics and went into several editions. By July Marsh was able to send £3 to each of the contributors from the profits. But the financial situation of *Rhythm* and its editors had deteriorated. By June, 1913, Gibson's sub-editorship came to an end as the magazine 'metamorphosed' into *The Blue Review*. He had started to make some money from *Daily Bread* and was paid £10 by an American magazine for 'Flannan Isle'. In October he was invited to stay in R. C. Trevelyan's villa in Italy (near Florence) with Lascelles Abercrombie, where they met D. H. Lawrence and Frieda. Lawrence described Wilfrid as 'one of the clearest and most loveable personalities I know'.

In November Gibson married Geraldine Townsend, Monro's secretary at the Poetry Bookshop. Her parents lived in Dublin, where the wedding took place. Marsh reported him as 'radiant. . . the picture of health and happiness', but deserting his poetry for 'Miss T'. The couple moved to the country, to Dymock in Goucestershire, and gradually he settled down to writing again. Marsh visited them at their cottage, as did Brooke. Marsh described the new Mrs Gibson as 'a very nice woman – without physical charm but very intelligent and as good as gold, evidently a supreme house-keeper, their cottage is very nice, all with a perfect sense of style – he couldn't possibly have done better for himself.' A colony grew around the village: Lascelles Abercrombie, the American poet Robert Frost and Edward Thomas all lived near the Gibsons. Their meetings were social as well as intellectual, the drink often flowing as freely as the ideas.

At one meeting in July, at which Marsh was present, a scheme for a new poetical publication was hatched. It developed into the quarterly magazine *New Numbers* and Wilfrid became its keen editor. Like so many things in the poets' lives, it was subsidized by Marsh. Throughout the winter the magazine grew, publishing works by Abercrombie, Drinkwater and Brooke. But the subscription price of seven shillings and sixpence probably inhibited its circulation, despite good reviews.

When the war broke out on 4 August, 1914, there was consternation in the Georgian ranks. Would it be appropriate to go ahead with their second anthology? Marsh decided to cancel. Alone, Gibson maintained that it was 'essential to do all we can to keep our flag flying during the triumph of barbarism'. The group was dispersed by the war. Sassoon, who entered the periphery of the set in March, 1914, enlisted in August, Brooke in September. Hulme also enlisted early. Murry and Lawrence were pacifists, and would not go. Others like Thomas went later. Abercrombie was declared not strong enough for military service and worked as a shell inspector for the Ministry of Munitions in Liverpool.

Gibson's attempts at enlistment were rejected four times because of his poor eyesight. His muse returned, however, invigorated by the war, and before the year's end came 'Before Action'. It is written in Georgian mode, with daffodils and frisking lambs, but it demonstrates Gibson's under-stated power to make a point: that young men may not live to see next year's daffodils and lambs. It is the poem 'Breakfast', from the same period, that leads so many anthologists and critics astray. There is such a convincing atmosphere of men under dangerous shell-fire, and such powerful incongruity in the contrast between the men discussing the chances of their local football team and making bets with the things that matter most to them in the front line – rashers and a loaf of bread – and the killing of one of them, 'Ginger raised his head/ And cursed, and took the bet; and dropt back dead.' No wonder readers assume that it was written by a soldier in the front line from personal experience.

'The Bayonet' is a cruder poem, but another feat of vivid imagination: the story of killing a man with a bayonet, hearing him squeal and then wiping clean the blade. The squeal remains to haunt the narrator. 'The Question' shows the quintessential Gibson: simple, direct, written in the demotic, with sympathy for the humble farm labourer in private's uniform as he wonders, did 'the old cow die or not'? One instinctively understands that the questioner is engaged in some cataclysmic struggle, but what concerns him is the fate of the old cow. It is the same syndrome as Tommy giving familiar names to dangerous places to make them less frightening, such as 'Hyde Park Corner', 'Clapham Junction' and 'Tower Hamlets'. The great question is so terrifying that it cannot be faced, so an accept-able replacement question is substituted. A similar rejection of reality is demonstrated by the wounded soldier, 'with both legs shot away' who keeps a tenuous hold on sanity in 'In the Ambulance' by constantly muttering, 'Two rows of cabbages,/ Two of curly-greens,/ Two rows of early peas,/ Two of kidney beans'.

The poems are short and economical: Gibson had the rare gift of being able to paint a whole scene and convey deep emotions with a few inspirational words. He even used his titles to give information, like 'In the Ambulance', where the fact that the soldier is in an ambulance is not mentioned in the text. The poems convincingly convey Tommy's daily lot in the trenches and between the lines. There are the marches ('Comrades'); the bird song between the sound of battle ('The Lark') and the 'peacock dragon-flies' which hover 'beneath the hurtling shells' ('The Dancers'); the mundane thoughts and conversations of home, of sweethearts, of country pursuits – all juxtaposed to images of soldiers dropping dead from bullet or shell-fire, or lying bleeding to death or losing their minds. In 'His Mate' (a very different story to Studdert Kennedy's equally moving poem of the same name) the narrator puts his battle-crazed pal out of his misery with a bullet. The shock of the last line, 'I struggled to my knees and pulled the trigger' is the greater because of the comforting familiarity of the first two, 'HI-DIDDLE-DIDDLE/ The cat and the fiddle'.

The critics admired Gibson's collection, *Battle*, published in 1916. *The Athenaeum* said they were, with Brooke's *Sonnets*, 'the only English poems about the war – so far – for which anyone would venture to predict a future on their own merits'. *The Herald* critic felt that 'Each separate vision, though realized in the particular case, has universal range – that is where the greatness of the art lies.' Abercrombie, writing in *The Quarterly Review*, showed a perfect understanding of his friend's mind: 'They are extremely objective; a series of short dramatic lyrics written with the simplicity and directness which Mr Gibson chiefly studies in his exceptional art, expressing, without any implied comment, but with profoundly implied emotion the feelings, thoughts, sensations of soldiers in the midst of modern warfare. The emotion they imply is not patriotic, but simply and broadly human; that is what war means, we feel; these exquisite bodies insulted by agony and death.' *The Times* and *The Nation* were equally complimentary, and *The Literary World* said, 'When we write down the word "genius" in connection with Mr Gibson's latest book of poems we do so advisedly. . . . Frankly, it is the finest verse the war has inspired.'

One wonders how a poet who was so acclaimed in 1914–18 could have become so desperately underrated and ignored in the second half of the century. Most anthologies content themselves with including 'Lament', probably his best-known war poem, with 'Breakfast' sometimes appearing to prove that he was 'a realistic poet of the trenches'.

Gibson's reputation as a war poet was enhanced by his second collection, *Friends*, in 1916. The main inspiration was the shattering death of

Rupert Brooke. 'When I was with him,' wrote Wilfrid, showing all the natural sweetness and genuine humility that made him so lovable, 'I used to wonder and wonder – is it possible that this radiant creature can really care for me? I always thought of him as one of the Sons of the Morning.' The dedicatory poem, untitled, starts 'He's gone'. It is followed by the poem 'Rupert Brooke', a hymn of love to his brilliant friend. The next lament in the book is for 'William Denis Browne (Gallipoli, 1915)'. Browne, a favourite of Marsh and a great friend of Brooke's, was a talented musician, and the poem recalls listening to music together 'night after night'. But 'The Friends' were not all killed. 'Trees' is dedicated to Lascelles Abercrombie and in 'To E. M. [Marsh] (in Memory of R.B.)' Gibson recalls the night he, Marsh and Brooke watched the fire at King's Cross.

The collection ends with some tender and delightful love poems to his wife (to whom he had dedicated the earlier collection, *Battle*). The many facets of married love are pictured – the contentment, the depths of happiness and passionate love. The shared love of the home they had created together is described in the four-part 'Home'. The poems are utterly charming in their simplicity and the depth of love that they show. The Gibsons had two children, a son (Michael, to whom 'Casualties' is dedicated) and a daughter (Audrey, to whom *Livelihood* is dedicated). Apart from these poetical references to his loved ones, however, Gibson was determined to keep his private life just that – private.

Brooke had made a generous gesture in his will. Knowing the penurious state that Abercrombie, de la Mare and Gibson normally lived in, he made them legatees of his literary estate. They received his royalties, which amounted to considerable annuities – Brooke's works were immensely popular in the ten years after the war, selling nearly three hundred thousand copies. Gibson's financial worries were over. He could write with single-minded confidence. In 1916 his verse play 'Hoops' was performed at a charity matinée at His Majesty's Theatre, together with works by Brooke and Gordon Bottomley.

In 1917 he was invited to do a lecture tour on Brooke in America, which was so popular that it was extended, and Macmillan of New York printed his *Collected Poems* (not published in Britain until 1926, when later poems were added). Finally, in that year, his fourth attempt at enlistment was successful (probably aided by strings being pulled by Marsh). Gibson's service career was undistinguished. He joined the Army Service Corps as a driver in the London area and then became clerk to a medical officer.

His personal, by and large boring, war experiences are described in some of the poems in the section 'In Khaki'. In 'Medical Officer's Clerk', Gibson bemoans the drudgery of poring over sordid records of soldiers with scabies and syphilis. 'The Chart' shows the boredom of:

> Drawing red lines on a chart
> With a diligent ruler and pen,
> Keeping a record of men,
> Numbers and names in black ink–
> Numbers and names that were men. . .

He feels that his heart would break if he dared translate those cold numbers into real people. That same concern is shown for 'The Conscript', who, even had he been Christ himself, complete with stigmata, would not have been noticed by the indifferent medical officers.

This so-called 'poet of the trenches' disliked service life. He missed his wife and his home and there is an unconfirmed report that he soon tried to get Marsh to get him out again. He was finally demobilized in 1919. After the war, financially secure because of Brooke's thoughtful bequest, Gibson went from strength to strength, publishing a further twenty books. His last work, *Within Four Walls*, was published in 1950, and he died on 26 May, 1962, at the age of eighty-three.

As a 'war poet' Gibson remains woefully underestimated. He need not have feared being dazzled by Brooke's 'sunset glow' – his own true evening star shines as brightly and as enduringly.

Siegfried Sassoon M.C.

LIEUTENANT, ROYAL WELCH FUSILIERS

TO LEONIDE MASSINE IN 'CLEOPATRA'

O beauty doomed and perfect for an hour,
Leaping along the verge of death and night,
You show me dauntless Youth that went to fight
Four long years past, discovering pride and power.

You die but in our dreams, who watch you fall
Knowing that to-morrow you will dance again.
But not to ebbing music were they slain
Who sleep in ruined graves, beyond recall;
Who, following phantom-glory, friend and foe,
Into the darkness that was War must go;
Blind; banished from desire.

            O mortal heart
Be still; you have drained the cup; you have played
    your part.

London, October 1918.

LIEUTENANT SIEGFRIED LORRAINE SASSOON, MC

Siegfried Sassoon was born on 8 September, 1886, in Brenchley in Kent, the middle son of Alfred, from a wealthy Jewish banking family, and Theresa, an intelligent, artistic woman who was ambitious for, and protective of, her talented son. She was a strong character, and needed all that strength when her husband left her with three young boys. Alfred died soon after this desertion, and these events were the only black spots in Siegfried's otherwise idyllic childhood. He enjoyed the balmy Kentish days, with the backdrop of hop kilns, meadows and orchards, and described these pastoral pleasures in the fictionalized *Memoirs of a Fox-Hunting Man* (1928) and his straight autobiographical accounts, *The Weald of Youth* (1942) and *The Old Century* (1938). Siegfried loved the solitary pursuits of reading, music, nature and writing poems for his mother, with whom his bond strengthened.

In 1900 he went to prep school in Sevenoaks, where cricket was his main love, but he worked hard enough to pass the Marlborough entrance exam. His time at this distinguished school was undistinguished: he preferred the sports field to the classroom and suffered from ill health. In 1905 he went up to Clare College, Cambridge to read Law. University didn't fulfil Siegfried any more than school had done, despite a transfer to History, and he left without a degree but with a love of romantic poetry, especially Tennyson and Keats. His years of education gave little indication of the literary career to follow.

Back home with his mother, he led an idle, aimless, desultory, 'country squire's' life. His principal occupations were cricket, buying books, golf, reading *Horse and Hound, The Field* and Surtees ('Mr Jorrocks was an all-pervading influence'), and dashing off the occasional verse, but his passion was for horses – especially point-to-point racing and hunting. His friends were typified by an old colonel with a parrot which squawked, 'Tear 'im and eat 'im' and other hunting noises.

The emphasis changed when his mother introduced him to a more literary environment, and the critic Edmund Gosse read his youthful poems (Siegfried had written several volumes which he had privately printed). Gosse thought enough of them to advise Siegfried to send them to Edward Marsh. As the verses were essentially Georgian in nature (and heavily influenced by the romantic poets he admired) they appealed to

Marsh, who wrote an encouraging and constructively critical letter: 'I think it certain that you have a lovely instrument to play upon and no end of beautiful tunes in your head, but that sometimes you write them down without getting enough meaning into them to satisfy the mind' (Hassall, *Edward Marsh*).

Marsh advised Sassoon to take a London apartment to be in the literary swim. Siegfried 'had visions of Mayfair in June, and all the well-oiled ingredients of affluence and social smartness.' In March, 1914, Marsh found him rooms in his own block. In *The Weald of Youth* Sassoon describes meeting Rupert Brooke there on 9 July: they discussed Conrad and Kipling, with Sassoon feeling somewhat overawed by this god of poetry. But the excitement was marred by his now limited allowance, and his lack of income soon put him into debt in the more expensive life of the city.

The outbreak of war was Sassoon's salvation. He enlisted, according to *Memoirs of a Fox-Hunting Man*, on the previous day, 3 August, as a trooper in the Sussex Yeomanry, selling his horse to the army so that they could stay together. His days with the Yeomanry were an extension of his idyllic civilian country life – like a hunt with a cause. He was acutely conscious of what he had to lose – 'the homely smells of the thriving farm. . . the apple-scented orchards' – but 'so far the War had been a mounted infantry picnic in perfect weather'. He was a patriot, and his poetry of this period reflects his feelings; later he regarded these early poems as 'too nobly worded lines', expressing 'the typical self-glorifying feelings of a young man about to go to the Front for the first time. . . . The more I saw of war the less nobler-minded I felt about it' (*Siegfried's Journey*). A riding accident in which he broke his arm kept him from the front, however.

When his arm mended he transferred to the infantry and was commissioned in the Royal Welch Fusiliers in May, 1915. After the normal period of training, he left for France on 24 November and joined the 1st Battalion in Béthune. Here he met Graves: both were writing poetry and compared notes, and Sassoon commented on some of Graves's verses, 'war should not be written about in such a realistic way'. Sassoon's first front-line poem, 'The Redeemer', was, he said, 'inspired by working-parties at Festubert, Nov 25 and 27.' But despite his advice to Graves he was already using phrases like 'horror and pain' and 'soaked, chilled and wretched' men.

Literary critics have frequently discussed the element of radicalism and realism in Sassoon's war poems. Bergonzi felt that 'whatever radicalism he manifested during the war was forced upon him by events, not temperamental; and in his moments of most bitter anger his poetic methods remained traditional, however startling his sentiments'. Hugh Massingham, reviewing *The Old Huntsman*, wrote, 'Realism is not objectionable, on the contrary it is fashionable'. But, he maintained, it paralyses art, whereas truthful art imposes its own laws. Sassoon was not a realist, but was writing 'modern epigrams, thrown deliberately into the harsh, peremptory, colloquial kind of versification which we have so often mistaken for poetry'. Virginia Woolf, on the contrary, seems to acknowledge his realism, as she 'knows no other writer who has shown us as effectively as Mr Sassoon the terrible pictures which lie behind the colourless phrases of the newspapers' (*The Times Literary Supplement*, 11 July, 1918).

The realism became personal when on 18 December, 1915, Sassoon wrote a moving, grieving poem for his younger brother, buried at sea on 1 November after being mortally wounded at Gallipoli. It has the memorable first line, 'Give me your hand, my brother, search my face'.

In January, 1916, he dedicated a poem, hopefully called 'Victory', to his patron, Edmund Gosse. First published anonymously in *The Times*, it is typically Georgian, filled with longings for colour and flora as a respite from the 'greys and browns and the leafless ash'. He was becoming a good officer who cared about his men, far removed from the carefree squire of 1914. On 10 February he wrote what he called 'the first of my "outspoken" war poems', 'In the Pink', in which he tries to empathize with a soldier as he writes a banal letter to his sweetheart. '*The Westminster* refused the poem,' he wrote bitterly, 'as though they thought it might prejudice recruiting!!'

The battalion moved up to the Somme area in February and, after home leave from 23 February to 6 March, Sassoon regularly took up rations from Bray to the Citadel, 'the camp. . . situated in a vast plain devoid of landmarks and bare and desert-like', and the British front line. He was living dangerously. On 18 March his friend, his love, Second Lieutenant David Thomas, was killed. Thomas appears in three poetic tributes: 'A Subaltern', 'A Letter Home' (to Robert Graves), and the sensual 'The Last Meeting'. Sassoon attended his burial: 'So Tommy left us, a gentle soldier, perfect and without stain. And so he will always remain in my heart, fresh and happy and brave.'

On 31 March he writes of creeping about in front of the British wire 'trying to spot one of their working parties and chuck some bombs at them. I am living in a sort of morose hunger for the next time I can get over the wire and look for the Germans with a bludgeon.' The war was becoming a personal crusade.

In April, 1916, he was sent to Fourth Army School at Flixécourt for a four-week course. Here, inspired by a 'famous Scotch Major who came and lectured on the bayonet' he wrote 'The Kiss', one of his most reproduced poems, about 'Brother Lead and Sister Steel'.

On his return came the famous 'Raid' on Kiel Trench, near Fricourt, of 25/26 May, so graphically described in his diaries and in *Memoirs of an*

Infantry Officer. With a good trench map, Holts' Battle Map of the Somme and the *Memoirs*, the route of the raiding party can easily be travelled today, cart tracks between fields more or less following the line of communication trenches from Point 71N across the field called Les Moulins à Vent to Maple Redoubt (now the site of Point 110 Old Military CWGC Cemetery where, incidentally, David Thomas and David Pritchard are buried.) The route then turns left to the Bois Français and rejoins the main road below Fricourt. The aim of the raid was for four parties of five men to enter Kiel Trench, take prisoners, bomb dugouts and kill Germans. At 10pm Sassoon, armed with his nail-studded knobkerrie, led his face-blackened men to the start point, but was forbidden to accompany them as he had to count them in on their return. At midnight the Germans began shelling with 5.9's and Sassoon moved up to within 20 yards of the trench, where he could see men lying on a ridge, between craters. Then a message came back from his trusty Corporal, O'Brien: the raid was a failure, they couldn't get through the German wire and were going to throw some bombs and retire. There were the sounds of scuffles and rifle shots, curses and groans and sixteen men, some of them wounded, scrambled back over the parapet. Corporal O'Brien was left, badly wounded, in a crater and Sassoon, ignoring orders, went to find him. He left him to get help and on returning, pulled out the unconscious man. Sadly he died as he was being brought in. This loyal NCO had been with the battalion since November, 1914, fighting through Neuve Chapelle, Festubert and Loos. His death had a profound effect on Sassoon who wrote, 'I would have given a lot if he could have been alive. . . but when I go out on patrol his ghost will surely be with me.' O'Brien is buried in the nearby Citadel CWGC Cemetery.

In June Sassoon won the MC and established his reputation as the derring-do 'Mad Jack'. For ninety minutes he remained under rifle and bomb fire, bringing in the wounded. 'Owing to his courage and determination,' the citation read, 'all killed and wounded were brought in.' Sassoon was a bystander during the great 1 July attack: from his 'opera box' support trench at Kingston Road he watched through field-glasses as the Manchesters took Montauban and Mametz, and observed the next few muddled days until the 'jostling company of exclamatory Welshmen' launched their suicidal attack on Mametz Wood on 7–10 July. Then his battalion was withdrawn to Heilly; on returning to the front he met up again with Graves, who on 20 July was erroneously reported killed. 'Robert died of wounds yesterday,' he wailed to Marsh. 'Won't they leave anyone we are fond of?' He wrote 'To His Dead Body' in his grief. When he heard that Graves was still alive, Sassoon sighed in relief. 'I felt a sort of glow spreading all over me.'

A couple of days later Sassoon came down with trench fever. In hospital at Amiens he was distressed by the delirious young soldier in the opposite bed 'calling out for "Dickie", and "Curse the Wood!",' who died the next day and became the subject of the poem 'Died of Wounds'. Moved to No 2 Red Cross Hospital in Rouen, Sassoon was fortunate that the 'genial doctor' recognized his name in the list of MCs in *The Times* and sent the decorated hero home. Soon he was in the tranquil environment of the hospital in Somerville College, where he 'whispered the word Paradise'. Asking himself whether he had earned it, he answered, 'I was too grateful to care'.

But with time to think of the horrors he had seen on the Somme, Sassoon became increasingly unsure of his beliefs. The change from acceptance to bitterness had begun. Poems like 'The One-legged Man', 'Stretcher Case', 'The Hero' and 'The Death-Bed' express his ironic anger and feelings of increasing hopelessness. His anger became more and more directed at the Establishment (who kept the war going) and the Staff (who incompetently carried out their dirty work) in poems like 'They', which Marsh pronounced as 'too horrible'.

After convalescent leave at home, during which the news from the battalion still at the front was a series of obituaries and casualty lists, he spent September with Graves (also on sick leave) in Harlech. In October Graves wrote to Marsh that 'Siegfried's verses are getting infinitely better'. Examined by a medical board in London in November, Sassoon felt ambivalent at the news that he was fit to return to duty, but duly reported in on 4 December, 1916.

Throughout the winter he told of his pain, his torment, his hatred of the corps commander with puffed-out chest covered in red and gold ribbons. He remembered his dead friends, his mutilated and maddened friends, and exploded with rage in the poem 'Blighters' at the occupants of the House of Commons chortling about 'our dear old Tanks'. Passing through Rouen on his way back to the front in early March, he wrote 'Base Details', one of his best-known poems of hate against staff officers, and in 'Return' described going back to the regiment to be greeted by the dead, who invite him to join them.

He was sent not to his own 1st Battalion, but to the 2nd, where a colleague reported, 'Mr Sassoon, who was wearing the ribbon of the Military Cross, was soon very popular with the men of the Company.' In April the battalion went into action on the Hindenburg Line, and Sassoon was wounded in Tunnel Trench. It was a careless accident. Sassoon thoughtlessly stood up ('I popped my silly head out of the sap'), and caught a bullet between the shoulders from a sniper. The bullet marked the death of the image of 'Mad Jack', or 'Kangaroo' as he was also known in the battalion.

He was sent to hospital at Denmark Hill, where Edmund Gosse pronounced him to be suffering from 'severe shock'. This Sassoon later disputed, as at this time he wrote what he considered to be 'a strong poem', 'The Rear-Guard', about the Hindenburg Line action. 'The Warmongers' and 'The General' express virulent hatred for those who prolonged and ran the war and were also written at this time.

In July he sent Marsh a letter enclosing his infamous protest statement, which began, 'I am making this statement as an act of wilful defiance of military authority because I believe that the War is being deliberately prolonged by those who have the power to end it. . . . On behalf of those who are suffering now I make this protest against the deception which is being practised on them.' The protest had been gestating for some time. His 'mental inquietude achieved some sort of climax,' his 'aggregated exasperations came to a head,' he was suffering a 'psychological thunderstorm' and he was influenced by the distinguished liberal journalist, Hugh Massingham, editor of *The Nation*. Graves saw a copy and agitatedly wrote to Marsh, 'It's an awful thing – completely mad – that he has done.'

Sassoon's influential friends conducted a concerted damage limitation exercise to avert a court martial. Graves rushed to Liverpool to meet Siegfried, who completed the gesture by throwing his medal ribbon into the Mersey. Marsh managed to get the War Office to agree to a medical board examination, which pronounced that there were 'no physical signs of any disorder of the nervous system. . . . He discusses his recent actions and their motives in a perfectly intelligent and rational way, and there is no evidence of any excitement or depression.' It looked hopeless, but an emotional Graves gave evidence to the board and Sassoon was eventually pronounced to be suffering from shell-shock and sent to Craiglockhart War Hospital ('Dottyville', according to Siegfried), where he built up a reassuring relationship with his psychologist, William Rivers.

Here he had his famous meeting with Wilfred Owen, whose work he encouraged and influenced. They were an ill-matched pair – the upper class fox hunter and the ill-at-ease failed teacher. Yet the collaboration worked to both their advantages. By 26 November, 1917, Sassoon was passed fit for general service once more. Although his famous protest was a refusal to fight, Sassoon suffered from the guilt feeling at not being in the fighting zone with his friends, so often experienced by soldiers confined to home service, expressed in the poem 'Banishment'.

Poetry had continued to pour from him throughout the Craiglockhart period, perhaps stimulated by his encounter with Owen. In May *The Old Huntsman* had been well received, and he was working on a new collection, *Counter-Attack* (published on 27 June and admired for the power of the poems). Amongst the best-known of the Craiglockhart poems is the bitter 'Does it Matter?', in which he ironically shrugs off the loss of legs, mind or sight as 'people will always be kind' to those who fought for their country. 'Glory of Women' attacks the mothers who love their wounded sons even when they have been mutilated, provided it is in a 'mentionable' place. A German mother is included, to prove that men of both sides were victims and women around the world are equally unrealistic.

In January, 1918, he was posted to Limerick, where he found 'something closely resembling peace of mind'. The soothing Irish countryside, the opportunity to hunt again, the warm and amusing Irish people, all worked magic, and a new posting to Palestine came as an anti-climax, as he felt mentally prepared to return to France.

On 13 February Sassoon sailed from Southampton to Cherbourg, noting that it was the third time in three years that he had been in France on 13 February. After a long journey by ship and train he arrived in Jerusalem on 12 March. 'Not a very holy-looking place,' he commented. He was second-in-command of C Company of the 25th Battalion, the RWF, but did not feel physically well in the hot climate and drew a great deal of support from the MO, whose love of ornithology he shared. This relationship, and the fun of a concert party (recalled in a poem of the same name) seem the only bright spots of this posting and he was glad to return to Alexandria, from where he sailed to Marseilles on 1 May.

The battalion moved towards Arras, and when in June he was involved again in battalion attacks he began to feel 'jumpy and nerve-ridden'. His nerve seemed to return in July, when he volunteered to lead a patrol to maintain their supremacy in no-man's-land. Touching the fire opal, the good-luck charm he always carried, Sassoon led a terrified corporal and stayed out with him for over two hours, returning literally slapping his thighs with excitement. The euphoria was short-lived. Standing up in a trench, he was hit in the head and thought he was going to die, but recovered to discover that the shot had been fired accidentally by his own sergeant. Philosophically, Sassoon concluded that to say he 'was well out of it is an understatement of an extremely solemn fact'.

Once more he went through the medical ritual of passing down the line from aid post to CCS to base hospital. By 20 July he was in London in the luxury of the American Red Cross Hospital at Lancaster Gate, followed by the Lennel House Convalescent Home in Berwickshire. He ended the war on permanent sick leave and was officially retired from the army on 12 March, 1919.

From the end of the war until the end of his life he sought to reconcile himself with the turbulent years that changed his life so dramatically. Had it not been for the war he might have continued his dilettante existence of sport and amateur Georgian poetry, a secret homosexual. During the war, in the increased emotion of shared danger and horror, his homosexual feelings were heightened. Yet, after one of the *volte-faces* that characterized his life, he married in 1933 and had a son in 1936. In August, 1957, he converted to Catholicism. He flirted with politics, even becoming literary editor of the socialist *Daily Herald*, but it was a short-lived appointment. Once he had expiated the war through his long series of memoirs, his inspiration waned. He died on 1 September, 1967, a week before his eighty-first birthday.

The recent cult of Owen tends to push Sassoon into a second-class position in the league of war poets. But if power, raw, truthful feeling and memorability are legitimate criteria, he must be classified as one of the 'greats'. He was also capable of the unexpected, like the charming poem reproduced here. But perhaps his finest, most sympathetic and powerful work is 'Aftermath', written in March, 1919:

> Have you forgotten yet?. . .
> Look up, and swear by the green of the spring that you'll
> Never forget.

SELECT BIBLIOGRAPHY

Abdy, Jane and Gere, Charlotte. *The Souls*. Sidgwick & Jackson, 1984.
Adcock, A. St John. *For Remembrance*. Hodder & Stoughton, 1918.
Allinson, Sidney. *The Bantams*. Howard Baker, 1981.
Ashmead-Bartlett, Ellis. *The Uncensored Dardanelles*. Hutchinson, 1928.
Balcon, Jill. *The Pity of War*. Shepheard-Walwyn, 1985.
Barker, Pat. *The Eye in the Door*, 1993; *Regeneration*, 1995. Viking.
Bergonzi, Bernard. *Twilight of the Gods*. Constable, 1965.
Blunden, Edmund. *Undertones of War*. Cobden-Sanderson, 1929.
Boden, Anthony. *Stars in a Dark Night*. Alan Sutton, 1986.
Brittain, Vera. *Testament of Youth*. Victor Gollancz, 1934.
—*Chronicle of Youth*. Victor Gollancz, 1981.
Brodrick Thompson, A. and Watts Moses, E. (eds). *The War Record of Old Dunelmians*. Robert Youll 1919.
Brooke, Rupert. *Poetical Works*. Faber, 1946.
Coulson, Leslie. *From an Outpost*. Erskine Macdonald, 1917.
Cross, Tim. *The Lost Voices of World War I*. Bloomsbury, 1988.
De la Mare, Walter. *Rupert Brooke and the Intellectual Imagination*. Sidgwick & Jackson, 1919.
Desborough, Lady Ethel. *Pages from a Family Journal 1888–1915*. Eton College, 1916.
Dunn, Captain J. C. *The War the Infantry Knew*. Cardinal, 1987.
Feilding, Rowland. *War Letters to a Wife*. Medici Society, 1929.
Frankau, Gilbert. *Self-Portrait*. Macdonald, 1940.
—*The Poetical Works*, Vols I & II. Chatto & Windus, 1923.
Frankau, Pamela. *Pen to Paper*. Heinemann, 1961.
Fuller, Simon. *The Poetry of War*. Longman, 1990.
Fussell, Paul. *The Great War and Modern Memory*. Oxford University Press, 1982.
Gibson, Wilfrid. *Collected Poems*. Macmillan, 1929.
Giddings, Robert. *The War Poets*. Bloomsbury, 1988.
Girouard, Mark. *The Return to Camelot*. Yale University Press, 1981.
Glenconner, Pamela. *Edward Wyndham Tennant*. The Bodley Head, 1919.
Graves, Robert. *Goodbye to All That*. Guild Publishing, 1979.
—*Poems About War*. Cassell, 1988.

Grey, Major. *The Second City of London Regiment in the Great War.* Regimental HQ, 1929.

Gurney, Ivor. *Selected Poems* (ed. P. J. Kavanagh). Oxford University Press, 1990.

Haig-Brown, A. R. *The OTC and the Great War.* George Newnes, 1925.

Hassall, Christopher. *Edward Marsh.* Longmans, 1959.

—*Rupert Brooke.* Faber, 1964.

Herbert, Alan Patrick. *The Secret Battle.* Methuen, 1919.

Hibberd, Dominic. *The First World War.* Macmillan, 1990.

—*Wilfred Owen: The Last Year.* Constable, 1992.

Hibberd, Dominic and Onions, John (eds.). *Poetry of the Great War.* Macmillan, 1986.

Hodgson, William Noel. *Verse and Prose in Peace and War.* Smith Elder, 1916. 2nd. ed. John Murray, 1917.

Holt, Tonie and Valmai. *Battlefields of the First World War.* Pavilion, 1993.

Jerrold, Douglas. *The Royal Naval Division.* Hutchinson, 1927.

Jolliffe, John. *Raymond Asquith: Life and Letters.* Collins, 1980.

Lambert, Angela. *Unquiet Souls.* Macmillan, 1984.

Ledwidge, Francis. *The Complete Poems of Francis Ledwidge.* Herbert Jenkins, 1919.

Longworth, Philip. *The Unending Vigil.* Constable, 1967.

McCrae, John. *In Flanders Fields.* William Briggs, 1919.

McPhail, Helen. *Wilfred Owen: Poet and Solder.* Gliddon, 1993.

Mackintosh, Ewart Alan. *A Highland Regiment.* John Lane, Bodley Head, 1917.

—*War, The Liberator.* John Lane, Bodley Head, 1918.

Marsh, Edward (ed.). *Georgian Poetry.* Vols 1–4. Poetry Book Shop, 1915–19.

Moorcroft Wilson, Jean. *Isaac Rosenberg: Poet and Painter.* Cecil Woolf, 1975.

—*Charles Hamilton Sorley.* Cecil Woolf, 1985.

Mosley, Nicholas. *Julian Grenfell.* Holt, Rinehart & Winston, 1976.

Nichols, Robert. *Anthology of War Poetry.* Nicholson & Watson, 1943.

Officers Died in the Great War. HMSO, 1919.

Parker, Peter. *The Old Lie.* Constable, 1987.

Pound, Reginald. *A. P. Herbert.* Michael Joseph, 1976.

Powell, Anne. *Bim.* Powell, 1990.

—*A Deep Cry.* Palladour Books, 1993.

Prescott, John F. *In Flanders Fields.* Boston Mills Press, 1985.

Purcell, William. *Woodbine Willie.* Hodder & Stoughton, 1962.

Quiller-Couch, Sir Arthur. *Oxford Book of English Verse.* Oxford University Press, 1949.

Raw, David. *It's Only Me.* Frank Peters, 1988.

Reynolds, Michael. *Hemingway's First War*. Basil Blackwell, 1987.

Salmond, Monica. *Bright Armour*. Faber, 1935.

Sassoon, Siegfried. *Memoirs of a Fox-Hunting Man, Memoirs of an Infantry Officer, Sherston's Progress* and *War Poems*. Faber, 1928–83.

Seeger, Alan. *Poems*. Constable, 1919.

Seymour-Smith, Martin. *Robert Graves: His Life and Work*. Hutchinson, 1982.

Silkin, Jon. *First World War Poetry*. Penguin, 1981.

—*Out of Battle*. Ark, 1987.

Soldier Poets: Songs of the Fighting Men. Erskine Macdonald, 1916.

Soldier Poets; Second Series: More Songs by the Fighting Men. Erskine Macdonald, 1917.

Sorley, Charles. *Marlborough and Other Poems*. Cambridge University Press, 1916.

—*Letters*. Cambridge University Press, 1919.

Streets, John William. *The Undying Splendour*. Erskine Macdonald, 1917.

Studdert Kennedy, Geoffrey Anketell. *The Unutterable Beauty*. Hodder & Stoughton, 1927.

Studdert Kennedy By His Friends. Hodder & Stoughton, 1929.

This England. *Salute to the Soldier Poets*. 1990.

Thomas, Edward. *Collected Poems*. Faber, 1936.

—*The Childhood of Edward Thomas*. (ed. Roland Grant). Faber, 1983.

Thornton, R. K. R. *Ivor Gurney's War Letters*. Carcanet New Press, 1983.

Vernède, R. E. *Letters to His Wife*. Collins, 1917.

Vernède, R. E. *War Poems and Other Verses*. Heinemann, 1917.

Wavell, Field-Marshal Earl. *Other Men's Flowers*. Jonathan Cape, 1944.

Webb, Barry. *Edmund Blunden*. Yale University Press, 1990.

Winton, Edward. *Gilbert Talbot*. Sidgwick & Jackson, 1917.

Ziegler, Philip. *Diana Cooper*. Hamish Hamilton, 1981.

SUMMARY OF THE POETS' LIVES/MILITARY SERVICE

NAME	AWARD	REGT	RANK	ENLISTED	TYPE	DIED	BURIED	FOUGHT	EDUCATION
Blunden, Edmund	MC	Royal Sussex	Lt	Aug 1915	Vol	20 Jan 1915	—	Somme, Third Ypres	Christ's Hospital, Oxford
Brittain, Vera		V A D	Nurse	June 1915	Vol	1970	—	Malta, Etaples	St Monica's, Oxford
Brooke, Rupert		RNVR-RND	Sub-Lt	Aug 1914	Vol	23 April 1915	Skyros	Antwerp	Rugby, Cambridge
Coulson, Leslie		Royal Fusiliers	Sgt	Sept 1914	Vol	7 Oct 1916	Grove Town	Gallipoli, Somme	Local Kilburn area
Frankau, Gilbert		East Surreys/RA	Capt	1914	Vol	4 Nov 1952	—	Loos, Ypres, Somme	Eton
Gibson, Wilfred Wilson		ASC	Ranks	1917	Vol	26 May 1962	—	Home Service	—
Graves, Robert		R W F	Capt	Aug 1914	Vol	1985	—	Loos, Somme	Charterhouse
Grenfell, Hon Julian	DSO	Royal Dragoons	Capt	1910	Reg	30 April 1915	Boulogne E	Eton, Oxford	Eton, Oxford
Gurney, Ivor		Gloucesters	Ranks	Feb 1915	Vol	26 Dec 1937	—	Somme, Ypres	King's Gloucester, RCM
Herbert, Alan Patrick		RNVR-RND	Sub-Lt	Sept 1914	Vol	11 Nov 1971	—	Gallipoli, Somme	Winchester, Oxford
Hodgson, William Noel	MC	Devonshire	Capt	Sept 1914	Vol	1 July 1916	Devonshire	Loos, Somme	Durham, Oxford
Ledwidge, Francis		Inniskillings	L Cpl	Oct 1914	Vol	31 July 1917	—	Third Ypres	Local school, Slane
Leighton, Roland Aubrey		Norfolks/Worcs	Lt	Oct 1914	Vol	22 Dec 1915	Louvencourt	Plugstreet, Somme	Uppingham
McCrae, John		Arty/Medic	Lt Col	Aug 1914	Vol	28 Jan 1918	Wimereux	First Ypres, 2nd Ypres	Guelph, Toronto
Mackintosh, Ewart Alan	MC	Seaforths	Lt	1914	Vol	Oct 1917	Orival Wood	Somme, Cambrai	St Paul's, Oxford
Owen, Wilfred E Salter	MC	Artists/Manchs	Lt	Oct 1915	Vol	Nov 1918	Ors	Somme, Sambre-Oise	Shrewsbury Tech
Rosenberg, Isaac		Kings Own R L	Pte	Oct 1915	Vol	1 April 1918	Bailleul Rd	Arras	Slade School of Art
Sassoon, Siegfried	MC	RWF	Lt	Aug 1914	Vol	1 Sept 1967	—	Somme	Marlborough, Cambridge
Seeger, Alan		Foreign Legion	Legionnaire	Sept 1914	Vol	4 July 1916	Lihons	Somme	Tutor, Harvard
Sorley, Charles Hamilton		Suffolks	2 Lt	Aug 1914	Vol	13 Oct 1915	Loos Mem	Loos	Marlborough, Jena
Streets, John William		Sheffield Pals	Sgt	Aug 1914	Vol	1 July 1916	Euston Rd	Somme	Whitwell Elementary
Studder-Kennedy, G A	MC	Chaplains Dept	Asst Chap	1915	Vol	1929	—	Somme, Messines	Leeds, Trinity Dublin
Tennant, Hon Edward W		Gren Guards	Lt	Aug 1914	Vol	22 Sept 1916	Guillemont	Loos, Somme	Winchester
Thomas, Edward		Artists/RGA	Lt	July 1915	Vol	9 April 1917	Agny	Vimy	St Paul's
Vernede, Robert Ernest		R Fus/Rifle Bde	2 Lt	Sept 1914	Vol	9 April 1917	Lebuquiere	Somme, Cambrai	St Paul's, Oxford